SIR ARTHUR HEYWOOD
&
THE FIFTEEN INCH GAUGE RAILWAY

To Anna Dawson

*'As you light up the stage
in your cabaret
shine on in radiant manner,
may you carry on through
to creation's last day
our dearest beloved Anna.'*

SIR ARTHUR HEYWOOD

AND
THE FIFTEEN INCH GAUGE RAILWAY

MARK SMITHERS
M.A. (OXON) M.B.A.

To Iain
On the occasion of his Christening

Mark Smithers

PLATEWAY PRESS
ISBN 1-871980-22-4

SIR ARTHUR HEYWOOD AND
THE FIFTEEN INCH GAUGE RAILWAY

© Mark Smithers & Plateway Press 1995

ISBN 1-871980-22-4

British Library Cataloguing in Publication Data
Smithers, Mark
Sir Arthur Heywood and the Fifteen Inch Gauge Railway
I. Title
385.52092

*All rights reserved. No part of this publication may be
reproduced or stored in a retrieval system or transmitted in any
form or by any means, electronic or mechanical including
photocopying, recording or information storage and retrieval
system now known or to be invented without prior permission
in writing from the copyright holders.*

Book Design, Jacket Design & Typesetting by:
*Roy C. Link, 1 Station Cottages, Harling Road, East Harling
Norwich NR16 2QP*

Jacket Photograph Coloured by:
Dean Smith

Printed by:
*Postprint, Taverner House, Harling Road, East Harling
Norwich NR16 2QR*

Published by:
PLATEWAY PRESS, PO Box 973, Brighton BN2 2TG

ALTE VOLTO
I Fly High

ACKNOWLEDGEMENTS

My grateful thanks are due to the following persons who provided assistance during the preparation of this book:

G. Barlow; B. Brickell; J. Brown; R. Butterell; M. Colborne;
M. Decker; B. Gent; A. F. Harris; P. Ingham;
the late Sir Oliver Heywood; Sir Peter Heywood;
P. Hodge; M. Jacot; J. Kimber; S. A. Leleux; Roy C. Link;
E. Lloyd; B. G. Markham; W. J. Milner; A. Neale;
A. S. Reen; G. K. Ridley; D. M. South; P. Stileman;
S. Townsend; P. Van Zeller; J. G. Vincent and C. R. Weaver.

Special thanks are due to Mr. and Mrs. H. Pilkington for allowing the author to explore Doveleys and for allowing access to certain previously unpublished Heywood family photographs, and to Mr. T. G. Finn for allowing access to the site of the Duffield Bank Railway.

CONTENTS

Acknowledgements vi

Introduction 1

Chapter 1 ....The Heywood Family Before 1872..3

Chapter 2 ....Estate and Garden Railways Before 1870....................................5

Chapter 3 ....The Duffield Bank Railway 1874-98...7

Chapter 4 ....Locomotives of the Duffield Bank Railway..............................19

Chapter 5 ....Duffield Bank Railway Rolling Stock 40

Chapter 6 ....The Commercial Impact of Heywood's Early Work................48

Chapter 7 ....The Heywood Family 1872-1897 53

Chapter 8 ....The Eaton Hall Railway..56

Chapter 9 ....The Railway at Doveleys 81

Chapter 10 ......The Role of the Minimum Gauge Railway................................85

Chapter 11 ......Decline and Fall of the Duffield Bank Railway 89

Chapter 12 ......Heywood Equipment on the R.&E.R. 97

Chapter 13 ......The Eaton Railway After 1916 111

Chapter 14 ......The Heywood Legacy and Renaissance...................................122

An Eaton Hall Album 153

Appendices
- 1 131
- 2 133
- 3 135
- 4 141
- 5 141
- 6 144
- 7 146
- 8 148
- 9 150
- 10 151
- Belgrave – An Architectural Study 179

INDEX ix

INTRODUCTION

RITAIN'S RAILWAY HISTORY has been shaped by many distinctive and diverse personalities over the last two centuries and one of most distinctive must surely have been Sir Arthur Heywood. Born in 1849 at Doveleys near Uttoxeter as Arthur Percival Heywood, he was the grandson of a baronet and former M.P. from whom he was destined indirectly to inherit the baronetcy in 1897.

From an early age, he showed an interest in both fortification techniques and railway engineering but he was prevented by the social conventions of the period from pursuing a career either in the Royal Engineers or with one of Britain's then numerous private railway companies. As a result, he was merely able to pursue his railway engineering activities at a purely amateur level and in particular to address two transportation problems of the period. Following his marriage in 1872 he was able to put some of his later theories into practice after settling into his new home at Duffield Bank in Derbyshire, his principal residence for the next twenty-five years.

During the 1860's it had been shown that the steam locomotive could make a useful technological and economic contribution to the working of functional railways constructed to gauges of two feet and less. The leading historical landmarks of the period were the introduction of single wheelbase and articulated 'Double Fairlie' locomotives (respectively in 1863 and 1869) on the 1 FT. 11½ IN. gauge Festiniog Railway under the auspices of Charles Easton Spooner, and the construction of an 18 IN. gauge steam 'works tramway' in the L.N.W.R.'s Old Works at Crewe under John Ramsbottom's direction in 1862.

Prior to the mid-1870's, however, the railway of less than 18 IN. gauge had always been regarded as a toy for the amusement of the well-to-do who owned private estates of sufficient size to lay out such a railway. One miniature line, of unknown dual gauges at Alresford in Hampshire, is recorded as being constructed as early as 1843 although few details of it now survive.

The pursuit of amateur metalwork as a hobby amongst the upper classes was given a major boost after the Great Exhibition of 1851 by the availability of the Holtzappfel ornamental turning lathe, together with its ancillary tools, and the publication by John Jacob Holtzappfel, 'Turning and Mechanical Manipulation'. Sir Arthur's father, Sir Thomas Percival Heywood possessed a Holtzappfel lathe and Sir Arthur certainly used this machine in his early endeavours with toy railways. Unlike his contemporaries, however, he was not content with merely building models. Instead, he decided to experiment with the small gauge railway and to show that it was an economic alternative to the horse and cart for the carriage of loads insufficient to justify the building of a

Sir Arthur Percival Heywood 1849-1916.

functional railway of 18 IN. gauge or greater. This was the rationale behind his choice of a track gauge of 15 INS. for the Duffield Bank Railway and the use of locomotives of a functional nature, rather than their simply being actual or purported scale models of real or imaginary standard gauge main line designs.

The other transportation problem of the period in which Sir Arthur was interested was the design of a suitable locomotive for the Royal Engineers for use on their trench railways. From surviving publications and other records of the 1879-83 period it is clear that Sir Arthur was in close contact with events at the School of Military Engineering at Chatham where tests were being carried out with the unsuccessful 18 IN. gauge Fox Walker 'Handyside' locomotives constructed in 1878. In the design of equipment for the Duffield Bank Railway, Sir Arthur drew not only upon Spooner practice, but also upon lessons learned at Crewe Works, the Royal Arsenal at Woolwich and at the School of Military Engineering.

Despite Sir Arthur's repeated attempts to gain commercial acceptance for his functional 15 IN. gauge railway system,

INTRODUCTION

particularly during the period from 1881-1898, only one external customer was found during his lifetime for a railway of this type and this was the first Duke of Westminster at Eaton Hall. A combination of technical and economic factors, the most important of which was the advent of motorised road transport, helped to put an end to Heywood's ambitions. In its latter years the Duffield Bank Railway became merely an amusement for invited guests, as the earlier small gauge model railways had been, and it was eventually dismantled following Sir Arthur's death in April 1916.

The story of Sir Arthur Heywood and his distinctive railways and railway equipment holds a fascination for many enthusiasts, particularly those whose preoccupation is with the narrow gauge sphere. During their own era the Heywood railways attracted interest from the technical and military press but from the point of view of Sir Arthur's objective of widespread adoption, they could only be regarded as unsuccessful. In more recent times, however, largely as a result of research carried out from the 1960's to the present day, they have acquired a following which has resulted in the preservation of various artifacts, the construction of working locomotive models and most recently the formation of more than one enterprise with the object of building full size replicas of locomotives and other Heywood equipment.

As a result of the accumulation of much relevant and important material unknown to the majority of enthusiasts during recent years, it has been felt appropriate to prepare this new history of the Heywood Railways. For the reader already familiar with the subject, it is hoped that he or she will find interest in a fresh assessment of the efforts of Sir Arthur Heywood's endeavours. For the reader previously unfamiliar with the subject, this volume will offer an insight into one of the more unusual facets of Britain's long and varied railway history.

Mark Smithers *January 1995*

CHAPTER ONE
THE HEYWOOD FAMILY BEFORE 1872

IR BENJAMIN HEYWOOD, BART., who was the first holder of the Heywood Baronetcy, was born on DECEMBER 12TH 1793. During his lifetime he succeeded in building up a highly successful banking business and on OCTOBER 22ND 1816 he married Sophia Ann Robinson. In 1831 he was elected to the House of Commons as a representative for undivided Lancashire but illness forced him to resign his seat during the following year. The Baronetcy was conferred on AUGUST 9TH 1838 as a gesture of gratitude for assistance with the passage of the 1832 Reform Act. Sir Benjamin eventually retired from banking in 1860 and he died on AUGUST 11TH 1865, his wife having predeceased him by nearly thirteen years.

According to the Memoirs of Sir Benjamin's son Thomas Percival, Benjamin Heywood's main residence during most of the 1820's was at Acresfield, a country house situated approximately three miles from Manchester. Upon the death of Benjamin's uncle, Ben Arthur Heywood, Benjamin moved to an even earlier family possession in the form of Claremont which was also situated in the Manchester locality. In 1831 it was decided to purchase a country retreat and the location chosen was Doveleys, then a relatively modest estate situated between Rocester and Norbury in Staffordshire.

Sir Benjamin and Lady Heywood were destined to have fourteen children of which three died in infancy and a further three during 1836, all before attaining the age of twenty. The Baronetcy passed to Thomas Percival Heywood who was born at Acresfield on MARCH 15TH 1823. Important aspects of Sir Thomas Percival Heywood's life were arranged for private publication by his daughter Isabel Mary in 1899 and from the resulting Memoirs it is possible to appreciate much of the early life of, and influences upon, Sir Arthur Percival Heywood.

From a relatively early age, Thomas Percival Heywood took considerable interest in the affairs of the Church of England, donating much wealth during his lifetime to Ecclesiastical causes. In 1841 he went to Trinity College, Cambridge but was unable to complete his degree owing to poor health. In 1844-5 he became a Life Governor of the Royal Agricultural Society and on MAY 19TH 1846 he married his cousin Margaret Heywood. In view of subsequent events, it is important to mention at this stage that Margaret's sister Mary Elizabeth married the Reverend George Henry Sumner, the Rector of Alresford and eventually the Bishop of Guildford.

Sir Thomas Percival's eldest son, Arthur Percival Heywood was born at Doveleys on Christmas Day in 1849 and christened on FEBRUARY 12TH during the following year. He was one of eight children of whom only Francis Graham (1854-1865) was destined to die in childhood, after a short illness.

In the Memoir, there are four letters written by Sir Thomas Percival Heywood to his eldest son during the latter's school days during the mid-1860's (some of which were spent at Eton). The last of these was written from the Rectory at Old Alresford. The Alresford connection with the Heywood family was thus established by this time and it was to have an important influence upon the subsequent life of Arthur Percival Heywood as we shall shortly see.

From the age of seven, Arthur Percival Heywood had shown an interest in metal and other turning and he remembered watching his father performing ornamental turning on a Holtzappfel lathe. This lathe had been bought at Sir H. Fleetwood's sale at Rossall and Sir Thomas had turned an ivory napkin ring on it, which contained a slight inequality. Sir Thomas was rather ashamed of this imperfection and did not persist with the hobby but the lathe and its tools were kept by Arthur Percival until his death in 1916.

At about the age of eleven, Arthur Heywood obtained the only practical instruction in this field that he received during his lifetime. This was from an old fishing rod maker in the skill of chasing metal screw threads.

Recollections by Arthur Heywood about his father in the Memoirs reveal that his father was approached by Major Du Cane in the mid-1860's to allow him to join the Royal Engineers. As early as 1864, Arthur had shown a considerable amount of interest in the subject of fortifications and he subsequently obtained, through the offices of Major Du Cane, a book on this subject. The social conventions of the period dictated, however, whilst a career in the Church, the legal profession or banking was regarded as respectable, an engineering career, be it military or civil, was inappropriate for a member of a family of the Heywoods' standing. Arthur Heywood's interests, therefore, could only be pursued at an amateur level. This did not prevent him from taking a keen interest in the activities of the Royal Engineers during the ensuing decades and these activities were to greatly influence the course of subsequent events at Duffield Bank.

The earliest experiments conducted by Arthur Heywood in the field of small railways were conducted at Dove Leys in the 1860's. Here, with the assistance of his father he set up a workshop in which the tools were driven by a half-horse power steam engine. At the age of eighteen, he completed a 4 IN. gauge brass-railed railway with a steam locomotive weighing some 56 LB. and about a dozen wagons.

CHAPTER 1

In OCTOBER 1868 Arthur Heywood followed in his father's footsteps and went to Trinity College Cambridge to read the then newly established degree of Applied Science. In 1871 he attained a First in this subject and his father's reactions were recorded in the Memoir: 'The degree which Arthur had taken at Cambridge caused us the greatest satisfaction and delight'. I remember my old friend, Captain Gooch, as soon as he saw the class list in the morning papers, came up to our rooms, in Thomas' Hotel, to offer us his warmest congratulations'. Arthur Heywood was less impressed on his own account, however, and recorded in 'Minimum Gauge Railways' in 1898 that: '…in 1871 I had the doubtful credit of appearing alone in the first class. Doubtful because the papers were absurdly simple, and the examiners hardly educated beyond the bare theories of the mechanical processes…'

During his time at Cambridge, Arthur Heywood made several visits to the G.E.R. locomotive sheds there and had illicit turns at locomotive driving. It is also possible that he was present at the experiments carried out on JULY 8TH 1870 on the Festiniog Railway comparing the performances of the locomotives WELSH PONY and LITTLE GIANT operating in tandem with those of the new Fairlie double bogie engine LITTLE WONDER, although this cannot now be shown for certain. It is highly unlikely that he witnessed the earlier locomotive trials carried out on FEBRUARY 12TH 1870 as these would have been within term time at Cambridge. On AUGUST 14TH 1872, Arthur Percival Heywood married his cousin Margaret Effie Sumner, who was the daughter of the Reverend George Henry Sumner previously mentioned. In order to provide a home for the newly married couple, Sir Thomas purchased a house and grounds at Duffield Bank, situated approximately five miles North of Derby. He said of this acquisition: 'There could hardly ever have been a happier purchase, Arthur and Effie made it their home, and each addition and development seems to have endeared it more to them. Arthur's railway and workshop are now known far and wide, and have always been the greatest interest to me'.

The purchase of Duffield Bank ensured that Arthur Heywood now had an extensive site at his own disposal for railway experiments. After the initial settling in period, he lost little time in pursuing these ends.

CHAPTER TWO
ESTATE AND GARDEN RAILWAYS BEFORE 1870

IN THIS CHAPTER IT HAS been decided to set the scene for detailed consideration of Heywood's 15 IN. gauge railways by considering some of the garden railways which existed prior to the commencement of construction of the Duffield Bank Railway. Although the concept of the small gauge steam operated pleasure railway for public amusement, as exemplified by the work of Greenly and Bullock, is associated with the first half of the twentieth century it should be remembered that from the first half of the nineteenth century there were known examples of private small gauge railways constructed for the amusement of their proprietors. As early as MARCH 27TH 1843, the 'Hampshire Chronicle' describes 'a curiosity in railway engineering… now in progress in a meadow in the parish of New Alresford, where Captain Robert Rodney of the Scots Guards has constructed at great expense, a railway in the form of a circle approximately 400 YDS. across… including a tunnel 70 YDS. long, under the trees by the side of the Alton Road… A loco engine and two beautifully finished coaches are being built for the line, which is expected to be opened for use soon after Easter'.

A guide to Alresford of FEBRUARY 1896 referred to 'Lord Rodney's Underground Railway' which had existed 'some few years since' and which was constructed 'on the principle of the present roundabouts now in use at the few remaining fairs' (a possible reference to the circular fairground railways produced by such manufacturers as Fowler and Savage during the late nineteenth and early twentieth centuries). It appears that the line was constructed mostly in a cutting, a view confirmed by Henry Spary, the son of its engineer, Mr. William Spary, in a notebook compiled shortly before the former's death in 1917.

The details given in the notebook are difficult to reconcile with the known facts about the field in which the line was situated, and when referring to the locomotives they are contradictory. It appears that the railway in its mature form was mixed gauge and had two locomotives, one of which was named FORMIDABLE (after the flagship of Captain Rodney's grandfather, Admiral Rodney, at the Battle of the South in 1781) and was constructed by J. Warner & Co. of London. There were approximately ten items of rolling stock, each capable of holding four persons and speeds in operation reached from between 20 and 25 M.P.H.

The Alresford line would have been an interesting example of an early garden railway and it is sad that more exhaustive documentation of it has not currently come to light. The aesthetic properties of the locomotives and rolling stock would have been most definitely 'miniature' in character as the purely functional sub-2 FT. gauge steam locomotive had not evolved at this early stage in railway history. As we have seen, the Heywood family had an Alresford connection even prior to Arthur Percival's marriage in 1872 and it is possible that some the carriages in use at Alresford may have run on a gauge of 15 INS. If Heywood had visited this railway before or at the time of his marriage, then it could have influenced his choice of 15 IN. gauge for the Duffield Bank although this can be only a matter for conjecture.

Another early passenger carrying small gauge garden railway, of which little appears to be known, was referred to in an advertisement in 'The Engineer' for NOVEMBER 26TH 1858: 'For sale – a perfect model engine, tender, two carriages holding 5 or 6 persons, about ¾ mile rails, switches, turntables etc. and engine house. Very complete and new. Power of engine about 1½ H.P. – enquire at Elliot Bros., 30 Strand'. This advert further emphasises the nature of the locomotives and equipment used on garden railways of the period, namely that they were very much examples of early model engineering constructed for no other purpose than amusement.

During the 1860's, as has been recorded elsewhere, a 300 YD. garden railway ran in the woods above Far Sawley in what is now Cumbria. This was owned by the steam launch engineer Charles Fildes and used a long wheelbase 2-2-2 locomotive, LAVINIA, which was rather reminiscent in its appearance to the toy locomotives of the period produced for children. The engine was an early railway application of the cylindrical firebox boiler, a feature which, as we shall see, was to be adopted by Heywood although his inspiration in this field was gained from elsewhere.

During the mid-1860's another estate railway was constructed and this, as with the Alresford line, may have had a an influence upon Heywood's activities at Doveleys and at Duffield Bank.

The Ardkinglas Estate in Argyll, which had a shoreline on Loch Fyne was owned by James Henry Callander M.P. of Craigforth and Ardkinglas prior to his death at the age of 48 in 1851. The estate was inherited by the elder of James Callander's two sons, George Frederick William, who was born in 1848. Estate records show that materials for a narrow gauge railway were being bought in 1866 and an Ordnance Survey Map surveyed in 1870 and published in 1874 shows the Ardkinglas Railway to have been approximately 500 YDS. long at this time. An account of the line appeared in the 'Oban Times' for 9TH OCTOBER 1875: 'During Her Majesty's stay in the West, the Royal Party drove out to Ardkinglas and

5

visited the property of Mr. Callander which comprehends an immense district. Mr. Callander is not only known in the West as a wise and generous landlord but as an enthusiast in mechanical contrivances which at first sight seem to be of little value but which on closer inspection are not only beautiful working models but really useful in various ways. For instance, Mr. Callander has, at considerable expense, erected a model railway nearly a mile in length, along the shore of Loch Fyne. Over this miniature line, a pigmy engine draws a handsome carriage capable of accommodating two persons. At intervals, stations have been erected and the line is worked on the most approved principles, these being on a small scale all the requisites of large railway system. The above carriage was designed and built by a native of Montrose, Mr. Charles Thompson, Coachbuilder, Glasgow. In addition to the above mentioned, Mr. Callander has on his lake models of the Cunard steamers on which one might cross the lake, also men of war, and quite a fleet of boats besides a steamer and sailing yacht'. Another contemporary source describes 'a bijou railway, a mile in length, with stations at intervals, and every railway requisite in miniature' and goes on to describe 'a diminutive engine, of I don't know how many donkey-power – perhaps two – which draws a handsome railway carriage in which two persons can be luxuriously accommodated'.

These accounts indicate that the railway had been enlarged between 1870 and 1875, probably in order to fulfil increased estate transportation needs, and that the carriage was probably 'one passenger wide' (i.e. that the two passengers sat facing one another). The lake on the estate was a representation of the Caspian Sea upon which mock sea battles were fought for the amusement of invited visitors. According to a letter from a Dr. Allan Macartney in the 'Scottish Field' for SEPTEMBER 1952, the station buildings were blown down in a storm on 28TH DECEMBER 1879, the same night as the Tay Bridge disaster. Dr. Macartney apparently saw a small locomotive in a garden, along with some lengths of track, in 1912 and photographed its rusting boiler, sans smokebox, on the shore of Loch Sween at Tayvallich to accompany the letter in 'The Scottish Field'. This engine has been described as an 0-4-0 with a wooden lagged boiler. The boiler at Tayvallich had a depending firebox, apparently waisted-in at the outer wrapper to fit between the mainframes, and a large dome placed centrally on the barrel proper. Any attempt to scale the Tayvallich boiler from the 1952 photograph is likely to be subjective but it would appear to be approximately 18 IN. diameter and a little over four feet long.

The gauge and date of dismantling of the Ardkinglas Railway are not easy to ascertain but it seems probable that it had fallen out of use by 1890. George Callander suffered from mental illness during the last three decades of his life and by 1891 Ardkinglas House was being tenanted by a Mr. Herbert Strutt of Mackeney House near Derby. Local tradition has it that possibly as a result of the legal difficulties inherent in disposing of any of the plant to be found on the estate, the railway's equipment was not disposed of until a few years later and, taking into account locomotive practice of the 1860's and the contemporary descriptions of the carriage, it would appear that the gauge was in the region of 18 INS.

The suggestion that the Arkinglas line was an influence upon Heywood's railways rests upon two basic observations. Firstly George Callander, who finally died in 1916, was a contemporary of Heywood's at Eton in the 1860's and it is possible that the two of them compared notes on the subject of estate railways whilst in their school days. There is at present, however, no known documentary evidence to prove that any such meeting took place but the possibility has never been conclusively disproved.

Secondly, a valuation roll for the County of Argyll for the year 1891/2 shows Sir Thomas Percival Heywood of Doveleys as being tenant of the shootings and lodge at Glenfyne on the Ardkinglas Estate and the fact that Sir Percival enjoyed his visits to Glenfyne during the period from 1891 to 1895 is recorded in the Memoir. As will be discussed later, Sir Thomas was unable to participate in shooting at this late stage and he was simply content to enjoy fishing and other relaxation but nowhere in the Memoir does any reference appear to a small railway on the Ardkinglas estate. It seems probable, therefore, that the little railway had fallen out of use by this stage although it was possibly still in situ. Although the Memoir also records that Sir Thomas made visits to Scotland during the 1866-9 period, it refers in this connection to Deskrie in Aberdeenshire. There is unfortunately no suggestion in any part of the Memoir that Arthur Percival Heywood ever accompanied his father on a visit to Glenfyne during the years prior to 1874, although the possibility cannot be ruled out as the travels of Arthur Percival Heywood are not exhaustively documented. The question also remains as to what prompted Sir Thomas Heywood to rent a portion of the Ardkinglas estate in 1891 as his Scottish holidays during the previous nine years were recorded as being taken at Inveran. Was the decision to rent the shoot at Glenfyne simply a spontaneous consequence of Mr. Callander's illness or had Sir Thomas made previous visits to the Ardkinglas estate? If so, did young Arthur Percival accompany him on any of these visits? If the answer to both these questions is yes, then Arthur would have seen a track gauge of approximately 18 INS. being insufficiently utilised together with a locomotive boiler with a depending firebox and, possibly, a consequently disproportionate rear overhang. Would such observations have prompted him in his quest for an optimum 'minimum gauge' and for locomotives with equal front and rear overhangs? From the historian's point of view there is insufficient evidence to prove that the Ardkinglas Railway was a direct influence upon Heywood's work although this remains an intriguing and tantalising possibility.

CHAPTER THREE
THE DUFFIELD BANK RAILWAY 1874-98

AS A CONSEQUENCE of his early observations, Arthur Heywood decided upon a gauge of 15 IN. for the line that he was to construct at Duffield Bank. In support of his decision to adopt this dimension, Heywood later cited the decision of Paul Decauville to adopt a gauge of 400 MM. (approximately 16 IN.) as the smallest dimension for his portable railway system but two important differences between the two railway systems was to prevail. Firstly, Paul Decauville designed his 16 IN. gauge lines exclusively for use with animal traction or hand motive power whereas Heywood's line at Duffield Bank was to use steam traction from the outset. Secondly, the Duffield Bank Railway was always intended to be 'permanent' rather than 'portable' in nature. A 9 IN. gauge line built at Doveleys was found (as will be seen later) to be adequate in terms of locomotive power but deficient in terms of stability when passengers attempted to ride on the ends or near the edges of carriages.

Duffield Bank was situated on an escarpment on the Eastern bank of the River Derwent by which it was separated from the village of Duffield. The property was to remain Heywood's principal residence until his succession to the Baronetcy in 1897 and the terrain would have presented a major challenge to any prospective railway builder. A view of Duffield Bank taken from the level of the River Derwent circa 1907, but which can not be reproduced here, shows the nature

This view shows EFFIE, probably about 1879, photographed from a position within the original open signal box protecting the southern loop of the Duffield Bank Railway. This box is not shown on the First Edition Ordnance Survey Map surveyed during this period (probably because this would not have shown an unroofed structure) although it certainly existed by this time. The stretch of line which eventually passed through the 'long tunnel' had yet to appear at this stage.
(Courtesy the late Sir Oliver Heywood).

CHAPTER 3

A southwards facing view of Tennis Ground Station circa 1883 showing the waiting shelter and the three road carriage shed. EFFIE is seen on the Eastern loop road with a train consisting of the early experimental wagon with a 6 ft. long floor, two standard 'top' wagons adapted to take bolsters for the carriage of logs, the open twelve seater carriage and the four wheeled brake van. ELLA is shown emerging with the closed sixteen seater carriage from the South tunnel. (Minimum Gauge Railways Plate 1).

of the inclination of the two mile long escarpment. The difference in level between the Duffield Bank Workshops and the eventual course of much of the experimental railway was between 70 and 80 FT.

Construction work on the Duffield Bank Railway commenced in 1874 and the earliest reference to the line in the engineering press appeared in the correspondence section of 'Engineering' for AUGUST 10TH 1877. In this letter, the Duffield Bank Railway was described by Heywood as: 'a short circular line three quarters of a mile in length with 22 LB. rails on a 15 IN. gauge'. The weight of rail quoted in the 1877 letter appears, in the light of later information, to have been the heaviest calibre in use at Duffield Bank at this time and lighter rail sections were also in use.

The course of the railway in its 1879 guise is shown on the First Edition 1:2500 Ordnance Survey Map published in 1881. This is reproduced in an accompanying Figure and shows that by this time the pitch pine trestle viaduct, constructed as a prototype for military railways, was in place and the formation on the northern section had been re-aligned to accommodate it. Two signal posts were in place, of which the northernmost at least appeared to be of a style influenced by Festiniog Railway practice of the period, and two tunnels were present, of which the southernmost was to remain in use until the line's eventual closure.

A letter written by Heywood in 'The Engineer' for JULY 25TH 1879 (and which will receive further consideration in this book) clearly indicates the importance of the influence of C. E. Spooner upon events at Duffield Bank at this time. The relevant extract reads: 'I was once told by Mr. Spooner of the Festiniog Railway that the Duke of Sutherland had expressed great regret to him that he had not known the capacities of a narrow gauge line at the time he planned the railway on his Scotch estates; and I feel sure, from what has been carried out

8

THE DUFFIELD BANK RAILWAY 1874-98

EFFIE with a train, probably taken on completion of the trestle viaduct in 1878.
The leading item of rolling stock is the twelve seater bogie carriage mentioned in Heywood's letter in 'Engineering' in August 1877.
The four wheeled brake van is at the rear of the train, whilst the remaining wagon is probably the early experimental 6 ft. wheelbase wagon.
(Minimum Gauge Railways Plate III).

by others, and from what I have been able to demonstrate on half a mile of line of my own, only 15 IN. gauge, that a railway even narrower, and lighter, than the Festiniog itself, is capable of working with ease and expedition all the traffic that would commonly be required in cases where the standard gauge is out of the question...'.

In describing the Duffield Bank Railway in 'The Engineer' for JULY 15TH 1881, Arthur Heywood stated: 'A certain length of line having been finished, a locomotive, carriages and wagons were built in the writer's amateur workshops, and experiments carried out over several years. Later, the line was extended and developed and a long timber viaduct erected in connection with a scheme for military railways. The workshops, situated 70 FT. below, were connected with a line by a branch having a gradient of 1-IN-10; the total length of the whole, including sidings, being at the present time about a mile; of which half is arranged in the form of a pair of spectacles to admit of a continuous run. The maximum gradients on this part are 1-IN-25 and the minimum curves half a chain. During the last year a six coupled locomotive, with radial axles for traversing sharp curves has been built, and also a closed bogie carriage to hold sixteen persons...'.

During the late 1870's, as will be discussed in the section devoted to D.B.R. locomotives, Heywood followed closely the experiments carried out by the Royal Engineers at Chatham to find a suitable locomotive design for use on 18 IN. gauge trench railways, or 'tramways' as the Royal Engineers termed them, and certain extensions were made to the Duffield Bank Railway. Minute 4847 (2ND MAY 1879) of the Royal Engineers Committee mentions an 18 IN. gauge test railway at Chatham incorporating a circular portion of approximately a mile in length and an approach section with 1-IN-10 and 1-IN-11 gradients. The layout of this line (which included three bridges and several turnouts) certainly influenced Heywood's

CHAPTER 3

A northwards facing view of Tennis Ground Station showing ELLA with a train comprised of nine four wheeled wagons, the early twelve seater carriage and the four wheeled brake van. The early pattern of roofless signal box, situated within the loop, is visible in this view. A distant signal arm has been added to the right hand side of the signal post since the earlier view of EFFIE at Tennis Ground Junction was taken. (Minimum Gauge Railways Plate II).

work at Duffield Bank. From the wording used by Heywood in the Third Edition of 'Minimum Gauge Railways', and from the previously mentioned Ordnance Survey Map, it can be seen that the final formation of approach incline from the Workshops, which incorporated a curve of 25 FT. radius and gradients of 1-IN-10 and 1-IN-12, was probably constructed during 1880. Prior to this date, EFFIE and the early rolling stock had probably been moved up on road vehicles to the experimental 'Main Line' by means of a steep pathway running from the Workshops directly up the escarpment and making a junction with another road which met up with the 'Main Line'. It is only to be presumed that horses were used for haulage up the escarpment, but, given the steep gradient involved, this would have been an extremely hazardous operation. The second locomotive, ELLA would have reached the 'Main Line' from the outset by means of the approach rail incline constructed according to military test principles.

The Duffield Bank Railway in its mature form retained EFFIE's original road-to-rail transit site for the junction between the approach incline and the 'Main Line'. By 1894 at least this junction was close to the halt known as Gorse Station. The experimental line then followed what was basically a figure-of-eight layout (also described, as we have seen, as 'a pair of spectacles'), of which approximately a quarter of a mile was on the level and the remainder of which contained numerous gradients. Much of the railway was built on the site of former quarry workings and the timber viaduct carried its associated section of the line over such terrain. The southernmost loop of the 'Main Line', which included Tennis Ground Station, was constructed inside a large former quarry working and this is very much in evidence in accompanying Plates.

There were three tunnels on the Duffield Bank Railway in its mature form, of which the earliest was situated on the south-eastern portion of the Tennis Ground loop. This was approximately 15 FT. long, being hewn from solid rock and

This photograph, taken by Lt. J.J. Galloway R.E. in 1894, shows ELLA after the engine's first major rebuild circa 1889-91, together with seven four wheeled wagons and the four wheeled brake van. The first two wagons from the engine are standard (5 ft. by 2 ft. 6 in floor space) wagons equipped with two tier 'tops' and loaded with cinders. The next two are wagons of the same type fitted with swivelling bolsters for carrying logs, whilst the fifth wagon from the engine is carrying a heavy load of stone with the aid of only one 'top'. Immediately behind is a larger (5 ft. 9 in. by 2 ft. 9 in. floor space) wagon with a 'top' of approximately 15 in. height, whilst the seventh wagon is once again of the 5 ft. by 2 ft. 6 in. variety with a single tier 'top' but this time carrying an oil tank. This train appears to have been made up to demonstrate the adaptability of the multi purpose Heywood four wheeled wagon. (Minimum Gauge Railways Plate V).

lined with bricks and masonry. Tennis Ground loop had, prior to 1880, been divided into two loops by another much longer tunnel just to the south of the station, but this had been removed by 1881.

The largest tunnel on the mature formation, the 'Long Tunnel', was situated on one of the lines forming the larger loop of the 'Main Line' immediately to the south of a pre-1881 carriage shed. This lined tunnel was approximately 60 FT. in length with a bore 4 FT. wide and it was constructed by the 'cut and cover' method. The precise date of completion of the 'Long Tunnel' is uncertain but this is likely to have been a short time before the Open Session of 1881.

The shortest of the three tunnels on the mature formation, some 12 FT. in length, was situated on Tennis Ground loop between the two smaller bridges. This tunnel was constructed with attractive portals and seems to have been provided in late 1880 or early 1881 as a measure of scenic mitigation for the loss of the earlier long tunnel necessitated by the provision of a single, enlarged, Southern loop at this time. Once again, it was an example of the 'cut and cover' principle.

Initially, the permanent way used on the Duffield Bank Railway consisted of 14 LB. rails without fishplates and spiked to elm and Spanish chestnut sleepers. These sleepers were 5 in. wide, 2 IN. deep and 2 FT. 6 IN. long and they were set at 1 FT. 6 IN. between centres. By 1877, this arrangement had been found to be unsatisfactory as the 12 CWT. maximum axle loading was taking too great a toll on the trackwork. It was therefore decided to re-lay the 'Main Line' with sleepers 6½ IN. wide 2½ IN. deep and 3 FT. long. The rail sections in use in 1881 varied in calibre from 9 LB./YARD to 22 LB./YD although by 1898 only four different sizes were in use: 12, 14, 18 and 22 LB. per yard. The sleeper length, Heywood thought,

CHAPTER 3

MURIEL with a train on Tennis Ground loop, probably during the latter half of 1894. From left to right the rolling stock consists of the 1881 sixteen seater; the dining car; the sleeping car and the bogie brake van. (Minimum Gauge Railways Plate VI).

was a factor of considerable importance and he felt that a sleeper should project beyond the rail a distance of rather more than half the track gauge. This was so as to obtain an adequate supporting moment on the side of the rails external to the track gauge to prevent the sleeper assuming a curvilinear shape in use. The centre spacing of the sleepers on the re-laid road varied from 1 FT. 6 IN. for rail of a 12 LB. section to 3 FT. for rail of a 22 LB. section. The joints on the revised permanent way formation were effected by means of fish-plates laid on the sleeper and concurrent with their counterparts on the opposite rail (on this point, Heywood was adamant as he was extremely critical of cross-jointed permanent way). The design of sleeper latterly in use on most of the revised Duffield Bank system was of unusual in the fact that it was of cast iron. Possibly influenced by the use of this material in tests carried out by the Royal Engineers in 1880 (see R.E. Committee Minute 5449 concerning the Travis/Day system of cast iron sleepers), Heywood decided to test its load bearing capabilities at Duffield Bank and evolved a design of 28 LB. sleeper with integrally cast rail chairs. The rail was secured in the chair by means of a steel spring. In use, Sir Arthur recorded in 1898 that with a 14 LB. steel rail and sleepers spaced at 2 FT. 3 IN. centres and 1 FT. 3 IN. either side of the suspended fishplates the road would be able to stand axle loadings of $1/4$ TONS with relatively little wear. He also stated that such track at Duffield had needed little in the way of repairs in five years despite constant service during that period.

In order to obtain the concurrent fish-plate arrangement which Heywood wanted, he would order a proportion of his rails some 3 IN. to 6 IN. shorter than the rest, depending on the desired curve radius. For weights of up to 18 LB./YD. he found a basic stock rail length of 15 FT. to be convenient.

Three basic methods were employed on the Duffield Bank Railway to shape rails to the required configuration on curved stretches of track. Where the rail length was relatively long and the curve was of relatively large radius (i.e. greater than 110 FT. for 14 LB. rail and 220 FT. for rail of 18 LB. section), it

12

THE DUFFIELD BANK RAILWAY 1874-98

A specially posed view of ELLA and a train on the 'hairpin bend' portion of the incline leading from the Workshops to the 'Main Line'. This train, which would have weighed in excess of five tons, could not have been hauled by the engine over this stretch of the Duffield Bank Railway. (Minimum Gauge Railways Plate IV).

was possible to screw the fish-plates up tight and spring the rail. The drawback with this practice was that the joints at the fish-plates tended to work into a dog-leg shape under the influence of traffic and changes in temperature. The second method of rail bending was by means of a rail press wagon. This wagon was also equipped with a drilling machine for fish-plate bolt holes, additional tool-boxes and a brake. The rail press screw worked in a horizontal plane and the rail was run on adjustable rollers at each end of the wagon. The screw would then be applied at the required intervals to give a curve that was, in reality, a succession of dog-legs but these would not normally be perceptible if the pressure intervals were greater than 1 FT. 2 IN. apart. For relatively sharp curves a three-roller bender was employed and this, Heywood claimed, was of a type designed by him for field railway experiments by the Royal Engineers (probably during the 1870's). The use of a vehicle of this type is indicative, once again, of the influence of Charles Easton Spooner as Spooner had designed a four-roller rail bending trolley for use on the Festiniog Railway. The use of sleepers more than twice the track gauge in length, referred to earlier, was justified by Heywood in "The Engineer" for JULY 15TH 1881 by reference to the use of 4 FT. 6 IN. long sleepers on the Festiniog Railway. As will be seen in other parts of this volume, much of Heywood's work was influenced by Spooner and other contributors to the two main engineering journals of the period, 'The Engineer' and 'Engineering'.

On the Duffield Bank system, the curves on the experimental 'Main Line' were as sharp as 40 FT. radius whilst the 'hairpin bend' on the approach line from the Workshops incorporated a minimum radius curve of 25 FT. and curves in sidings could be as tight as 15 FT. One of the major engineering features of the Duffield Bank line was the previously mentioned pitch pine viaduct. The inspiration behind the viaduct was John Barraclough Fell's elevated trestle railway which was tested by the Royal Engineers at Aldershot in 1872-3, but Heywood dismissed this line as 'a hopelessly inconvenient and ridiculous plan'. The viaduct at

13

Duffield Bank was constructed of pitch pine and it is to be presumed (and this assumption is supported by photographic evidence) that the meaning of Heywood's statement that 'each (trestle) member is a multiple of the height' was that the angle of the side members in relation to the horizontal was kept constant, regardless of the trestle height. One important difference between the trestles used by Heywood and those used at Aldershot for larger clearances was that the side-members on the former were not vertical throughout any portion of their height (this was probably the principal reason behind Heywood's belief that his trestle was an improvement over Fell's design). As originally constructed, the roadway on the viaduct was carried on four timbers 11 IN. deep and 3 IN. wide. These were bolted together in pairs so that one pair supported each rail. The two pairs of timbers were kept parallel by stretchers and through bolts positioned at 5 FT. intervals. The trestles were approximately 15 FT. apart and within each pair, the roadway timbers broke joint with each other on alternate trestles so that the unit length of roadway timbers was approximately 30 FT. It was possible for these timbers to be 'run forward' during construction without the aid of scaffolding and the method of assembly mitigated the effect of a single trestle trying to sink out of alignment when under load.

The cost of the original viaduct was £30 including every item of expenditure and its average height was 15 FT. The connections between timbers were made entirely by means of bolts and cast angle-plates (this latter constructional feature is interesting in the light of the fact the Royal Engineers Committee had expressed a preference for wrought iron brackets in correspondence with the Inspector-General of Fortifications concerning Fell's system). Two carpenters completed construction of the trestles within five days and, with the assistance of three labourers, completed the remaining work to enable the viaduct to be ready for traffic within three further days. A platform and railing were added after initial construction for the convenience of pedestrians and shortly after the completion of the eight coupled locomotive MURIEL in 1894, the roadway timbers were upgraded to a section 13 IN. deep and 3½ IN. wide, the original trestles being retained. It is also possible that the viaduct was re-aligned at this stage in order to accommodate a revised track formation at its northern end.

At the time of its eventual removal, as per the 1916 Auction Catalogue, the viaduct was described as being 89 FT. long and with an upper width of 4FT. 6 IN. The pedestrian right of way was facilitated by 107 cross planks each 9 IN. by 2 IN. by 4 FT. 6 IN. and the five trestle supports had an average height of 12 FT. 6 IN. The base timber of each trestle was 12 FT. wide and 11 IN. by 6 IN. section, the side members each 12 FT. 6 IN. by 8 IN. BY 6 IN., whilst the stay members were 4 IN. square section and each trestle used, according to the catalogue, 36 FT. of this material, although the one surviving relevant photograph does not appear to support this proposition. One modification necessitated by the fitting of the cross boards in 1894 was that the rails needed to be supported on these items rather than directly by the road timbers. By 1916 each running rail had an angle iron guard (1¾ IN. by 1¾ IN. by ¼ IN.) and these were held in place by thirteen 2 FT. long cross-ties of 2½ IN. by 1½IN. by ⅜ IN. T-section, presumably fitted in the inverted position with the apex of the T located between cross boards. The quoted figure of 178 linear feet of angle iron suggests that only the outer sides of the rail were protected by guard irons.

In addition to the long viaduct, there were two further pitch pine bridges. These were also described in the 1916 catalogue and one of these was of the trestle pattern and crossed a gully. This bridge was 24 FT. long and 1 FT. 8 IN. wide, whilst the road timbers were of 11 IN. by 4 IN. section. The two trestle supports were 7 FT. high with side members of 7 IN. by 5 IN. section and 3½ IN. square section stays.

The other bridge was a simple cantilever and crossed the pedestrian route from Duffield Bank House to the Tennis Ground. As with the long viaduct in its final form, this was 4 FT. 6 IN. wide, although there was no pedestrian access rail. Its quoted length in 1916 was a mere 9 FT., which is not consistent with an early surviving illustration showing the locomotive EFFIE at this location. The cross-boarding, as per the 1916 description consisted of 16 planks each 8 IN. by 2½ IN. by 4 FT. 6 IN., whilst the full length road timbers were of 9 IN. by 4½ IN. section. Unlike the long viaduct, the 42 quoted linear feet of angle iron (together with a similar amount of supporting flat iron) suggests that both sides of each rail were protected by guards. There were ten T iron cross-ties.

Semaphore signalling was employed on the Duffield Bank Railway along with interlocking signals and points for the important junctions. Heywood appears to have been an enthusiast for semaphore signalling even before the second locomotive, ELLA, was constructed as the signals at this stage were useful as point indicators. No signal boxes are shown on the First Edition Ordnance Survey Map, but by the time of surveying the Second Edition (1898), a signal box was shown at Manor Copse Station. Photographic evidence shows that this was an enclosed structure with externally visible timber framing, certainly influenced by Midland Railway practice. A similar signal box, situated just to the north west of Tennis Ground Junction, appears in an Edwardian photograph and on the Third Edition Ordnance Survey Map surveyed in 1913 but this had certainly been preceded by an earlier open-topped box situated in the vee of the junction and probably constructed before 1879. This was constructed to give an attractive 'Mock Tudor' appearance and the waiting shelter at Tennis Ground Station was given a similar styling, although this building was provided with a flat roof. The 1916 catalogue stated that one of the later signal boxes had seven levers and the other eleven, whilst there were latterly twelve signals and nine gradient posts. The two signal boxes are recorded as being linked by telephonic communication by 1898 and it

THE DUFFIELD BANK RAILWAY 1874-98

would seem that this facility was utilised as part of signalling practice during the last two decades of the line's existence.

Of the stations on the line, the most ostentatious was Tennis Ground, which boasted not only a passing loop but also the signal boxes mentioned above and a three road carriage shed. This latter building was described in 1916 as being 45 FT. by 19 FT. in ground area with a corrugated iron double slope roof and two skylights.

Further rolling stock accommodation was provided at Manor Copse Station where the eastern side of a passing loop was covered by a shed. The corrugated iron roof of this shed was described in 1916 as being 76 FT. 6 IN. by 17 FT. 6 IN. whilst the wooden boarding consisted of 105 linear feet of 9 IN. by 3 IN. timbers and 300 linear feet of 7 IN. by 2½ IN. timbers. There were twelve upright supports of 5 IN. square section.

By 1913 the passing loop had been relegated to the status of a siding and an alternative Northern turning loop had been created by reinstating the disused pre-1881 track formation in that vicinity.

The 1916 Auction Catalogue records the existence of a shed at Gorse Station, this being approximately 41 FT. by 10 FT. 9 IN. at ground level, a corrugated iron roof and wood supports of three different calibres: 53 linear feet at 7 IN. by 2½ IN.; 41 linear feet at 7 IN. by 2 IN. and 82 linear feet at 4½ IN. by 3 IN. This structure is also recorded as a large pair of folding doors and a glazed front partition 43 FT. 6 IN. wide and 7 FT. high.

There were, by 1898, a total of six stations on the Duffield Bank Railway: Tennis Ground, Manor Copse, The Rough, Viaduct, Gorse and Edgehill. It is not certain from surviving evidence precisely when each of them came into use but a 'slow' train run during the visit of Lt. J. J. Galloway R.E. in 1894 is recorded as making four stops and so it may be that only two of the four smaller stations (Gorse and The Rough) were in use for demonstration purposes at this stage. The practice of only using four stations for demonstration 'slow' trains was adhered to on JULY 27TH 1898 for the visit by representatives of the Institution of Mechanical Engineers in order to gather information for the Leslie S. Robertson Paper, 'Narrow Gauge Railways – Two Feet and Under'. Whilst the names of four of the D.B.R. stations were self explanatory in relation to the railway's terrain, it should be mentioned that Manor Copse and Edgehill both took their names from neighbouring properties; the former referring to Duffield Bank House proper (which was situated to the north-west of Heywood's property) and the latter to a property situated almost due south from the Duffield Bank Railway.

Duffield Bank Workshops

The First Edition Ordnance Survey Map shows that the bulk of the structure of Duffield Bank Workshops had been completed by 1879. This was doubtless a consequence of the fact that workshops were required to produce the equipment necessary for the operation of the railway and also certain other items necessary for the maintenance of the Duffield Bank estate and other Heywood family properties. In 1898, the Workshops at Duffield Bank were described in the Third Edition of Minimum Gauge Railways and this description is reproduced below.

'The machine-shop contains an 11 IN. lathe for wheel turning, cylinder boring, and the heavier work; an 8 IN. lathe for surfacing, sliding and general work; a 7 IN. lathe for screw cutting and fine work; a 4 IN. Pittler universal lathe with a variety of automatic and other fittings, chiefly used for smaller brass work, such as cocks, glands, lubricators, etc.; a 3 IN. sliding and screw-cutting lathe, for very light work; a

This view shows ELLA with a passenger train consisting of at least the four sixteen-seater open carriages and the 1881 closed coach. The photograph was probably taken during the 1894 'Open Session'. (Courtesy F. Wilde Collection).

planing machine to take work 4 FT. by 1 FT. 6 IN. by 1 FT. 6 IN.; an 8 IN. stroke double table shaping machine, fitted for hollow and circular shaping, specially used for machining coupling rods, etc.; a 4½ IN. shaping machine with circular motion, for light work; a milling machine; a 9 IN. stroke slotting machine with compound table, for heavy work; a 2½ IN. spindle drilling and boring machine; a 1¾ IN. drilling machine, for general work; a screwing and tapping machine, to 1½ IN. for bolts and 2 IN. for pipes; a cold-sawing machine to cut iron up to 2½ IN. square; a slot drilling machine; a twist drill grinding machine; two grindstones, three bench vices, and complete sets of screwing tackle and fitters' tools.

The smith's shop contains two fires, of which one is blown by a fan, and is suited for the heavier work; anvils for ordinary purposes and also for treatment of angle iron, etc.; a 2½ CWT. gas hammer; a punching and shearing machine; a bench vice, and complete set of smith's tools.

The erecting shop contains an overhead travelling crane; an engine pit; a 30 TON hydraulic press for putting axles into wheels, crank pins into cranks, testing samples, etc.; a hand screwing and tapping machine to ¾ IN. for bolts and to 1 IN. for pipes; standards for fitting up frame-plates; a rivet heating forge; two bench vices, and tools for tube extracting and other special processes connected with the construction and repair of locomotives.

The iron-foundry contains a 16 IN. cupola worked through a double tuyere by a 'Root's' blower; an overhead travelling crane; a core stove; charge-weighing scales; a large supply of boxes for general purposes, and special ones for cylinders, chilled-wheels, sleepers, gutters, etc., with all ladles and other appliances suitable for producing castings up to half-a-ton weight. Especial pains have been taken to turn out chilled wheels (13½ IN. diameter), for the rolling stock, of perfect smoothness and even depth of chill.

The brass foundry contains a furnace, a metal moulding bench, and the usual fittings.

The carriage shop has two lines of 15 IN. gauge formed of cast plates bolted together and bedded in concrete, and contains a wood morticing and boring machine; fitters and joiners' vices, with every convenience for erecting, finishing and painting two of the 20 FT. bogie cars simultaneously, or eight of the standard wagons, according to requirements; all bulky joiners' and carpenters' work is also done in this shop.

The pattern and joiners' shop contains a 5 IN. Holtzappfel lathe; and a small circular saw; 2 instantaneous grip vices; saw tooth-setting machine; and a variety of other special appliances, in addition to a full set of joiners' tools.

The saw-shed contains a 30 IN. circular saw bench; a band saw; a small general joiner; an 11 IN. planing machine, and a small emery grinder.

The engine house contains an 8 H.P. Otto gas-engine, of which the water circulation is effected by a small centrifugal pump.

The drawing office is fitted up with the usual appliances, and is in telephonic communication with my house and two of the stations on the railway.

The general stores comprise timber; foundry sand of various quantities; five kinds of pig-iron; copper, spelter, tin, etc.; bar, rod and angle iron; wrought iron tubing up to 2 IN.;

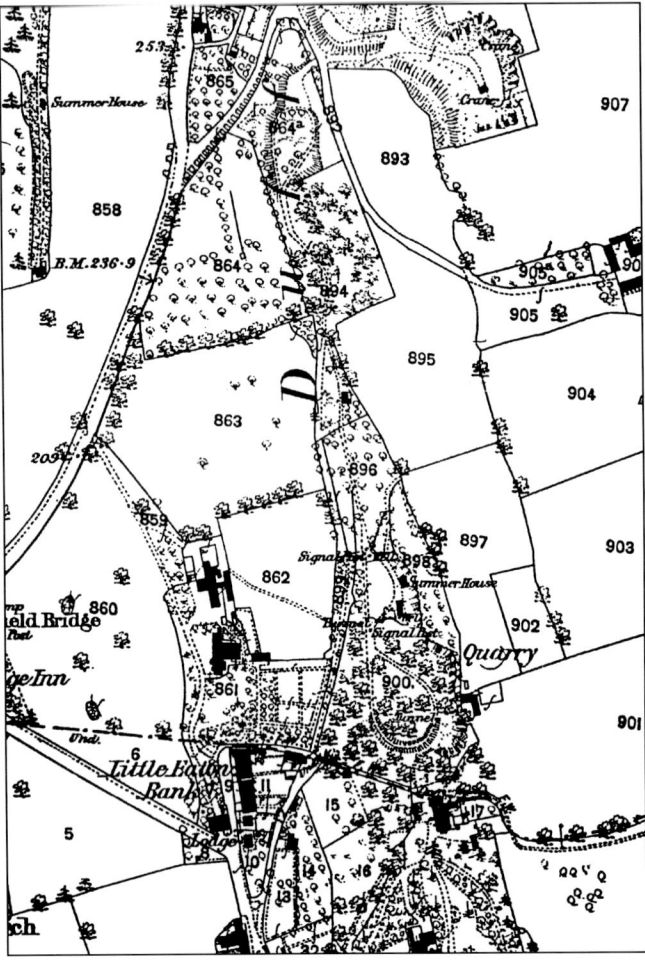

Figure 1. Duffield Bank and its surrounding area as shown in the Ordnance Survey Map of 1881. As this map was surveyed in 1879 it shows the course of the Duffield Bank Railway immediately after the construction of the viaduct. The track formation consisted at this stage of three basic loops, the centre one of which appears to have been 'double' (this latter feature being retained in the later formation). Access from the Workshops to the 'Main Line' at this time appears to have been gained by means of a steeply inclined pathway leading onto a gently curved approach road which met the 'Main Line' at what eventually became Gorse Junction. The booking office and waiting shelter of Tennis Ground Station are shown as a 'Summer House', whilst sheds for rolling stock (and presumably at this time also for EFFIE) are shown at Tennis Ground and just north of the eventual site of the 'Long Tunnel'. Two wells are shown close to the Station at Tennis Ground and these may have been EFFIE'S original water supply. The original course of the line, as first used by EFFIE in 1875, would have been similar to that shown here with the exception that the quarry working bridged by the viaduct would have been by-passed on its westernmost side. The 'by-pass' section of track was subsequently reinstated and the viaduct and its northern feeder line re-aligned by 1898.

THE DUFFIELD BANK RAILWAY 1874-98

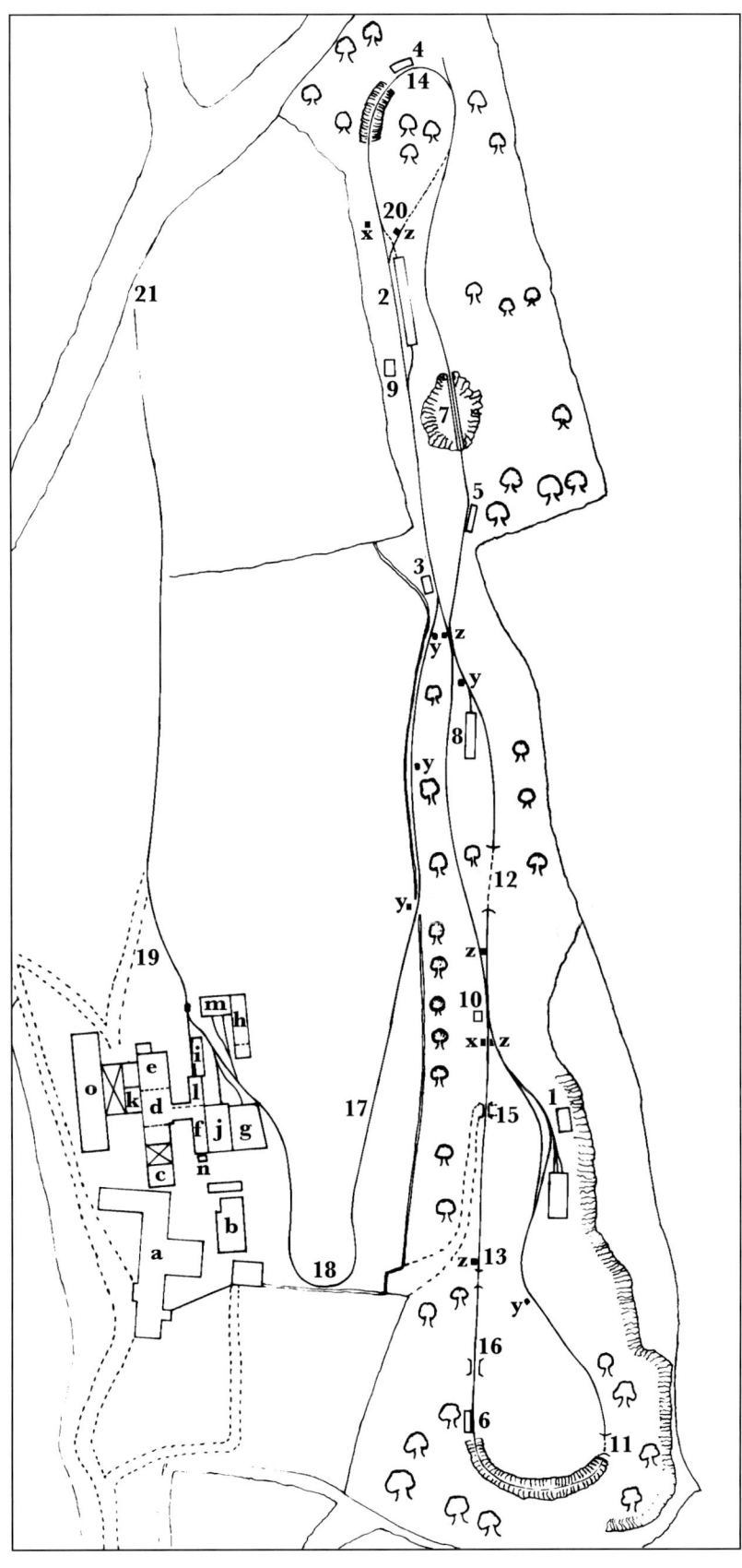

Figure 2. The Duffield Bank Railway in its mature form as extracted from the Second and Third Editions (surveyed respectively in 1898 and 1913) of the 1:2500 County Ordnance Survey Map. The numbered and lettered sections are described below.
No's. 1-6 (Stations): 1. Tennis Ground (oldest and largest station, constructed during 1875-9 period);
2. Manor Copse (second largest station which was, as with Tennis Ground, provided with rolling stock accommodation); 3. Gorse; 4. The Rough;
5. Viaduct; 6. Edgehill. So far as is known, No's. 4-6 were effectively just halts with platforms and never possessed any passenger accommodation.
No. 7: Viaduct constructed in 1878 as a prototype for Royal Engineers requirements. This was strengthened during the last quarter of 1894 following the completion of the locomotive MURIEL.
No. 8: Carriage shed constructed before 1879 and altered by 1898.
No's. 9, 10: Signal boxes, respectively at Manor Copse and Tennis Ground. Manor Copse signal box had been completed in its enclosed form by 1896 but the later enclosed signal box at Tennis Ground was probably not completed until about 1900. This replaced the earlier open box constructed about 1876, which does not appear on any of the Ordnance Survey maps.
No's. 11-13 (Tunnels): 11. South Tunnel (the oldest survivor of the three on the mature layout and cambered to match the superelevation of the rails);
12. Long Tunnel; 13 Short Tunnel.
No. 14: Northern loop upper curve incorporating 40 ft. radius stretch and gradient of 1-in-47.
No's. 15, 16 (small bridges): 15 simple cantilever spanning pedestrian access to the tennis ground; 16 trestle bridge spanning a gully. No. 17: 1-in-12 test incline originally constructed in 1880 for military-style locomotive testing. No. 18: 25 ft. radius test curve ('hairpin bend').
No. 19: Course taken by grooved flagstones, possibly linked at one stage to the D.B.R. proper.
No. 20: Alternative track configurations for 1898 and 1913. The northern portion of the Manor Copse run-around loop had been removed by 1913 in order to allow the re-instatement of a pre-1881 formation which crossed its course. No. 21: The probable site of the six ton transhipment crane. a:-The Heywood family's residence at Duffield Bank. b:-Squash Courts. c:-Design Office incorporating glass canopy. d:-Setting Out Room. e:-Machine Shop. f:-Locomotive Erecting Shop. g:-Carriage Erecting Shop. h:-Mess Room and Timber Store. i:-Smithy. j:-Foundry. k:-Joiners' Shop. l:-Gas Engine, House and Sawmill. m:-Engine Shed. n:-Weighbridge. o:-Farm buildings, separated from Joiners' Shop by a glass canopy. x:-Signal post on map surveyed in 1898 but not on the map surveyed in 1913. y:-Signal post on maps surveyed both in 1898 and 1913. z:-Signal post on map surveyed in 1913 only. (Author).

DUFFIELD BANK RAILWAY

CHAPTER 3

bolts, rivets, nuts, and pins; steam fittings of all kinds; every sort of requisite needed in the construction of small railways and rolling stock, and also for meeting house and farm requirements.

The pattern store contains patterns for all the locomotive, carriage, wagon, signal, permanent way, and general experimental work; and for drain grates, gutters, etc. which are supplied from Duffield for my other estates.

The shops are lit by gas, and the 15 IN. gauge line runs throughout. The construction, both in wood and iron, is done as far as possible to template, and every endeavour is made to turn out the very best work, which is perhaps the more easily attained in that there are no profits to be considered. At the same time it should be explained that the shops and machinery are, throughout, though good and sufficient for their purpose, in no way models of excellence. Their object is only to turn out the chiefly experimental work required, and the gradual additions that have been made during the twenty-five years of their existence have been done as cheaply as was consistent with efficiency.

Outside the shops are a weigh-bridge for weighing rolling stock and loads, and a six-ton crane to tranship heavy goods from drays to the 15 IN. gauge railway.

Adjoining the Workshops is the locomotive shed, with rails raised 30 IN. above the floor, so as to get more easily at the lower parts of these small engines. It is arranged for two locomotives, and is fitted with an air jet for raising steam, and with a water supply.

The carriage and wagon stock is, for the most part, housed in three sheds at various stations on the main part of the railway, 80 FT. above the workshops.

The layout of facilities within the Workshops is shown in an accompanying Figure which also shows that by 1898 a line had been constructed linking the Workshops with an adjacent public road. The date of construction of this line is not easy to ascertain but it was certainly prior to 1895, when the crane was required to assist with the transfer of ELLA to the Eaton Railway, and may (for a reason to be considered) have been as early as 1882. The photograph showing the newly completed parcels van for Eaton Hall in 1896 was taken on this stretch of track.

Certain additional information relating to the workshops can be gleaned from the 1916 Auction Catalogue. The gas engine was a Crossley product and drove onto the primary line shafting (1¾ IN. diameter) in the saw mill. From here, it can be inferred, the drive was taken to a secondary set of line shafting in the machine shop. The weighbridge had a plate – 4 FT. by 2 FT. 6 IN. – with rails laid on and a non-weighted headstock. It was manufactured by W. & T. Avery. The 5 TON transfer hand crane had a wooden jib, a baseplate bedded in concrete and was manufactured by R. C. Gibbins & Co.

A feature of note shown on the Second Edition Ordnance Survey Map (surveyed in 1898) is the course of a line apparently linking the farm building area with the road transfer line. Surviving remains show that a substantial part, at least, of this track was comprised of flagstones with grooves of 15 IN. distance between outer edges. This would have been a short handworked farm tramway, possibly using only one wagon and possibly not permanently linked to the D.B.R. system proper. Its course is marked on the accompanying Figure.

Amongst Heywood artifacts surviving at the time of writing is one of lathes from Duffield Bank Workshops. This was acquired by a U.S.-based purchaser during the 1970's and has a plate bearing the inscription 'A. P. Heywood, Duffield'. The lathe is currently in the care of the Riverside and Great Northern Railway Preservation Society, Wisconsin Dells, Wisconsin.

Figure 3. This notice was displayed at the site of the Duffield Bank Railway in readiness for the visit of members of the Institution of Mechanical Engineers on Wednesday 27th July 1898. As had been the case when Lt. Galloway visited the line four years previously, only four stops were made during the run although Sir Arthur Heywood recorded that six stations (including 'Edgehill' and 'Viaduct' not mentioned here) were in use at this time. The locomotive in steam to operate the train would have been MURIEL as ELLA was undergoing rebuilding in the workshops at this stage. (Collection W. J. Milner).

CHAPTER FOUR
LOCOMOTIVES OF THE DUFFIELD BANK RAILWAY

Arthur Percival Heywood with the newly completed EFFIE at Duffield Bank in 1875. This view illustrates the constructional features of the locomotive, such as the inside mainframes, outside cylinders and back dome boiler. The curved rail at the rear of the footplate is rather reminiscent of the one fitted to the 18 inch gauge Manning Wardle engine BURGOYNE, purchased by the School of Military Engineering at Chatham in 1873, but without a central pillar. In the background is the subsequent site of Tennis Ground waiting room and booking office, which was constructed at some stage between 1875 and 1879. The photograph also shows that the northern sub-loop at the Tennis Ground end of the line had a passing loop (the tunnel dividing the two sub loops at the Tennis Ground end of the line had been removed by 1881 and the two sub loops were replaced a single larger loop). EFFIE is standing on the approach line to the shed.
(Minimum Gauge Railways Plate XII).

N 1875 ARTHUR PERCIVAL HEYWOOD completed his first locomotive and it was named EFFIE after his wife. With construction of the Duffield Bank Railway already in progress it is perhaps not surprising that a relatively simple design of locomotive was chosen and the completed engine was of the 0-4-0 tank configuration. When assessing Heywood's work, it should be remembered that of the 18 IN. gauge functional steam operated systems which had been in use in the United Kingdom by 1875 and described in 'The Engineer' or 'Engineering', only the Aldershot system had by that time used a locomotive with more than two axles and this was of a peculiar design. This observation must have been in Heywood's mind at the time of writing his article in 'The Engineer' in 1881 as at that stage he still advocated a four wheeled locomotive in most instances for use on a narrow gauge railway of the type with which he had been experimenting.

Although relatively simple in design, EFFIE possessed some interesting features. Even at this relatively early stage in Heywood's amateur railway engineering career, he had a preoccupation with the view that narrow gauge locomotives should have fully adhesive wheel arrangements and equal overhangs at either end. Being an 0-4-0, EFFIE naturally

19

CHAPTER 4

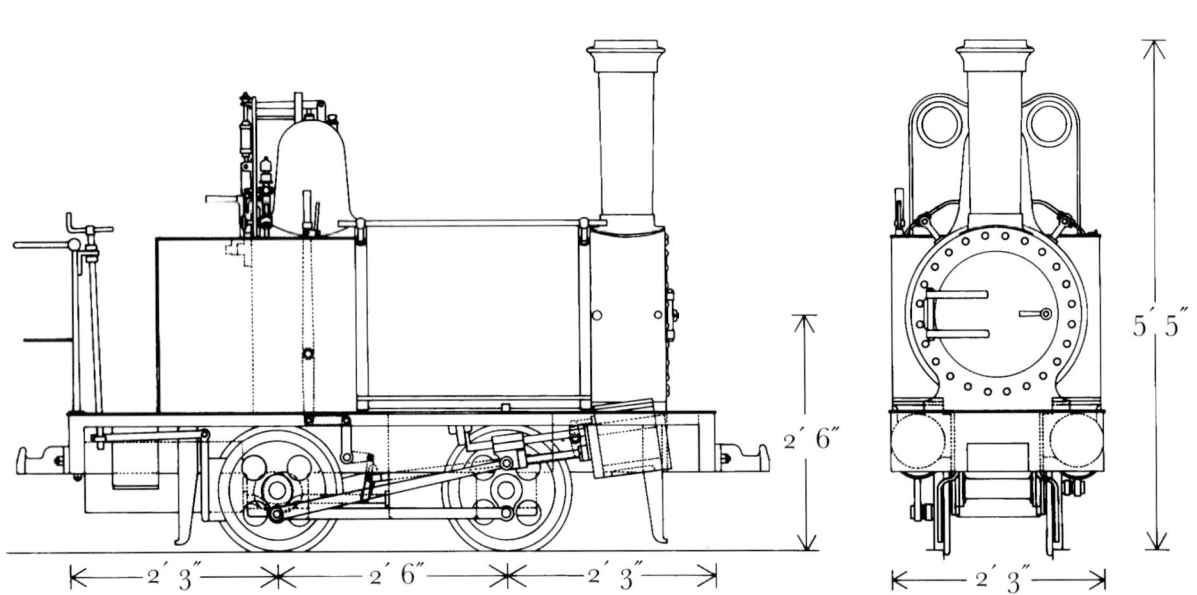

EFFIE

SCALE 1: 24

© MARK SMITHERS 11/93

Figure 4. A reconstructed side and front elevation view of EFFIE. From photographic evidence it can be seen that two of the three frame stretchers were water tanks (which would have required an interconnecting pipe beneath the rear axle). The upper surface of the rear tank effectively constituted a dropped footplate between the mainframes (another feature copied from BURGOYNE?) whilst two tubular recesses would have passed through the forward tank in order to take the valve gear rods linking the die blocks to the rocker shafts. The steamchest proportions are strongly suggestive of the proposition that there was no 'headroom' between the top of the slide valve and the inner surface of the steamchest lid (an effective prototype for the steam brake control valves used post-1889 on Heywood locomotives). Owing to the need for the die block to rocker shaft rods to be restrained in a linear travel, the rocker shaft bellcrank upper and lower holes would have been of an elongated configuration (was the same true of the Fowler locomotive HERCULES?). Close examination of photographs indicates that 24 pairs of staggered rivets secured the smokebox frontplate to the boiler/smokebox barrel. Only one of these rivets passing through the barrel is shown in the drawing as it would be easy for any prospective modeller to ascertain the position of the remaining 23. Similarly, only one of the front tubeplate rivets is shown, but as it can be discerned that there were 36 of these, it is once again an easy task to 'mark off' the remaining 35. Sadly, few rear footplate details are currently available for EFFIE and there is insufficient evidence from which to construct a rear elevation. The width of the boiler backhead is evidence to suggest that the injectors were mounted on the rear of this backhead and that the clack valves were also mounted there (this latter proposition is contrary to HERCULES but consistent with LITTLE BEAUTY). The early Fowler sub-2 ft. gauge locomotives, together with ELLA as built, offer the best guide to the rearward appearance of EFFIE. (Author).

satisfied the first of these criteria but the chassis of the engine was also designed so as to satisfy the second, giving a wheelbase of 2 FT. 6 IN. and an overhang at each end of 2 FT. 3 IN. from the wheel centre to the outer face of the timber bufferbeam. In order to ensure that no constraints were placed upon the wheelbase dimensions by reason of the firebox, EFFIE's boiler possessed a firebox of the non-depending variety similar to the design adopted by John Ramsbottom on his 18 IN. gauge Crewe Works locomotives and on some standard gauge 0-4-0T's (such as the preserved No. 1439). Heywood acknowledged his debt to Ramsbottom as regards boiler design (cylindrical firebox and slide valve regulator in the dome) but in the absence of further evidence it cannot be ascertained today whether his primary influence was the standard or 18 IN. gauge locomotives. The former were featured in a fine 'portfolio' drawing in 'The Engineer' whilst the latter appeared in a drawing in 'Engineering' in 1866. Unlike either of the previously mentioned Ramsbottom designs, however, EFFIE's boiler was of the back dome variety. The dome was surmounted by a Salter safety valve whose lever passed over the top of the spectacle plate.

The boiler barrel was made integral with the smokebox and, unique amongst the Heywood locomotives, EFFIE was fitted with a smokebox door of flat section with an externally mounted hinge. The total length of the combined boiler barrel and smokebox assembly was 4 FT. 6 IN. and its diameter was 1 FT. 10 IN. EFFIE's 23 boiler tubes were arranged so as to give vertical rows arranged in a 4:5:5:5:4 configuration. Unlike subsequent Heywood 15 IN. gauge locomotives, the steampipe union would have been within the smokebox and the steampipe arrangement symmetrical. This was because no displacement lubricator was fitted.

As regards the chassis, EFFIE was fitted with disc wheels of 1 FT. 3½ IN. diameter and the cylinders were 4 IN. bore and

Figure 5. An engraving of EFFIE first published in 'Engineering' in 1881.

6 IN. stroke. The steam chests were mounted directly above the cylinders and the valves were actuated through rocker shafts connected to inside motion of the Stephenson/Howe variety. Unfortunately, precise details of the rocker shafts do not appear to have survived and the known illustrations of EFFIE do not shed any light upon the manner of their configuration. They would appear to have had overhung bellcrank drive to the valve rods, rather than the underhung arrangement used later by Kerr, Stuart & Co. Ltd. Springing on EFFIE, as on subsequent Heywood locomotives, consisted of thick pads of India rubber fitted into the hornblocks above the axleboxes. The use of this material, as with the boiler design, suggested possible Ramsbottom/Crewe Works influence although Heywood did not acknowledge such influence in relation to the rubber springing. According to the letter in 'The Engineer' for JULY 25TH 1879, the working play for EFFIE's springing was ¼ IN. and the wheel flanges were ⅝ IN. deep. The engine had at this stage run over 2,000 miles.

According the 'The Engineer' for JULY 15TH 1881, the handbrake fitted to EFFIE was found in service to be too slow in its action and a tender was constructed for the engine with a much faster action brake. No details or illustrations of this tender have currently come to light but its main significance was in the fact that subsequent Heywood 15 IN. gauge locomotives were provided with steam braking at the time of their construction.

Heywood was critical of a number of features of EFFIE, not least in the standard of finish (which was dictated by the use of much material readily available during construction) and the heating surface which he felt was inadequate. On the positive side, however, he felt that the engine was reliable and pleasant to handle and by 1881, it had run approximately 3,000 miles. Although EFFIE appears to have been kept in working order during the 1880's in order to demonstrate the potential of the D.B.R. system for two train working, the engine had fallen out of use at Duffield Bank by the time of compilation, in August 1894, of the feature published in October and November of that year in 'The Royal Engineers Journal'. As will be described in a subsequent chapter, it is possible that the engine saw subsequent use on the 15 IN. gauge railway at Doveleys although there is conflicting evidence regarding this point. A surviving letter written by Miss Isabel Effie Heywood suggests that EFFIE had been dismantled by the time of the Edwardian era.

ELLA (Historical Observations)

In designing the second locomotive for the Duffield Bank Railway, Heywood was influenced by events which had transpired regarding the experiments carried out during the 1870's by the Royal Engineers in the pursuit of a suitable design for trench railways. With certainty, it can be said that the lack of commercial acceptance argument which helped to ensure rejection of J. B. Fell's design of elevated railway would also have put paid to any hopes that Heywood may have had of a military application for railways of 15 IN. gauge. With this historical consideration in mind, it appears that the primary purpose of the construction of Heywood's second locomotive was to interest the Royal Engineers in the adoption of a similar locomotive for 18 IN. gauge, rather than to persuade them to use such an engine on a track gauge of 15 IN. Be this as it may, the Duffield Bank line was featured in the Royal Engineers' Journal in 1894 to coincide with the production of the Second Edition of 'Minimum Gauge Railways' but this, together with a brief mention by Major J. R. Hogg in the Royal Engineers Professional Papers (Paper VII of 1883) appeared to be the greatest level of interest shown by the Royal Engineers in most of Heywood's work.

The period of construction of Heywood's second locomotive coincided with tests carried out by the Royal Engineers in connection with 18 IN. gauge trench locomotives of the 'Handyside' pattern. In brief, this principle enabled the use of a winch and special 'gripping struts' on the locomotive. By this means, it could ascend an incline as steep as 1-IN-10 light, grip the rails and haul its rolling stock up the incline in a 'stationary engine' mode. The use of gripping struts on the engine and rolling stock enabled such haulage to be undertaken in stages. As early as 1877, the year before completion of the six 18 IN. gauge Handyside locomotives (built by Fox Walker & Co. of Bristol as their Class HPTE and Works No's. 399-404 of 1878), two events had occurred which were of great significance as regards future developments at Duffield Bank. The first of these was that in January of that year, the Inspector-General of Fortifications had rejected a proposal by Henry Handyside for a double bogie locomotive design (this I.G.F. Minute was appended to R.E.C. Minute 3727 of 24TH NOVEMBER 1876). This may have been one of the reasons why Heywood decided to develop a single wheelbase system of articulation. This theory is particularly plausible in

CHAPTER 4

ELLA is seen here when new at Tennis Ground Station in 1881. This view shows several original features of the engine (compare the engraving in 'The Engineer') including the plain crank webs, straight swinging link for the valve gear and the vertical screw reverser. The conventional lever worked firehole door with which the engine was originally fitted is evident in this view. (Minimum Gauge Railways Plate XIII).

view of the fact that the second event of major significance was the August 1877 letter in 'Engineering'. In a locomotive costing for a 15 IN. gauge line Heywood describes a 'locomotive to draw 50 TONS on the level'. Such a requirement was laid down by the Royal Engineers for the Handyside locomotives but was certainly beyond the capabilities of the next locomotive which he built. The question thus arises as to what type of locomotive Heywood envisaged in his 1877 letter. It may be at this stage that he had come to hear of the rejection of the double bogie 'Handyside' design and may have been proposing an eight wheeled version of the six wheeled engine that he was shortly to complete. This had certainly been envisaged by 1883, in the Professional Papers of the Royal Engineers and became a reality, as we shall see, in 1894. Differences between a drawing published in the latter year in 'Royal Engineers Journal' and the eight coupled MURIEL as completed suggest that design work on this latter engine was a protracted affair.

Heywood's familiarity with the events concerning the testing and ultimate rejection of the Handyside locomotives by the Royal Engineers is clearly indicated by a sentence in his 1879 letter in 'The Engineer': 'Any engine will do on level ground but what every one wants, and especially the Army Field Railway Department, is a *simple* engine that will climb well' (italics added by author). The locomotives and other equipment used by the Royal Engineers during their early trench railway experiments are described more extensively in 'An Illustrated History of 18 IN. Gauge Steam Railways' (Haynes/O.P.C. 1993).

The second Duffield Bank locomotive was turned out during the first half of 1881, having been at the design stage in 1877 and under construction from late 1878 (the 1879 letter states: 'I myself am now building a six coupled locomotive, all the axles of which work radially so as to combine the greatest adhesion with the greatest flexibility'). It was named ELLA after one of Heywood's daughters and possessed a number of

LOCOMOTIVES OF THE DUFFIELD BANK RAILWAY

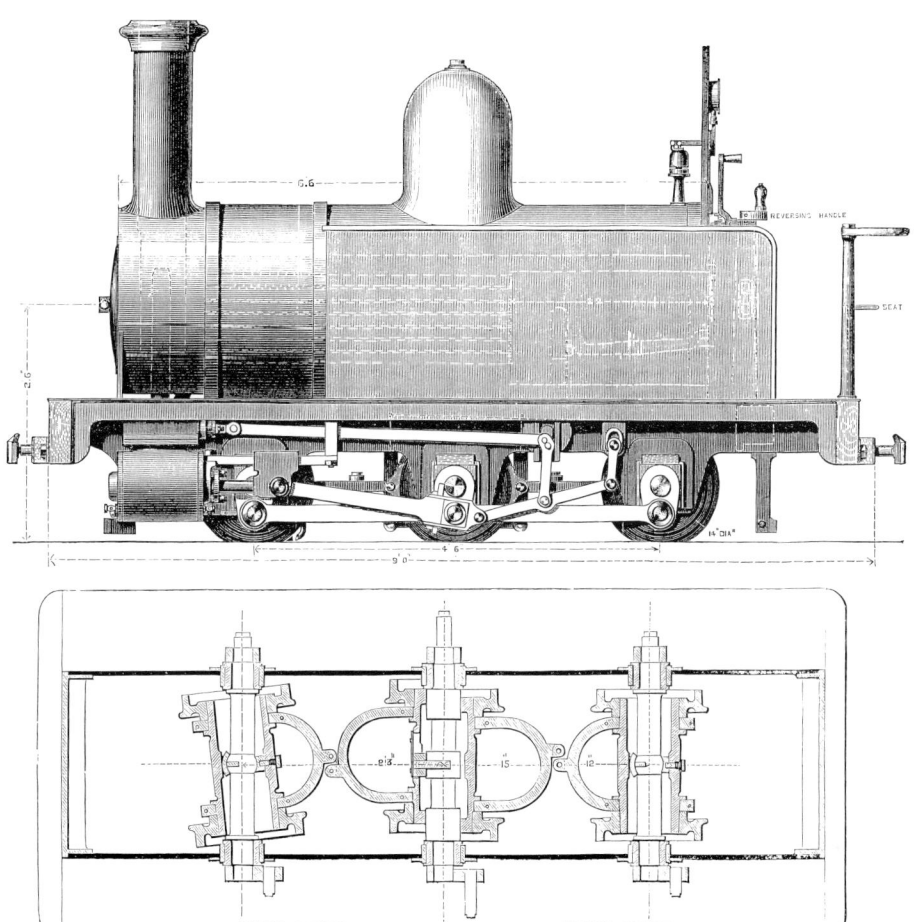

ELLA   SCALE 1:24

Figure 6. Side elevation of ELLA and an inverted plan of the flexible wheelbase system used on the engine. The side elevation shows several of the early details, particularly in relation to the valve gear. The swinging link as originally used was straight, and the 'dog leg' configuration adopted later was used in order to facilitate a lengthening of the distance between the two upper pivots on the vibrating link. The original Hackworth pattern straight slide is in evidence in this view, as is the straight rear valve rod. As originally constructed, the slide valves on ELLA could only be set in the conventional manner which requires the removal of the steam chest cover, but MURIEL as built incorporated two piece adjustable intermediate valve rods which could be lengthened or shortened by means of three bolts and elongated holes. The coupling rod bearings are not of the enclosed pattern adopted later on MURIEL and the original vertical pole reverser is also in evidence. The bufferbeams at this stage were timber although during 1897-1900 cast iron bufferbeams with integral recesses for the sandboxes were fitted. The early pattern of coupler incorporated an external boss for the spigot.

Certain dimensions scaled from this engraving show interesting comparisons with those on later Heywood locomotives. The outer chimney stack is 2 ft. high, some 2 in. shorter than on the Abbott boilers of 1903 onwards, whilst the spectacle plate is some 3 in. shorter than that originally fitted to MURIEL. The inverted plan of the wheelbase illustrates all too clearly the point which had been highlighted in "The Engineer" three years previously when the Cleminson flexible wheelbase system for carriages and wagons was discussed by correspondents. The transition from the straight to a curved portion of track will not be a smooth one when a flexible wheelbase working on this principle is adopted. In later diagrams prepared for the Royal Engineers Journal and the Institution of Mechanical Engineers the split form of representation for the flexible wheelbase was not used and the entire configuration was depicted either in the 'straight' or 'curved' mode. ELLA'S flexible wheelbase components were examined during the 1889 rebuild and were found to have suffered little wear as the tool marks were still visible on the ball joints. A feature which was not shown on the inverted plan, but which would have been necessary in practice, is some form of guide for brake linkage rod in order to keep this component in the vertical plane when the centre axle sleeve moved sideways. This was presumably a separate component which was bolted to the flexible wheelbase linkage to the front of the centre axle. ("The Engineer").

interesting features. One of these in particular was to raise the greatest controversy of Heywood's period of locomotive construction and this was concerned with the method by which a fully adhesive flexible wheelbase configuration was achieved.

ELLA'S Flexible Wheelbase

In discussing his flexible wheelbase system in 'The Engineer' for JULY 15TH 1881, Heywood first stated that he wished to avoid the complication of the double-bogie principle and instead he adopted a single wheelbase design in which the six cast steel wheels were mounted on sleeves surrounding the axles proper so that the end two wheelsets could pivot about ball-joints on the core axles and the middle wheelset was allowed limited lateral play. Hoops surrounding all three sleeves were connected by a linkage so that when on a curve, the sliding of the centre axle sleeve would pull the end two sleeves into a position approximating to normality to the curve. The arrangement is shown in an accompanying Figure.

The basic idea of sleeved axle single wheelbase articulation was not at that time a new one as a system designed for eight and ten coupled locomotives had been patented in 1870 (No. 1817) by John Clark, better known for his work in connection with the Clark and Webb 'chain brake'. The Clark system was, however, radically different to Heywood's and relied on only the axles at the extreme end of the wheelbase carrying sleeves, as did the later German Klien-Lindner principle. Unlike the latter, however, two divorced yokes were employed, one for each sleeved axle and each of these could pivot at their apices about fixed points. This was accomplished by a combination of suitably shaped core axles and play being provided between the driving pins on the sleeves and the faces of the slots through the core axles. No ball joints were therefore used.

As a result of the radical differences between Clark's sleeves and Heywood's, it can be stated that the former are unlikely to have influenced the design of the latter. In any case the use of sleeves with ball joints would certainly appear to have originated with Heywood's principle as used on ELLA.

The geometric principle behind Heywood's 'radiating gear', as he termed it, was certainly not original in substance, however. With one minor and unimportant difference in relation to the orientation of the small connecting links (as originally illustrated in the feature in 'The Engineer' discussing ELLA), it was identical to the system patented by James Cleminson in 1876-7 (No. 3029). This was used on a relatively small number of six-wheeled carriages and wagons during the late 1870's and the 1880's. The Patent Specification also covered variants for an eight wheeled chassis.

The classic Cleminson arrangement is depicted in an accompanying Figure and the drawing of this system which appeared in the Vignes' Technical Study of 1878 had already appeared in an 1877 publication, 'The Cleminson System of Radial Axles'. The possible relevance of this latter work is that Heywood in his 1898 Edition of 'Minimum Gauge Railways' cited the year 1877 as being the date when he thought out the idea for ELLA's articulation system.

The significance of Heywood's second 15 IN. gauge locomotive was not lost on James Cleminson and two weeks after the appearance of Heywood's 1881 feature in 'The Engineer', a letter appeared in that journal which was written by Mr. Cleminson. In this letter, he stated:

'As I am and have been for some years past engaged in the construction and working of a considerable mileage of railways of this character, and flexible wheelbase rolling stock, it will be readily understood that I take more than a passing interest in the results given by them. The attempt of Mr. Heywood to arrive at conclusions of practical value is commendable in the extreme, as much by reason of his aims as by the earnestness of his efforts to attain them, his deductions, however, are not of the worth they deserve to be. I am unable at this moment, owing to excess pressure of work, to give an analysis of Mr. Heywood's views, but with your

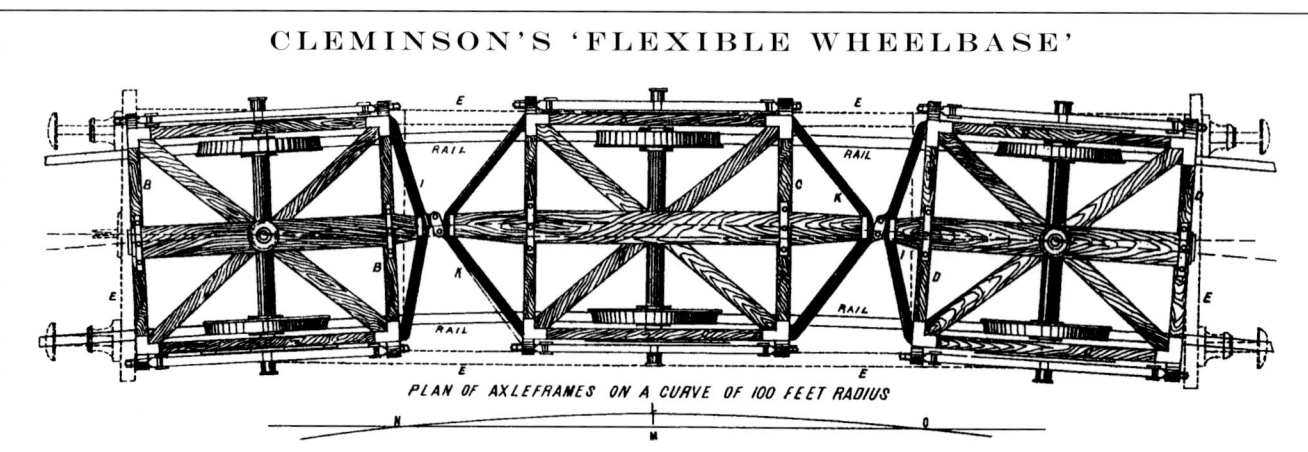

Figure 7. James Cleminson's Flexible Wheelbase (Patent 3029 of 1876) as illustrated in the Royal Engineers Committee Extracts of 1879. Although this system was designed for items of rolling stock rather than locomotives, the similarity of the geometric principle to the one used on ELLA is immediately apparent.

permission, I will return to the subject later on; in the meantime it is only just to say that whilst his example of my flexible wheelbase is exceedingly creditable to him, it lacks the impress of large practical experience and the latest mechanical principles involved'.

As no further analysis of Heywood's views was undertaken by James Cleminson, it is not possible to assign any real historical significance to the first part of the letter but there can be no doubt that Cleminson's view was that Heywood had copied the geometric principle of ELLA's radiating gear from his own system for carriage and wagon wheelbases. Sadly, from the historian's point of view, Heywood did not reply to Cleminson's letter to confirm or deny whether this was in fact the case and the matter received no further discussion in 'The Engineer'. What can be stated, however, is that James Cleminson's social circle at this time would have included Charles Easton Spooner from whom, as we have seen, Heywood copied a number of ideas. Another important point is that Heywood did not always state the inspiration behind ideas obviously taken from prior sources (see for instance the 'cloned' Roscoe pattern lubricators used on ELLA and his subsequent locomotives). These last two observations would tend to suggest that Cleminson's claim in his letter was justified. Further support for this proposition is suggested by the fact that Cleminson attempted to get his flexible wheelbase system adopted on 18 IN. gauge military rolling stock (see R.E. Committee Minute 5061 of DECEMBER 12TH 1879) but although some interest was shown by the Royal Engineers, the matter was not proceeded with.

The next important question to be considered concerning Heywood's 'radiating gear' is whether the claim made in 'The Engineer' in 1881 that when: '(the middle axle) slides laterally, as is the case on entering a curve, the other two hollow axles with their respective wheels, are radiated truly to the curve, no matter what may be its radius, providing it is within the lateral travel of the centre axle'. There was no direct criticism of this argument following Heywood's 1881 feature in 'The Engineer', largely on the ground that it had been considered at great length in letters published in the same journal following James Cleminson's own feature in 1878. It was stated by a correspondent, Mr. Midleton in 'The Engineer' for AUGUST 9TH 1878 that: '…in my opinion his (Cleminson's) system is only correct when all six wheels of a carriage are fairly on a curve and when entering or leaving any curve… Mr. Cleminson's plan is worse than a rigid six-wheel carriage and his system only begins to work after one-half of the total wheel-base has entered a curve and is not in full work till all six wheels are fairly on a curve'.

The basic tenor of Mr. Midleton's argument therefore was that on a vehicle fitted with a system of this type, the axles could not adopt a position of normality to the track direction throughout the vehicle's transitional travel from the straight to the curve. To this extent, his argument was clearly valid as the leading axle must rely on the motion of the middle one for its orientation and the middle axle cannot slide laterally until the body of the vehicle has been pushed into the curve by the action of the outermost rail upon the leading outermost wheel. At the very least, therefore, it can be said that upon entering a curve, the leading axle will tend to lag in its attempts to assume a normal position and the middle axle will be drawn into the curve at an earlier stage than would be required to assume a normal position. The difficulty which is readily evident with the Cleminson/Heywood geometry is that there can be no smooth guidance of such a vehicle into and out of a curve. This is because of the fact that, unlike the position where a leading sprung pony truck is employed, the longitudinal mid-point of the body of the vehicle must move concurrently with the lateral mid-point of the leading axle. Essentially, therefore, it can be said that although Heywood's flexible wheelbase enabled his six (and later eight) coupled locomotives to negotiate 25 FT. radius curves, their motion would have been less smooth than a conventional chassis with a pony truck and the apparent success of the system on Heywood's railways was due in some measure to the relatively low speeds of the trains and short wheelbases of the locomotives. Cleminson's six-wheel carriages and wagons failed to achieve lasting commercial success on railway systems at home and abroad although a few examples survive in preservation today.

The other major criticism levelled at Heywood's flexible wheelbase system was that its use would lead to instability on the ground that there was effectively only one point of suspension for each of the end axles and a sliding line of suspension for the centre one. In support of this proposition, it may be observed that on the Ravenglass and Eskdale Railway towards the end of ELLA's career, the ball-jointed axle sleeves were immobilised and it was said that the engine ran freer and steadier as a result. As an example of the limitations of this argument, however, it is constructive to look forward over two decades from the time of ELLA's completion. In 1905 the Matheran Hill Railway, a 1 FT. 11 1½ IN. gauge line linking Neral (a station on the South Eastern main line of the old Great Indian Peninsular Railway near Bombay) to Matheran was opened. This line incorporates a route length of approximately 12 MILES, and whereas the interchange at Neral is a mere 132 FT. above sea-level, the corresponding elevation at Matheran is 2495 FT.

The four locomotives built by the Berlin concern of Orenstein and Koppel for use on this railway were, like ELLA, outside framed 0-6-0 side tanks with a flexible wheelbase in which the sliding of the middle wheelset could effect angular displacement of the end two axles about vertical axes as a result of the action of an intermediate linkage. In the case of the M.H.R. locomotives, this linkage consisted of a longitudinal bar, mounted below the axles, to which three cranks were fixed. The intermediate of these was actuated by a collar mounted on the sliding middle axle sleeve and the outer two engaged, via suitable universal joints, in the apices of A-frames

CHAPTER 4

The four 60 centimetre gauge Orenstein & Koppel 0-6-0T's constructed in 1905-7 for the Matheran Hill Railway all had operating careers lasting into the early 1980's and one example, Maker's No. 2343 of 1907 was brought to the United Kingdom for preservation in 1986.
Photographed at Amberley Chalk Pits Museum on July 5th 1987, the locomotive moved to Railworld, Peterborough, before transfer to the Leighton Buzzard Railway in 1994.
(Author).

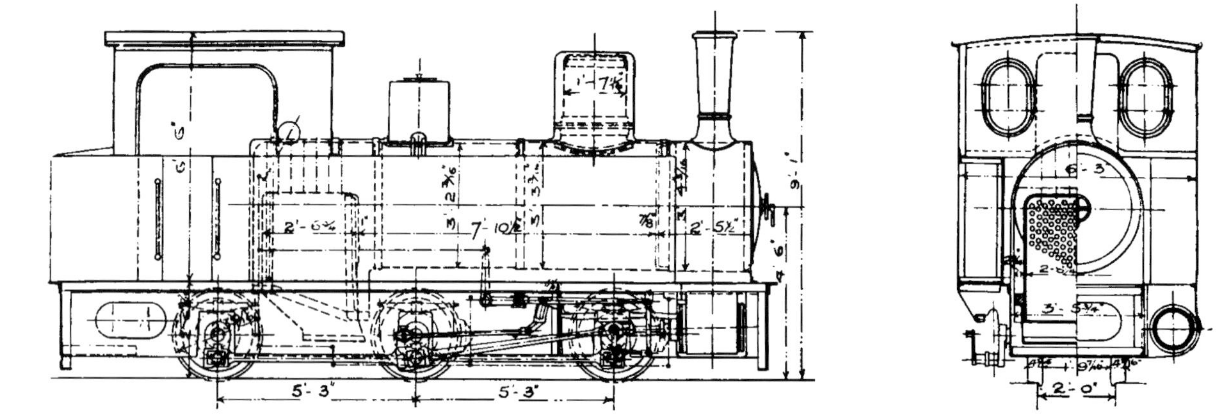

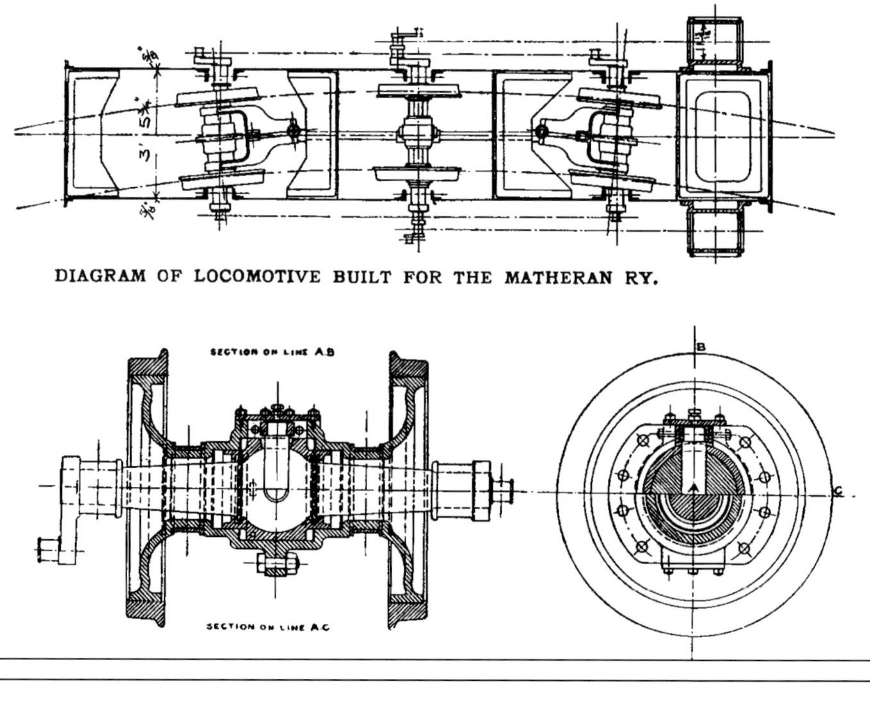

DIAGRAM OF LOCOMOTIVE BUILT FOR THE MATHERAN RY.

Figure 8. The six-wheeled flexible wheelbase locomotives for the Matheran Hill Railway as shown in schematic outline in 'The Locomotive' for March 15th 1907. The locomotives as built differed in a number of details but the wheelbase principle was not altered. The provision of a small amount of lateral play in the two extreme axles, as was to be expected in the light of normal Klien-Lindner practice, can be seen in this figure. The provision of such play would have mitigated to some degree the harshness of the locomotive's travel from a straight into a severe curve at the expense of dynamic stability of the frames and superstructure on straight and lightly curved track.

attached to hoops surrounding the sleeves on the extreme axles. Although the drawing showing the basic layout of these locomotives in the accompanying Figure differs greatly in detail from the locomotives as finally built, it can be seen that the basic articulation principle for these locomotives involved the use of a limited amount of lateral play in the front and rear axles as well as the middle one. In theory, these locomotives would have had a less stable wheelbase than ELLA, although they remained in active use for over seventy years and all four currently survive in preservation.

Although built under German Klien-Lindner patents, there remains the possibility that Heywood may have had an indirect influence upon the basic specification of the Matheran Hill locomotives. This possibility arises out of the fact that Sir Arthur was present at the official opening of the Leek and Manifold Valley Light Railway on 27TH JUNE 1904. The Consulting Engineer to this line was Everard Richard Calthrop who was shortly afterwards to fulfil the same function with respect to the Matheran Hill Railway. It may be, therefore, that Calthrop had been in communication with Heywood concerning the flexible wheelbase system used on ELLA and had this system in mind when laying out the specification for the M.H.R. locomotives. It is significant to note in this context that in the 3RD. Edition of 'Minimum Gauge Railways' that Sir Arthur felt that a six-coupled wheelbase was normally the most cost-effective application of his system, and that apart from the Matheran locomotives no other six-coupled revenue earning steam locomotives were ever built under Klien-Lindner patents.

The experience possessed by Orenstein & Koppel in the manufacture of sleeved axle locomotives of the Klien-Lindner pattern would have given this manufacturer an advantage over British concerns in the competition for the construction contracts for the Matheran engines. Further notes on the subject of the Klien-Lindner system will be found in Appendix Six.

Motion and Valve Gear

In addition to the 'radiating gear', ELLA possessed several other features of interest. As illustrated in the engraving which accompanied the feature in 'The Engineer' it can be seen that ELLA possessed a peculiar design of big end brasses. These were cylindrical about the main axis of the connecting rod so as to allow the big end bearings to rotate within limits about

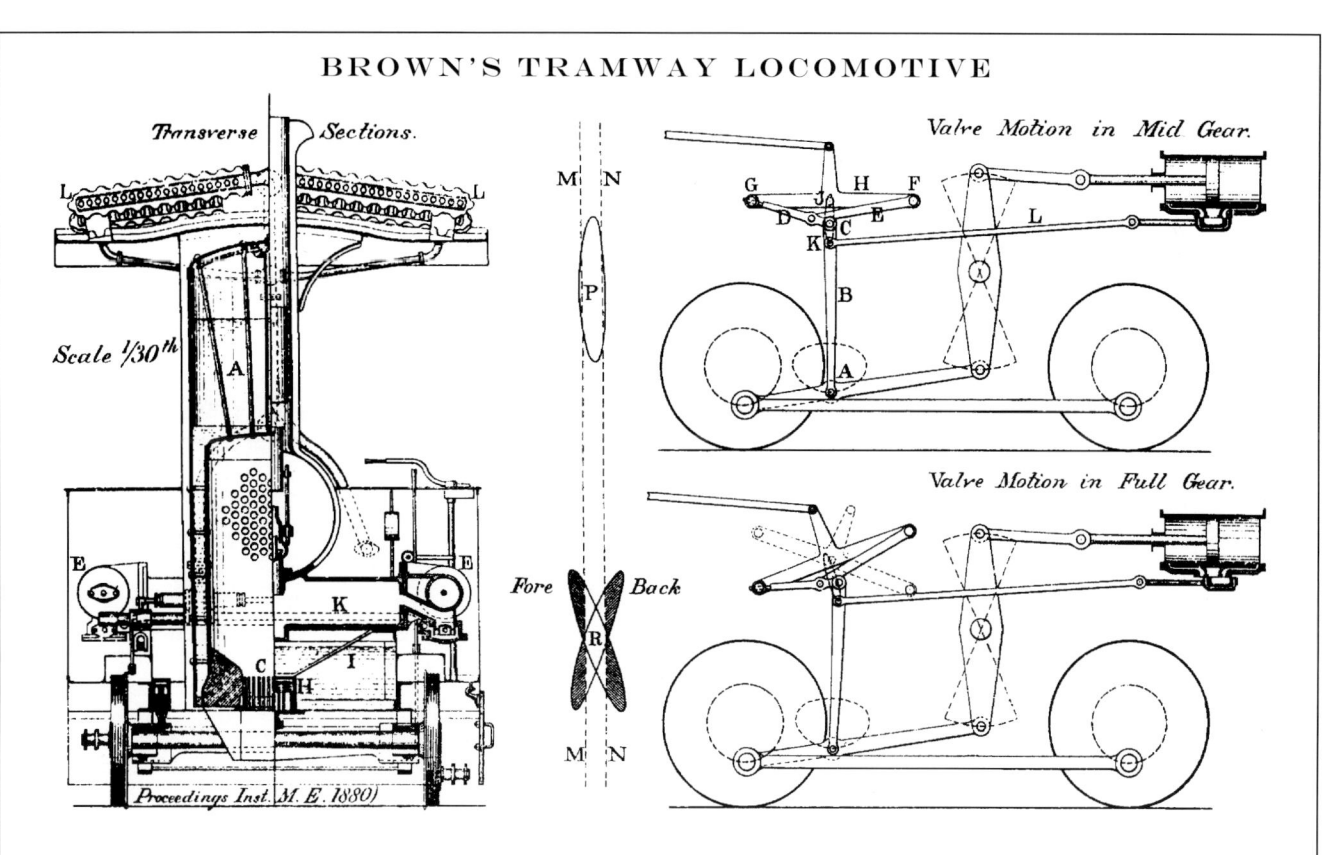

Figure 9. A drawing of the cylinder and valve gear arrangements for a Hawthorn indirect drive tramway locomotive with Brown valve gear as depicted in the 'Proceedings of the Institution of Mechanical Engineers' in 1880. The nature of the indirect drive ensured that the connecting rod could also constitute the 'swinging link' for driving the vibrating link of the valve gear. On a direct drive locomotive, a separate 'swinging link' was necessary. The vertical linear linkage is apparent and its mode of operation was slightly different from the one eventually adopted on ELLA when rebuilt in 1897-1900. A simple straight slide and die block were adopted on ELLA, MURIEL and KATIE when these engines were originally constructed. (Institution of Mechanical Engineers).

27

this axis when the core axles failed to remain perpendicular to the vertical axes of the mainframes, owing to road irregularities. By this means, twisting forces on the slide bars could be mitigated. Another interesting feature of ELLA's design was the valve gear. In describing this gear in its original form in 1881, Heywood described it as being a modification of Brown's valve gear and in arrangement very similar to Joy's valve gear. The truth of the matter was that the use of sleeved axles prevented the fitting of axle-mounted eccentrics of the type associated with most link motion arrangements and outside valve gear had to be adopted. At this relatively early stage, Walschaerts valve gear had yet to gain universal acceptance in the United Kingdom. It appears that ELLA may originally have been intended to have outside link motion of the type used on some Fowler narrow gauge locomotives constructed in 1879 but by 1880 Heywood wished to avoid using an externally mounted link motion requiring the fitting of overhanging eccentrics and/or return cranks (for further discussion of this matter, see Chapter Six).

The valve gear used on ELLA as originally constructed was in substance a combination of Brown's gear and the principle invented by John Wesley Hackworth in 1859. Despite this fact, Heywood himself was probably unaware of Hackworth's system owing to the latter's relatively late commercial adoption for locomotive usage. As far as the British railway historian is concerned, Hackworth valve gear is most commonly associated with the products of the Stoke locomotive manufacturer Kerr, Stuart & Co. Ltd. after 1915.

The basic Hackworth principle entails the valve motion being taken from an eccentric (or more commonly in locomotive practice, a return crank) set at 180 degrees to the driving crankpin. The eccentric rod transmits drive upwards onto a die block set within a straight slide, as opposed to the curved slide used on Joy's valve gear. At some point on the rod between the eccentric and the die block, a connection is made via a pin with the valve rod which transmits the motion to the valve spindle. 'Notching up' of the gear is accomplished by rotation of the slide: in mid-gear the slide is vertical and the travel of the valve spindle is restricted to twice the sum of the 'lap' and 'lead' associated with the valve.

By lengthening the eccentric rod so that it makes connection with the valve rod above the die block, it is possible to mount the eccentric so that its axis of offset is coincident with the crankpin. On the valve gear used by Heywood, this approach was taken a stage further by having the source of motion derived from the crank itself, but in order to reduce the vertical travel of the vibrating link to a dimension allowed by the proportions of other parts of the locomotive, a trailing swinging link was employed, which engaged with a hanging radial rod at its rearmost end. This measure was clearly influenced by Brown's valve gear where, because of that gear's application to indirect drive locomotives, the connecting rod could also 'double' as the swinging link. From the swinging link on Heywood's gear, an upwardly projecting vibrating link transmitted motion to the die block and performed the function associated with the eccentric rod in the original Hackworth layout. The loci of motion of the lower pin on the Brown and Heywood vibrating links were oval, in contrast to the circular locus of motion of the centre of an eccentric.

The main drawback with Hackworth valve gear in its original form from the point of view of railway locomotive usage is that the adverse effect of vertical movement of the driving axle, owing to road irregularities, upon valve events is more pronounced than on most other valve gears. This distortion is a function of the ratio of the vertical displacement of the axle to the vertical travel of the rod which moves the die block. Although the vertical travel of the vibrating link on Heywood's valve gear was reduced, by means of the swinging link, to about half of that of the driving crank, this reduced dimension was still greater than the typical eccentric throw on an equivalent Hackworth gear. The relative distortion caused by chassis springing to the valve events of an engine with Heywood valve gear will, all other parameters being equal, be less than that caused to an engine with equivalent Hackworth valve gear.

One of the characteristics inherent in the original Heywood valve gear, owing to the restrictions imposed by ELLA's general proportions, was that the pivots for the die block and valve rod connection were placed very close together. This both restricted the the valve travel and imparted a possible structural weakness to the vibrating link. As we shall see, a design alteration was subsequently made in order to circumvent these difficulties.

ELLA'S Boiler

ELLA's boiler followed the pattern of EFFIE's in its basic construction and as with that of EFFIE, it was probably supplied by Messrs Abbott and Co. of Newark. The safety valve spring was mounted within a vertical cylindrical recess in the dome barrel so as to discourage tampering. There were two major differences between the boiler designs of ELLA and EFFIE. The first of these was that the boiler on the former had much revised heating surface proportions, with the number of tubes increasing from 23 to 42 (arranged in a 5:6:7:6:7:6:5 configuration) and the firebox diameter being increased from 11 IN. to 1 FT. $2\frac{1}{4}$ IN. The Third Edition of 'Minimum Gauge Railways' recalls that ELLA was in a stripped down state for overhaul during 1889 and it seems certain that the boiler was renewed at this stage to the subsequent Heywood standard specification of 57 tubes ($1\frac{3}{8}$ IN. diameter), 1 FT. $3\frac{1}{4}$ IN. internal diameter firebox and 2 FT. 1 IN. external barrel diameter. This development involved the use of a close minimum inter-tube spacing of $\frac{3}{8}$ IN. and it may be significant to note that the 1880's decade subsequent to ELLA's completion had seen the appearance of two new narrow gauge locomotive designs employing a cylindrical firebox and closely packed tubes. The first of these, in 1882, were the Geoghegan Patent 0-4-0T's of the Guinness Brewery tramway (firebox tubeplate

1 FT. 7¼ IN. internal diameter: 64 tubes each 1½ IN. diameter), and the second, in 1887, were the Beyer Peacock 18 IN. gauge locomotives for Horwich Works (firebox tubeplate 1 FT. 5 IN. internal diameter: 55 tubes each 1⅜ IN. diameter). Both of these designs were discussed by the Institution of Mechanical Engineers in their Proceedings for the year 1888. The tube packing arrangement (equidistant hexagonal packing with vertical rows 4:6:7:8:7:8:7:6:4) used on the reboilered ELLA was the closest match the revised tube and firebox dimensions would allow to the tube arrangement of the Guinness engine (4:7:8:9:8:9:8:7:4), which was illustrated in the Paper.

The second major difference between ELLA's boiler and that of the earlier engine was to place the dome centrally on the locomotive rather than immediately forward of the spectacle plate.

ELLA's regulator control was arranged so that when the regulator was closed, the blower would be opened so as to maintain sufficient draught for the fire. This was accomplished by having a solid slide valve in the dome which, in the 'neutral' position, was of sufficient size just to cover entry ports to both the main steam pipe and the blower. The blower pipe passed directly through the front tubeplate. An internally mounted spring stop prevented the blower being opened inadvertantly when the regulator rod had been left in the 'neutral' position.

By 1881, Heywood apparently disapproved of the conventional externally mounted smokebox door hinge and consequently decided to mount the hinge on his last five locomotives within the smokebox. A reconstructed working arrangement for this hinge is shown in one of the accompanying illustrations, but it is difficult to see precisely what advantage such a system would have had in operation.

Other Miscellaneous Items

As had been the case with EFFIE, ELLA's suspension consisted of India rubber pads and according to the feature in 'The Engineer', it was found that so long as the quality of these components was sufficiently high, their resistance to destruction by oil would be satisfactory. Unfortunately, some deterioration did occur in Heywood rolling stock suspension many years later when some of his vehicles found their way to the Romney, Hythe and Dymchurch Railway in Kent and this resulted in his bogies being replaced there by the more modern Gibbins pattern with integral springing in their side frames.

At this stage in the discussion of Heywood's locomotives, an important point needs to be noted. The observation has sometimes been made that the use of sleeved axles would have precluded the use of a conventional depending firebox even if Heywood had not been opposed to the use of such fireboxes on minimum gauge locomotives as a general rule, regardless of whether sleeved axles were used or not. The use of a depending firebox on the Matheran Hill locomotives clearly

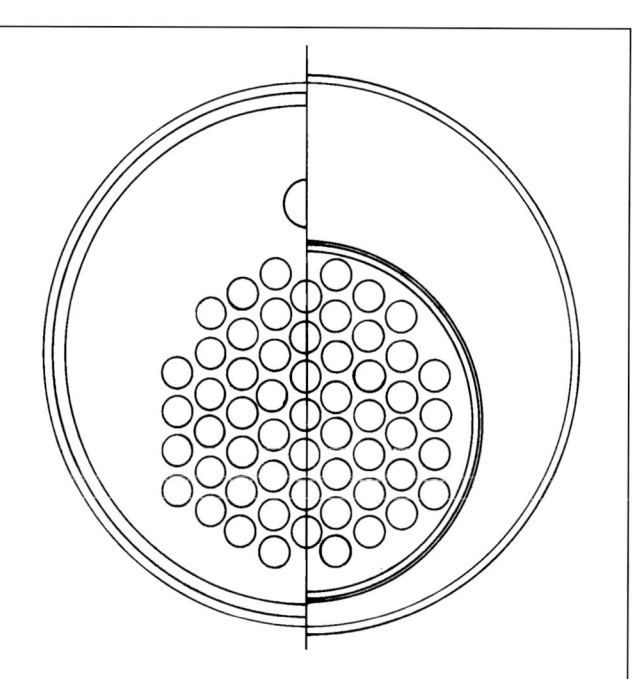

Figure 10. Above – Although the tube arrangement drawing which accompanied the Abbott boiler drawings has not come to light, it has been possible to reconstruct the standard Heywood tube arrangement using the surviving Abbott drawings and photographic evidence. This tube arrangement would have been common to all Heywood locomotives completed after 1894, having first been used on ELLA during this locomotive's 1889 rebuild. Below – As a comparison, the front tubeplate drawing of the Guinness loco from the 1888 Institution Paper is also shown (below). Removal of the seven tubes below the line X–X leaves the Heywood arrangement.

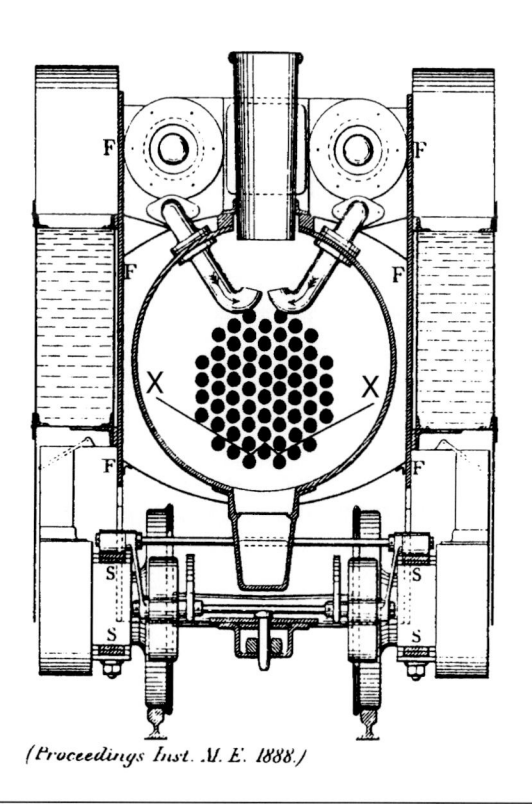

(Proceedings Inst. M. E. 1888.)

demonstrates that one could have been fitted to a Heywood type locomotive although this would have necessitated relocation of the steam brake cylinder. ELLA was equipped with a steam brake at the construction stage and originally this was the only form of braking used. The decision to use a steam brake may have been influenced by practice on the 18 IN. gauge at Crewe Works where a design had been produced in 1877 showing the Webb pattern 0-4-0T fitted with a steam brake. In 1878 a locomotive was built to this design by Fox Walker & Co. (Works No. 386) for the War Department. The Crewe-based 'BILLY' of 1875 (which had originally been propelled by a three cylinder Brotherhood steam motor) was also rebuilt around the same time in line with the 1877 drawings.

From examination of photographs taken throughout the engine's lifetime, it has been possible to ascertain the modus operandi of the steam brake as used on ELLA and subsequent Heywood locomotives. The brake cylinder (the outline of which is just visible in the 1881 'Engineer' engraving) was located equidistant between the mainframes and to the rear of the firebox backhead. One side of the piston was fed by the pipe connected to the control valve, whereas a relatively light spring was located between the other side of the piston and the adjacent end of the cylinder. By this means, the admission of steam from the control valve would actuate the brake and movement of the control valve so as to connect the pipe from the brake cylinder direct to waste would allow the spring to return the brake to the 'off' position. From examination of photographic evidence of the pipework associated with ELLA's steam brake, it appears that the piston pulled towards the rear of the engine in order to actuate the brake. The brake linkage utilized on ELLA was of a floating clasp type with four shoes acting on the centre axle only. There was no fitting of brakes, as had been accomplished on the Cleminson coaches used on the Manx Northern Railway, to the wheels on the pivoting axles of any Heywood locomotive as it was felt that the additional complication of the associated linkage was not justified.

According to correspondence from Mr. Bert Thompson, who drove the locomotive during its final years on the Ravenglass & Eskdale line, it would appear that allowance was made for the necessary swinging of the brake linkage on a curve by having universal joints on the uppermost pivots of the brake hangers. The brake hangers thus had limited lateral, as well as longitudinal, swing but the resultant upward displacement of the brake blocks on a 25 FT. radius curve on even the larger Heywood 0-6-0T's for the Eaton Railway would only have been in the order of $^1/_8$ IN.

In addition to the distinctive mechanical features, ELLA's aesthetic properties set the pattern for all of the subsequent Heywood locomotives, with the basic design of chimney, side tanks and weatherboard being found on all of his five later locomotives. Heywood had an intense dislike for the fitting of cabs to locomotives of the minimum gauge variety and even his last locomotive for the Eaton Hall Railway, completed in the year of his death, possessed only a weatherboard. In defence of his view that cabs on such locomotives were uncomfortable and dangerous owing to the contracted dimensions involved, it must be remembered that when home-based 18 IN. gauge lines are considered, the cabs on many of their locomotives were not enclosed at the rear. Cabs were never employed on locomotives used on the Crewe or Horwich narrow gauge works systems.

The cylinder draincocks on ELLA and all subsequent Heywood locomotives were operated by a bar which ran laterally in front of the cylinders and which was actuated by means of a single crank and a rod worked from the footplate.

As was stated by Heywood himself, ELLA was designed for tractive effort rather than speed and a number of performance tests were carried out with the locomotive for the benefit of the Royal Engineers, possibly during 1894. These included loading the locomotive to its utmost capacity on steep inclines; applying the steam brake when the locomotive was travelling at various speeds and over various awkward locations; and giving the engine a fifty mile run with the greatest possible load at an average speed of $7^1/_2$ M.P.H. allowing 12 minutes in each hour for watering. Shortly after this last-mentioned test was carried out, a continuous run was under-taken with the same load and this run took up approximately one hour and thirty-five minutes, the longest the water in the tanks would hold out. When considering the merits of these tests, however, it must be borne in mind that ELLA's haulage capacity was somewhat less than the Royal Engineers' requirements for trench supply railways and that even if the R.E. Committee had decided in favour of the adoption of some of Heywood's design proposals, any resultant loco-motive would have been significantly larger than ELLA. The tests do not appear to have enjoyed 'official' blessing as the R.E. Committee Minutes make no mention of them.

The net cost of ELLA's construction, exclusive of drawings and patterns was recorded as £309 and Heywood's only assistants during the two and a half years of actual construction work were a joiner and a casual labourer. All of the castings were made in the Duffield Bank Works, with the exception of the steel wheels cast by the Hadfield Steel Foundry Co. of Sheffield, and all of the machining required was also executed at Duffield Bank. As with the boiler, the frame-plates and sundry brass fittings were purchased from outside. It was reckoned that at commercial rates, if 10 per cent were added to ELLA's construction costs for drawings and patterns, and another 20 per cent for the manufacturer's profit, then £400 would have appeared to have been a fair trade price for such a locomotive. It is significant to note that in 'Minimum Gauge Railways' Heywood appeared to have made no revision of his cost calculations to compensate for the effect of inflation during the years from 1881 to 1898 when referring to ELLA.

The completion of ELLA in 1881 and the publication during

that year of the First Edition of Heywood's pamphlet 'Minimum Gauge Railways' coincided neatly with the holding of the Royal Agricultural Society's Show in Derby and members were invited to the Duffield Bank Railway during the Show. At this time farmers and estate managers both at home and in the colonies were showing a considerable amount of interest in the possibilities offered by narrow gauge railways from the point of view of internal transportation requirements and they had already been impressed by the properties of the Decauville portable track system. Unfortunately from Heywood's point of view, the 1881 Royal Agricultural Show was not to yield any commercial interest in the use of 15 IN. gauge railways and Heywood type locomotives for agricultural use at home or abroad.

As a result of an accident on JULY 3RD 1883 involving a steam tram locomotive in Huddersfield, Heywood wrote a letter to 'Engineering' which appeared in the 2ND AUGUST issue. The tram engine had run away whilst descending a steep incline and its trailer car had overturned at the bottom, resulting in loss of life. It transpired that the tram locomotive was not fitted with a handbrake and that the only means of control in such a situation was to reverse the locomotive. Heywood must have realised that if the steam brake on ELLA were to fail in similar circumstances, he would have been left with only a slow acting screw reverser to control the engine. It seems certain, therefore, that the final type of reverser and dual hand and steam braking were adopted on ELLA as a result of this accident. The final design of reverser used appeared to work on a modification of the principle originated by William Bouch of the Stockton & Darlington Railway in the 1860's and combined lever and screw actions for coarse and fine adjustment respectively. This was accomplished by having a sprung latch on the reversing lever which could be disengaged when the lever was being moved and which would engage in the thread of a leadscrew when the desired lever position had been selected. Fine adjustment could then be effected by means of a handwheel on the rear end of the screw, which was of the ordinary helical variety rather than the torpedo profile associated with the Bouch system. On a large main line engine, where precise control of the 'cut-off' timing paid tangible dividends in terms of economic operation, the complication inherent in such a device may have been justified but a conventional lever reverser would have suited Heywood's purposes adequately.

The steam brake lever after this alteration was mounted on the same column as the reverser and the latches for both were actuated by push rods working in hollowed out recesses within the levers. The control valve for the steam brake by this time at least appeared to be basically of a slide valve variety but with no scope for 'headroom' between the top of the valve and the lower surface of the steamchest lid. Examination of the surviving mainframes of ELLA and the Eaton Hall engine, KATIE, suggest that the rear of the reversing/steam brake control pedestal was supported by the top of the control valve chest, which in turn hung from two longitudinal angle irons, one attached to the mainframe and the other which formed the footplate valence.

The injectors were both supplied with steam from one common tap, which in turn was supplied from the front of the brake control steamchest. The control handle for the injector steam tap was a long T-shaped bar mounted in a bearing on the right hand side of the reverser/steam brake lever pedestal. Rather unusually, the delivery flows from the injectors were combined in a common manifold before being split up once again in order to feed the right and left 'clack' valves. This arrangement was presumably an attempt to equalize the water flows into each side of the boiler, but must have entailed some loss of kinetic efficiency, owing to the potential for eddy currents in the manifold. This latter problem would have been aggravated by the 90 degree displacement of entry flows into, and exit flows from, the manifold.

The handbrake pedestal was located on the left hand side of the engine and its associated rodding was connected to the rear pair of brake shoes. There would have needed to have been provision for taking up the 'lost motion' when the steam brake was applied without moving the handbrake handle. This was accomplished by means of the use of slotted crosshead rods actuated by pins and slotted bellcranks, the latter mounted on the transverse handbrake rod and shown in the drawings of MURIEL and URSULA.

In his letter of AUGUST 1883 in 'Engineering', Heywood also stressed the importance of good sanding arrangements and referred to 'some plan of steam sand ejector'. The close proximity of Duffield Bank to Derby may also have been a significant factor in the adoption of the Gresham principle of steam sanding by the Midland Railway on the famous 'Spinner' 4-2-2's constructed from 1887-1900. Sir Arthur did not patent steam sanding on his own account and his own experiments with steam sanding on ELLA were unsuccessful as sand was blown into bearing surfaces causing excessive wear.

The blast nozzle on ELLA was eventually modified to be of the adjustable variety, with adjustment being effected by means of raising or lowering an internal cone. This was operated from a bellcrank attached to a transverse bar which was rotated by a connecting rod worked from a lever on the reversing pedestal. It is not certain from surviving evidence precisely when this modification was carried out, and it may be that it was done after the construction of MURIEL. It was felt necessary to incorporate this feature on the ground that varying demands on the locomotive, and resultant varying strengths of the blast generated, would have an adverse effect upon the fire if no mitigating measures were taken. Even Heywood appeared to recognise that too strong a blast would result in some instances when the engine was running at a relatively high speed if a fixed size nozzle were used and that this would tend to pull the fire off the bars of the grate. The petticoat pipe was exceptionally long in relation to the smokebox diameter (a feature illustrated in the 1881 engraving

CHAPTER 4

MURIEL after receiving the standard Heywood lined out holly green livery as photographed by Lt. J. J. Galloway on his visit to the Duffield Bank Railway on September 8th 1894. (Minimum Gauge Railways Plate XIV).

in 'The Engineer') and perforated about its lower portion. It acted to some degree as a spark arrester.

MURIEL

In 1894, Heywood produced a Second Edition of 'Minimum Gauge Railways' and he made another attempt to interest possible commercial users of narrow gauge railways in his efforts. During August of that year another three day 'Open Session' took place and on this occasion it was possible for the invited visitors to view the last and largest of the three locomotives completed specifically for use on the Duffield Bank Railway. The locomotive completed in 1894 was named MURIEL and in addition to being of rather larger dimensions with regard to most important mechanical features than ELLA, the engine possessed a fourth coupled axle. As with ELLA, sleeved axles were fitted and these were arranged so that the extreme end axles had sleeves which could pivot and the intermediate axles had sleeves which could slide. The side play on the intermediate axles for MURIEL allowed a travel of 1-15/16 IN. either side of the central position, as opposed to one inch for ELLA. Linkages of a type similar to that used on ELLA connected the leading axle with the forward intermediate one, and the trailing axle with its adjacent intermediate counterpart. There was no linkage connection between the two intermediate axle sleeves and Heywood described this form of his radiating gear as 'practically equal to a double bogie'. When standing on a curve of 25 FT. radius, the clearance between the outermost intermediate wheels and the inner surface of the outermost side mainframe would have been approximately three eighths of an inch! In order to accommodate the increased side play in the intermediate sleeved axles, the tyre width dimension, which was 3 IN. on ELLA, was reduced to 2½ IN. on MURIEL.

A design refinement incorporated into MURIEL when new was the use of secondary suspension in the form of two cast iron frame stretchers with bearing surfaces on their lower edges. These bore against rubber pads carried in seatings in the upper portions of the hoops on the pivoting axle sleeves. This refinement was also incorporated into the two later 0-6-0T's for the Eaton Railway. It is unclear whether MURIEL was the first Heywood locomotive to have secondary suspension as photographic evidence shows that cast iron intermediate frame stretchers (as opposed to the forged bars originally fitted) were at some stage fitted to ELLA. The 16 CWT. difference between ELLA's weight when new and as given in 1894 may be partly accounted for by the fitting of cast iron intermediate stretchers during the locomotive's first rebuild, although this cannot be shown for certain.

Other standard Heywood constructional details, such as the use of Holden and Brooke's restarting injectors and the combined lever and screw reverser, which was fitted to ELLA a few years after construction, were present on MURIEL as built. The water cocks for the injectors were controlled, as with ELLA, by the use of a square spanner handle which engaged with the square shanks of the valves, whose upper ends protruded through the footplate.

In view of the R.E. Committee requirements stipulated for the Handyside locomotives in 1876 (for a more detailed discussion of these, see 'An Illustrated History of 18 IN. Gauge Steam Railways' O.P.C. 1993) and what has already been stated regarding ELLA's haulage capabilities, it is suggested here that MURIEL was built principally to give some idea how a suitably proportioned Heywood style locomotive would measure up to the demands of trench railway usage. The reference to an eight wheeled version of ELLA in the R.E. Professional Papers was also suggestive of this deduction, as were the comments made earlier in connection with the 1877 letter in 'Engineering'.

Sundry additional improvements to the basic specification were incorporated into MURIEL such as counter-balanced

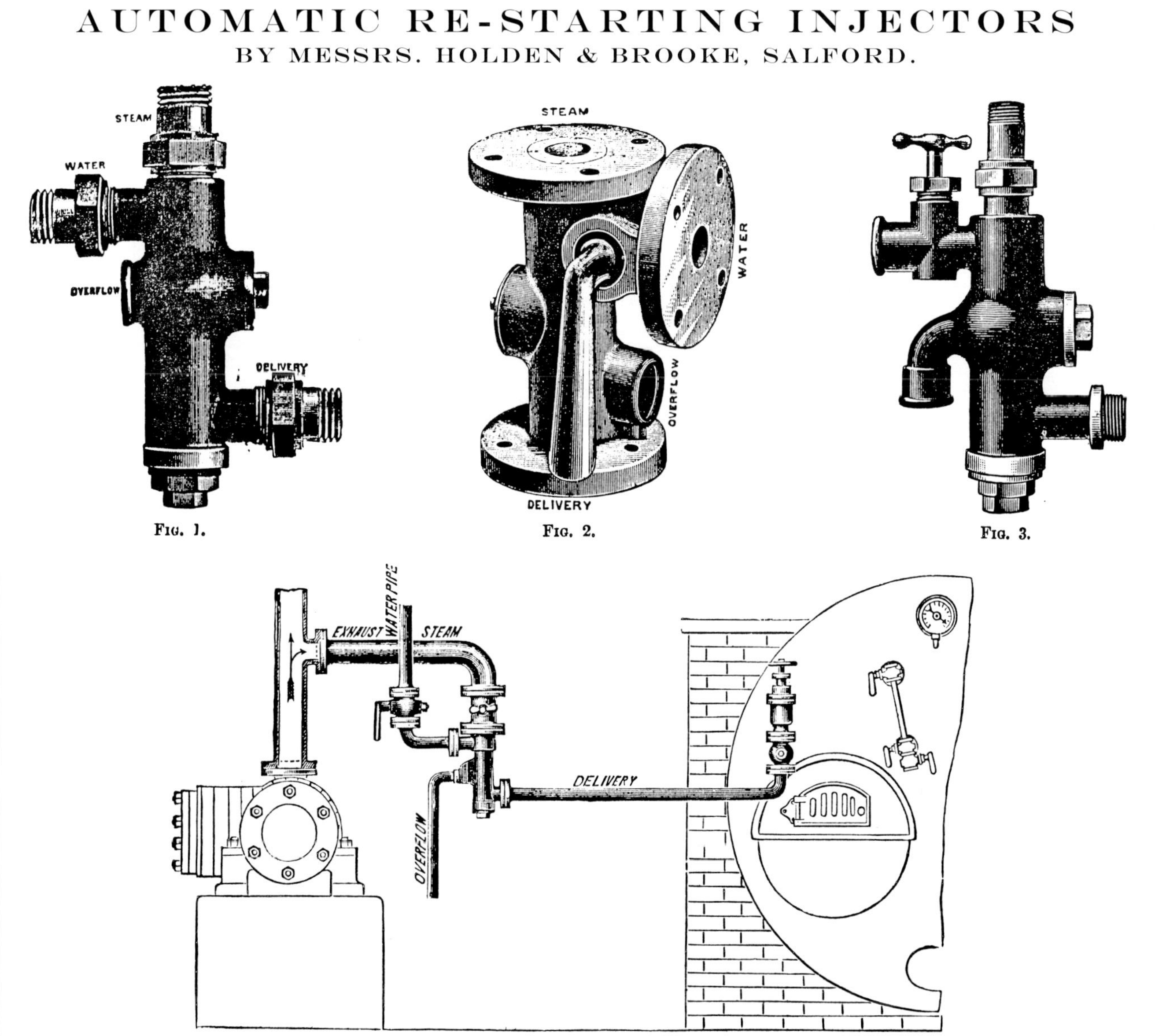

> # AUTOMATIC RE-STARTING INJECTORS
> ## BY MESSRS. HOLDEN & BROOKE, SALFORD.
>
> FIG. 1.   FIG. 2.   FIG. 3.
>
> *Figure 11. This engraving appeared in 'Iron' magazine for April 20th 1888 and shows a Holden & Brooke automatic restarting injector of the related design to that fitted to ELLA and MURIEL at the time of compilation of 'Minimum Gauge Railways' in 1898. The term 'automatic restarting' relates to the fact that the injector contained a valve which released any air trapped in its body during operation, which would otherwise have destroyed the partial vacuum necessary to allow propulsion of the feedwater into the boiler.*

flycranks, a steam water-lifter and redesigned coupling and connecting rod brasses so as to box in the ends of the crankpins and exclude dirt.

Coupling rod brasses of the type used on MURIEL were used on the Geoghegan patent locomotives of the Guinness Brewery tramway, being shown in plan in the 1888 Institution of Mechanical Engineers paper and described in 'The Locomotive' magazine in 1902. This fact gives further support to the suggestion made earlier that ELLA's second boiler, with its more closely packed tube configuration than the original, was influenced by the Geoghegan locomotives. These latter engines also employed another feature which Heywood advocated, namely equal front and rear overhangs, but this would appear to have been the result of operational experience in Dublin rather than suggesting any consultation between Heywood and Geoghegan prior to the latter's relevant patent (3296 of 1879). This patent, as a matter of interest, did not show enclosed coupling rod brasses and differed in several respects from the Guinness locomotives as built.

The use of a steam water-lifter once again betrays evidence of discussion with the Royal Engineers as the R.E. Committee

CHAPTER 4

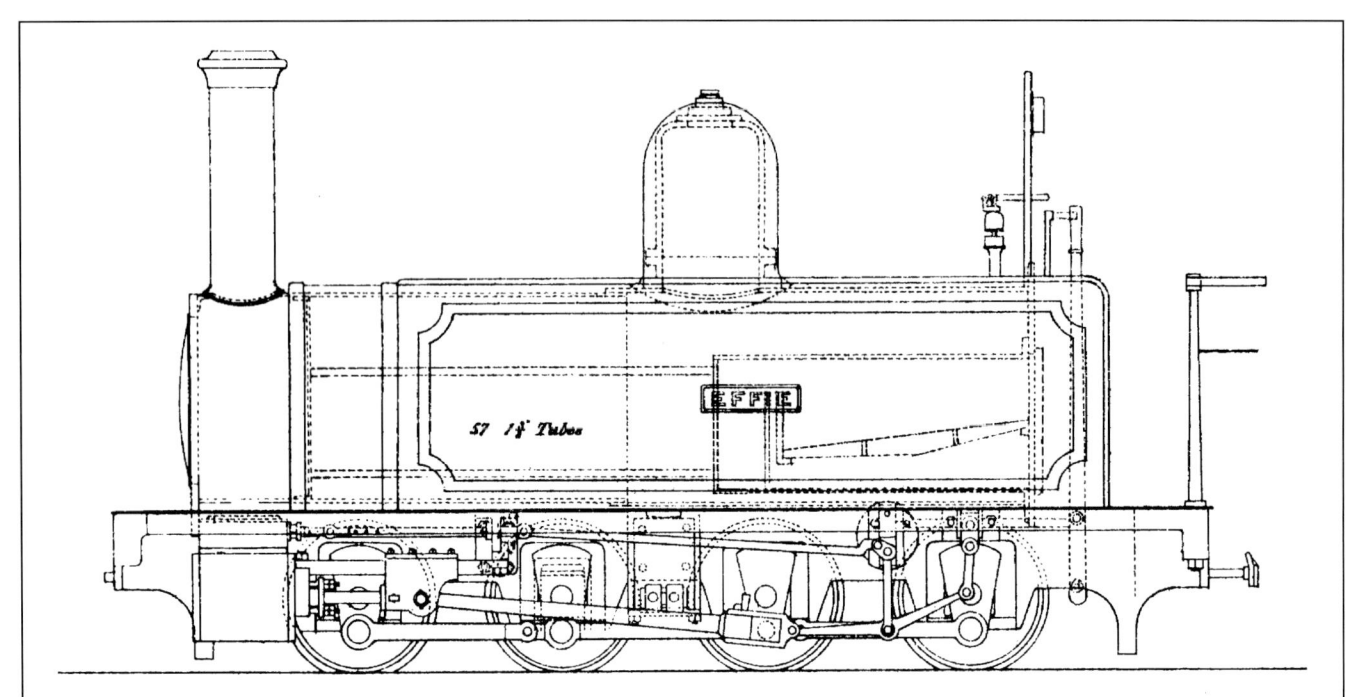

EIGHT COUPLED LOCOMOTIVE WITH FLEXIBLE WHEELBASE

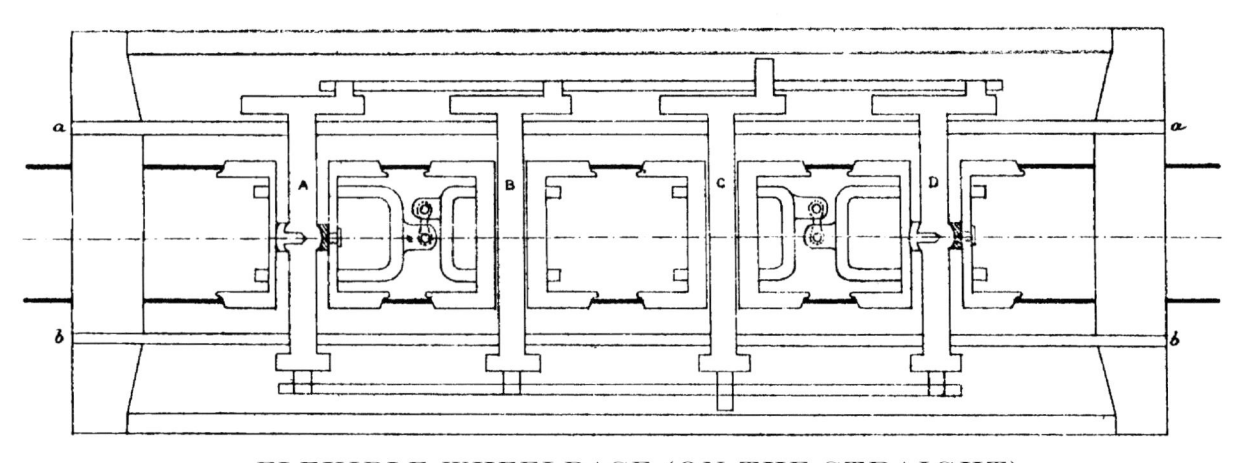

FLEXIBLE WHEELBASE (ON THE STRAIGHT)

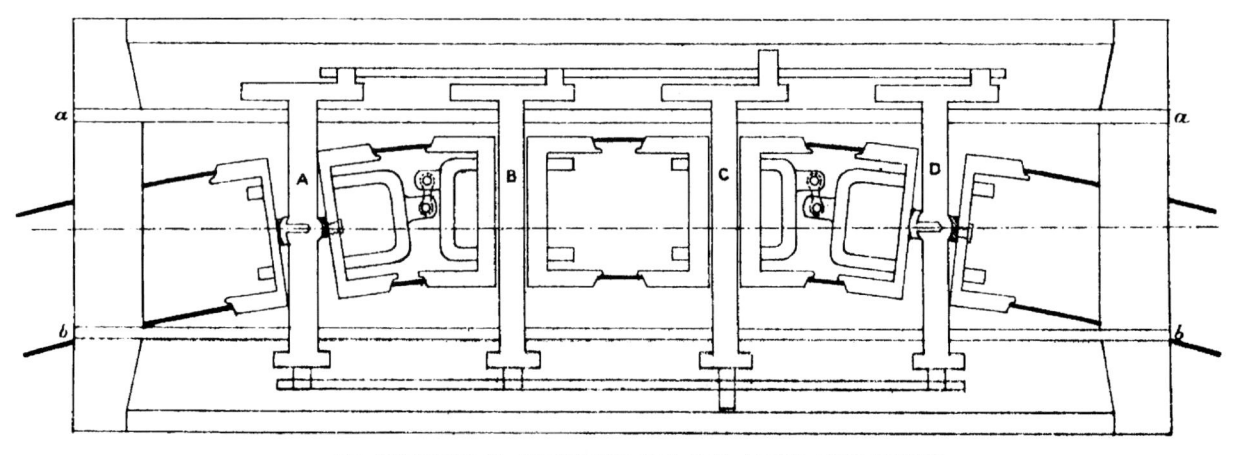

FLEXIBLE WHEELBASE (ON CURVE)

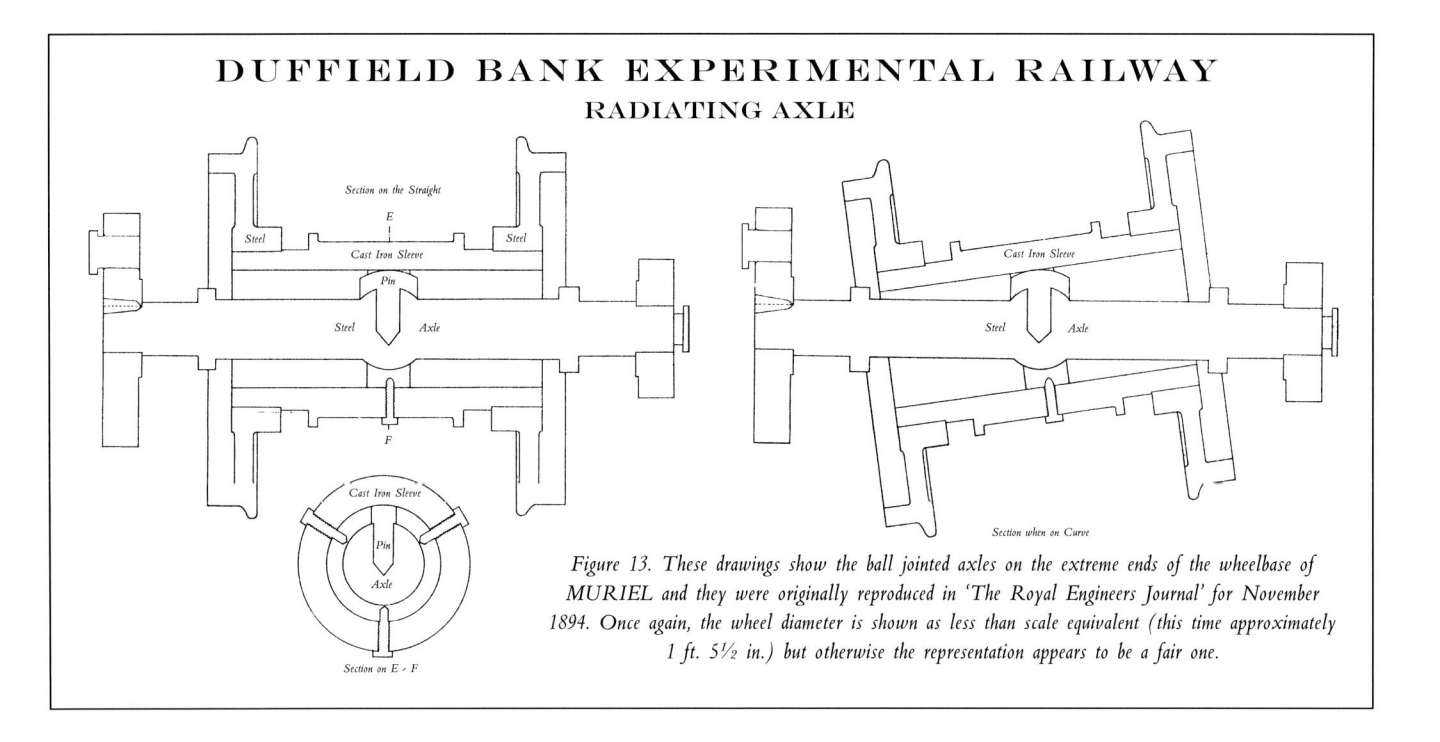

DUFFIELD BANK EXPERIMENTAL RAILWAY
RADIATING AXLE

Figure 13. These drawings show the ball jointed axles on the extreme ends of the wheelbase of MURIEL and they were originally reproduced in 'The Royal Engineers Journal' for November 1894. Once again, the wheel diameter is shown as less than scale equivalent (this time approximately 1 ft. 5½ in.) but otherwise the representation appears to be a fair one.

had investigated the possibility of using injectors for water lifting purposes some years previously. R.E. Committee Minute 4870 of 16TH MAY 1879 describes such tests with the Hancock Locomotive Inspirator (an appendage fitted after construction to at least some of the 'Handyside' engines). Water lifting apparatus was utilised on most steam locomotives used by the 60 CM. gauge War Department Light Railways during World War One.

The swinging link on MURIEL's valve gear was of a 'dog leg' rather than a straight configuration so as to facilitate the lengthening of the vibrating link below the level of the die block and allow correspondingly for the lengthening of the distance between die block and rear valve rod pivots when compared with ELLA's original layout. The drawback inherent in this alteration was that the valve events were slightly distorted, although all subsequent Heywood locomotives were fitted with the revised swinging link when new.

The water-gauge glasses were inserted during construction through the top cock and fastened with a top nut, thereby dispensing with the need for external glands. Circular nuts were used on the boiler fittings in preference to hexagonal ones as an aid to cleaning. The steam brake possessed a 5 IN. diameter piston and actuated, as with ELLA on the wheels mounted on the sliding axle sleeves. Four brake shoes were used once again, but this time they were arranged two per sliding axle and faced away from each other. The working principle of the brake linkage on MURIEL is not easy to deduce from photographic evidence but a suggested arrangement is shown in an accompanying figure.

The bufferbeams on MURIEL, and all subsequently built Heywood locomotives were cast iron and they incorporated sandboxes between the mainframes. The angle irons constituting the footplate valences were anchored at each end to the adjacent bufferbeam (securing rivets are visible in photographs of ELLA and MURIEL towards the end of their working careers in the 1920's). ELLA's original wooden bufferbeams had not been replaced by the time of Lt. Galloway's visit in 1894. Heywood was generally keen on the

Figure 12. PAGE LEFT. Contemporary side elevation view of eight coupled Heywood locomotive, together with views of flexible wheelbase on the straight and on a curve. Although inaccurate in some details when compared with MURIEL as built, several features of interest are shown, including the revised pattern valve gear. KATIE, the first of the Eaton Railway locomotives, was constructed with a similar arrangement of valve gear but ELLA did not go through this intermediate stage of evolution as it still retained its original valve gear layout in 1894. The revised design of reverser with lever and screw, adopted on ELLA circa 1884, was incorporated into MURIEL when new, as were counterbalanced flycranks and enclosed crankpin bearings on the connecting and coupling rods. Unlike ELLA, MURIEL was built with cast iron bufferbeams and ELLA'S were eventually replaced with bufferbeams of the same material in 1897-1900.
An important point about this drawing is that it shows the name EFFIE rather than MURIEL suggesting that it was originally intended to scrap the 0-4-0T EFFIE upon completion of the eight-coupled locomotive. The wheel diameter is shown under size (equivalent to 16¾ in.) on the side elevation drawing in comparison with the quoted dimension of 18 in., whilst in the inverted plan views, coned treads are erroneously shown. These drawings were originally published with a feature in the 'Royal Engineers Journal' for October 1st 1894 and at the time of the author, Lt. J. J. Galloway's visit to Duffield Bank on September 8th that year, only ELLA and MURIEL were in steam. ELLA had certainly been reboilered by this time as the engine's later boiler dimensions are quoted in the accompanying feature.

CHAPTER 4

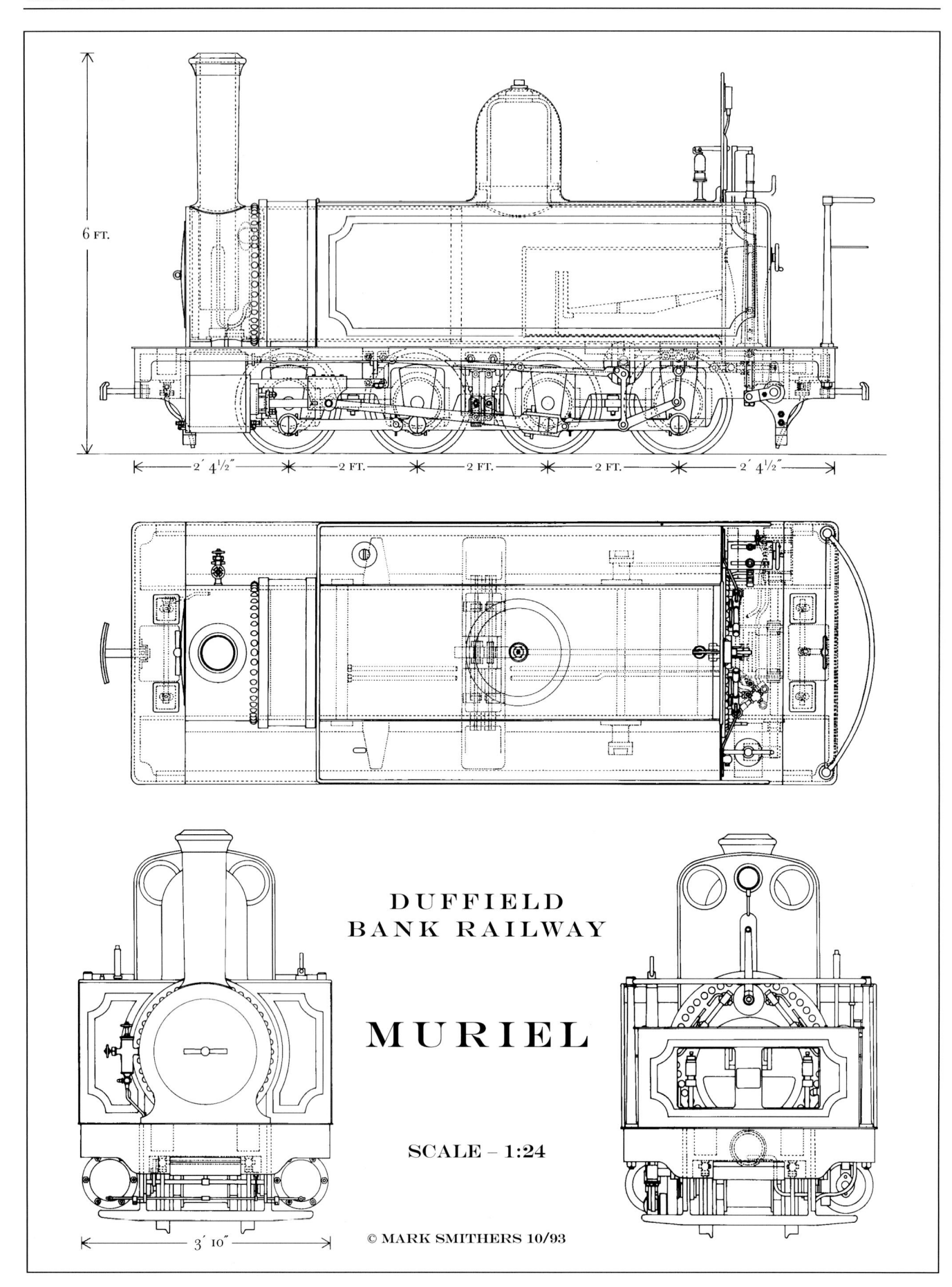

6 FT.

2' 4½" 2 FT. 2 FT. 2 FT. 2' 4½"

DUFFIELD
BANK RAILWAY

MURIEL

SCALE – 1:24

3' 10"

© MARK SMITHERS 10/93

The Engine Shed at Duffield Bank in June 1904 showing (from left to right) SHELAGH setting off for the 1 in 12 incline and 'Main Line', ELLA and MURIEL. As late as 1903, Sir Arthur had advertised an Open Session at Duffield Bank to which representatives of the Royal Engineers were invited (August 20th-22nd that year), but by this stage there was absolutely no prospect of the adoption of 15 inch gauge Heywood railways, or even an 18 in. gauge version, for military purposes. Within the wooden engine shed can be seen what was effectively a two road inspection pit (approximately 2 ft. 6 in. deep) and above ELLA'S running line, a cowling for the steam raising tube. Steam raising was accomplished by means of a compressed air supply piped from a compressor probably situated near the Otto gas engine in the group of buildings adjacent to the photographer. (Courtesy F. Wilde Collection).

Figure 14. PAGE LEFT. A reconstructed General Arrangement drawing of MURIEL as running immediately prior to rebuilding in the Edwardian period. This drawing has been compiled from information in 'The Royal Engineers Journal' for October 1894, Abbott boiler drawing No. 187D and measurements taken from the surviving components of the engine present in RIVER IRT at Ravenglass. As with the other two reconstructed Heywood locomotive drawings in this book, certain dimensions and component configurations have had to be inferred from photographic evidence. See also the reconstructed drawing of URSULA below. One particular difficulty is encountered with this locomotive, namely where was the steam water lifter located? Close examination of one of the later Duffield Bank photographs shows that an additional valence was located above the right hand side tank and it is suggested that the water lifter was concealed by this valence (which must have been hinged or removable to allow access to the tank filler cap). The water lifter seems to have disappeared by the time MURIEL reached Ravenglass. (Author).

use of castings in his work and, as we have seen, the Duffield Bank Workshops contained both iron and brass foundries.

As regards design proportions, Heywood recommended as long a cylinder stroke as possible, along with a relatively small wheel diameter, as speed was not of any great object on railways of the type which he advocated. In practice, it was found that his locomotives were unlikely in normal operating conditions to be called upon to reach speeds greater than 20 miles per hour. The steam water lifter was found to be of greatest use in frosty weather when elevated sources of water were likely to be frozen up, but in the Summer, it was found that its use would raise the feed water to a temperature which would impair the operation of the injectors.

MURIEL on one occasion between 1894 and 1898 took a

CHAPTER 4

A view showing the balanced flycranks, crosshead, steamchest and forward valve gear components on the left hand side (looking forwards) on RIVER IRT. These components are largely unaltered from the days when they formed part of MURIEL although the mechanical lubricator is a later addition. The 'kink' in the intermediate valve rod was necessitated by the running board support/brake rod bearing casting. Also evident in this view are the designs of crankpin bearing (made in two halves) adopted for the connecting and coupling rods which were in fact 'blind' to exclude dirt. Full enclosure of both connecting and coupling rod bearings was first adopted on MURIEL and was persisted with on all of the subsequent Heywood engines. (Author).

train consisting of eight bogie vehicles (four open sixteen seaters; the closed sixteen seater; the sleeping, dining and parcels vehicles) with 124 passengers around the northernmost loop which incorporated a curve of 40 FT. radius on a gradient of 1-IN-47. In order to accomplish this feat, an element of over loading was necessary as the nominal capacity of this train would have been about 100 passengers. It has to be said that the eight Heywood bogie vehicles would have given a train length (allowing for couplings and the shorter length of the parcels van as against the coaches) in the order of 180 FT., whereas the 1-IN-47 gradient was somewhat shorter than the train length.

At the time of the compilation of the 3RD Edition of 'Minimum Gauge Railways' in 1898, the year in which the Duffield Bank Railway was visited by the Institution of Mechanical Engineers, ELLA was undergoing another rebuild and, as will be seen, the decision had been taken to construct an enlarged version of the modified locomotive as the final development of Heywood's locomotive lineage. The decision to revert to the six coupled wheel arrangement for the last two Heywood locomotives was taken ostensibly on economic grounds.

One of the modifications made to ELLA during the 1897-1900 rebuild was the fitting of cast iron bufferbeam/sandbox units. A consequence of this alteration was the reduction in the engine's length over buffer beams by 4 IN. The opportunity was also taken to make another modification to the basic Heywood locomotive valve gear. On the rebuilt ELLA and on the two later locomotives, the vertical component of the motion was guided by a linear (sometimes wrongly termed a parallel) linkage. Forward and reverse settings of the gear were obtained by rotation of the body of the linear linkage through the required angle to the vertical. This principle was a slightly modified form of the one used on the Brown valve gear previously described and used on at least two designs of locomotive constructed by R. & W. Hawthorn during the

Above: The linear linkage as adopted by Sir Arthur Heywood in place of the straight slide and die block assembly on the valve gear. This modification was first adopted during the rebuilding of ELLA in 1897-1900 and it is now to be found on the Ravenglass and Eskdale locomotive RIVER IRT. The modification was carried out in order to reduce the friction and wear associated with the slide and die block. The upper portion of the fulcrum about which the body of the linkage could be rotated for reversal is clearly visible, as is the mode of operation of the linkage. The rod connected to the reversing lever can also be seen in this view. (Author).

1880's. After this modification, the Heywood gear greatly resembled Brown's valve gear, one major difference being that on the Heywood gear the drive to the valve rod was taken from the vibrating link at a point above, rather than below, the pin making connection with the linear linkage.

A new boiler was supplied for MURIEL from Abbotts in 1908 in connection with the rebuild which was then in progress on the engine. It seems likely that MURIEL's valve gear was altered during this rebuild as the 1907 photograph suggests that the earlier form of valve gear was still fitted at this time. The rebuild was completed, according to an entry in the Auction Catalogue, in 1910. The steam water lifter was certainly not present on the engine when it reached Ravenglass in 1917, and it would seem likely that it was removed circa 1904, once it had become clear that any prospect of MURIEL's design being adopted for military purposes was well and truly dead.

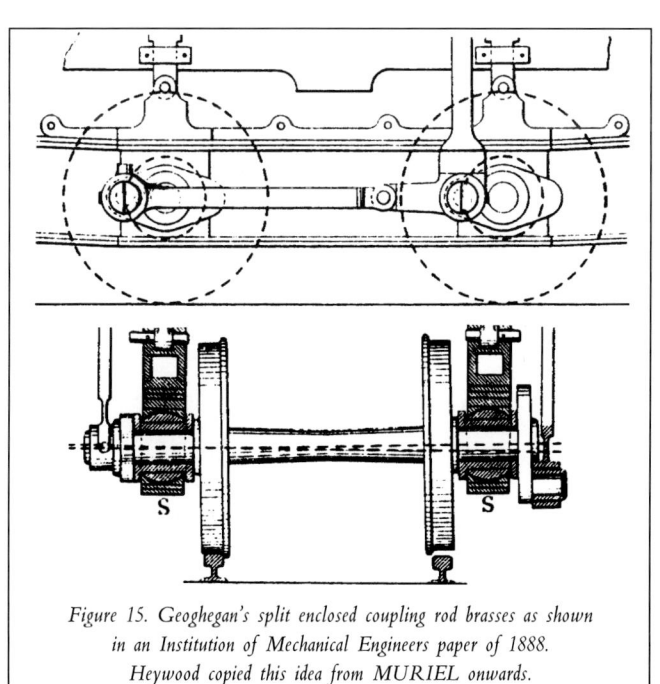

Figure 15. Geoghegan's split enclosed coupling rod brasses as shown in an Institution of Mechanical Engineers paper of 1888. Heywood copied this idea from MURIEL onwards.

CHAPTER FIVE
DUFFIELD BANK RAILWAY ROLLING STOCK

THE ROLLING STOCK designed by Heywood had, as with his locomotives, a very distinctive character but before any detailed discussion can be undertaken of the items used at Duffield Bank it must be understood that rolling stock proportions in general played a major part in Heywood's choice of 15 IN. as his ideal track gauge. It is recorded that the passenger carriages used on the experimental 9 IN. gauge line at Doveleys were 3 FT. long and 18 IN. wide inside their body portions and that passengers were seated one abreast. Even the four-wheeled wagons used on the Duffield Bank Railway were of larger dimensions than the 9 IN. gauge carriages and it is these early 15 IN. gauge wagons which must now be considered in detail.

Four-Wheeled Wagons
The first four-wheeled wagons used on the Duffield Bank line in the 1870's had an internal floor width of 2 FT. and an internal body length of 4 FT. The depth of the sides, according to the capacity of 8 cubic feet given in 'The Engineer' in 1881, would have been 1 FT. By 1881, the preferred internal body dimensions were 2 FT. 6 IN. width and 5 FT. length. The justification for this latter set of dimensions was stated at the time by Heywood to have been inherent in the fact that Charles Easton Spooner advocated an internal floor size with a length of four times the gauge and a width of twice the gauge. By 1877, the standard Heywood principle for four-wheeled wagons involving the use of a detachable 'top' comprising the four sides had evolved. The floor of the wagon was constructed with a rim approximately 1 IN. high so as to engage with the top. The angle irons holding the four sides of the top together were each augmented by a downward projecting iron so as to retain the top in its desired position when fitted upon the wagon. Each top additionally had an iron rim to facilitate stacking so that up to three tops could be stacked in order to carry relatively high loads. In order to empty the wagon, the top or tops could simply be lifted clear, if necessary, and the flat part of the wagon turned manually through the required angle in the vertical plane.

By 1898, the standard size of four-wheeled wagon adopted had an internal floor 6 FT. long and 3 FT. wide and box or 'top' sides 15 IN. deep. These dimensions appear to have been used for an experimental wagon on the Duffield Bank Railway and adopted from the beginning on the Eaton Railway before

An early Heywood four-wheeled 'top' wagon in the Museum Collection at Ravenglass. This vehicle, which passed successively through Eaton Hall and R.H.&D.R. hands, can be distinguished from later Heywood wagons by its plain axle bearings. The couplers have been removed at some stage. (Author).

EFFIE on the bridge that was (by 1895 at least) closest to Edgehill Station. The neatly rounded corners on the running plates of this and subsequent Heywood locomotives were probably influenced by Spooner's 0-4-0T designs of the 1870's. The rolling stock consists of some early 'top' wagons, fitted with plain axle bearings, and a single seat 'workman's car'. (Courtesy the late Sir Oliver Heywood).

eventually becoming standard at Duffield Bank. In most cases, the wheelbase on Heywood wagons of this type appears to have been half the internal floor length.

One important feature of the Heywood four-wheeled wagons was the fact that the 'tops' could be discarded altogether to create a flat wagon or allow a swivelling carrier to be fitted to a pair of wagons so treated so that particularly long loads could be carried. This latter aspect of the wagons' design could be traced back to Crewe Works for its origin, thereby exemplifying another feature borrowed by Heywood from existing minimum gauge practice. The fact that the workmanship on the earlier Heywood wagons was of good standard was illustrated by the comparatively late survival of some examples on the Ravenglass and Eskdale Railway and at Eaton Hall after 1916.

The materials used by Heywood in wagon construction consisted of pitch pine for the main structure and cast iron for the axle bearings. The rims for the 'tops' were made from angle iron. The early pattern of bearings utilised were of a plain description (a wagon with bearings of this type survives today in the museum at Ravenglass, having passed through the hands of the Eaton Railway and the R.H.&D.R.) but wagons constructed from about 1881 onwards used a pattern of suspension which, as with that used on his locomotives, relied on rubber blocks for flexibility. The bearings were of cast-iron and lubrication was effected by means of sponges placed in oil receptacles located below the level of the journals. Axle diameters varied between 2 IN. and 2½ IN. depending on the size of the vehicle and the load for which it was constructed, whilst the wheel diameter for Heywood's rolling stock was standardised at 1 FT. 11½ IN. with one wheel on each axle, as with Crewe and Chatham Dockyard 18 IN. gauge practice, being loose. By means of contrast, the opposite wheel was forced onto the axle by a hydraulic

CHAPTER 5

DUFFIELD BANK EXPERIMENTAL RAILWAY
AUTOMATIC COUPLER BUFFER

Elevation - In Position For Automatic Coupling

Plan View

Elevation - Left Hand shows Position when Automatic Coupling is Not Required

Figure 16. The standard Heywood coupling as used on the Duffield Bank and Eaton Hall Railways. Those used on the locomotives did not employ hooks. (Royal Engineers Journal).

pressure of approximately 15 TONS. The axlebox/oil reservoir assembly was retained within the hornblock by means of a single bolt and this was effected in such a manner as to retain the rubber block in a position immediately above the axlebox. According to information first published in 1881, the cost of each complete bearing, comprised of axlebox, oil cover, rubber block, bolt and hornblock was 5s. (25p) of which 1s. (5p) was for the rubber block.

Bogie Vehicles

The developments in passenger carriage design which were taking place during the 1870's on such 1 FT. 11½ IN. gauge lines as the Festiniog and N.W.N.G.R., and to a less sophisticated extent on the 18 IN. gauge lines at Woolwich Arsenal and Chatham Dockyard, could not have gone unnoticed by Heywood and shortly after the completion of EFFIE, a bogie carriage was constructed. This vehicle seated twelve passengers; two abreast in three compartments of equal capacity. According to Heywood in 1877, this carriage cost £25 to construct. As with the Chatham Dockyard carriages illustrated in 'Engineering' in 1875, there was no roof, although the compartment based superstructure of the Heywood vehicle was an improvement over the exposed longitudinal seating configuration of the Chatham carriages from the point of view of safety. The 'twelve-seater', which appears to have been withdrawn from Duffield Bank Railway service by 1894, was of interest in that its chassis construction was not of the well configuration favoured for subsequent passenger rolling stock constructed by Heywood.

According to the 1881 feature in 'The Engineer', one other

A Heywood coupling on a preserved wagon. The relief inscription reads 'DBR 1883'. (Author)

bogie vehicle existed on the Duffield Bank Railway by that stage. This was a sixteen seat closed carriage constructed in such a manner as to seat twelve passengers within the body and four (two on each end) over the bogies. The basic well configuration of the chassis on this vehicle owed much to Spooner's influence and this can easily be demonstrated by comparing two accompanying Figures, one of which shows a schematic design for a bogie carriage by C. E. Spooner in 'Engineering' for 18TH NOVEMBER 1870 and the other of which

SPOONER BOGIE PASSENGER CARRIAGE
FOR 2FT 9IN GAUGE

Figure 17. A schematic Spooner design for a bogie carriage as originally reproduced in 'Engineering' for 18th November 1870. The well configuration of the chassis can easily be seen, along with the drawgear mounted on the bogies. Both of these features were to appear on the standard pattern of Heywood bogie carriage.

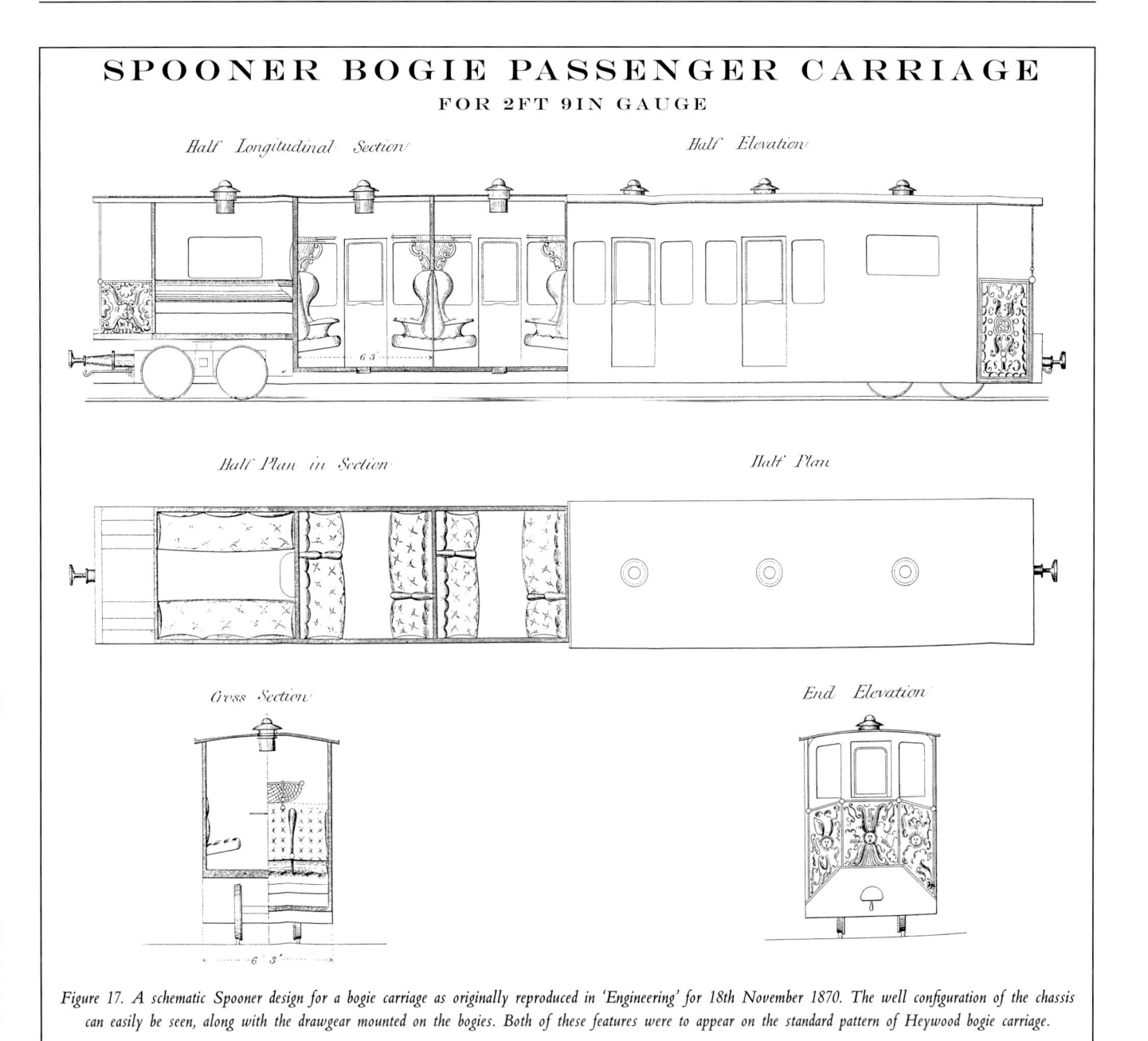

shows the design of the Duffield Bank Railway closed carriage as illustrated in 'Minimum Gauge Railways' and 'Engineering' in 1881. A point of interest to note about the design of Heywood's 16 seater carriages is that the Spooner well frame structure was also chosen for some 18 IN. gauge bogie convict carriages built circa 1880 by the Lancaster Wagon Company for use by the Royal Engineers on a construction line linking Forts Horsted, Luton, Borstal and Bridgewoods at Chatham.

The first Duffield Bank closed carriage was 19 FT. 6 IN. long over sole timbers and 3 FT. 6 IN. wide. The bogie wheelbase was 1 FT. 6 IN. and the bogie pivots were set at 15 FT. apart. The height to the top of the roof was 5 FT. 3 IN. and the main material used, for sole timbers and body was pitch pine, whilst the bogie frames (which incorporated the later standard Heywood axlebox) were of elm.

The closed carriage was soon joined by four open coaches of similar construction and dimensions, and seating the same number of passengers. These vehicles are recorded as being fitted with a footbrake acting on one bogie and they were reckoned to weigh one ton each as opposed to the 1.2 TONS for the closed carriage. The cost for each of the open carriages (presumably at early 1880's prices) was given as £37 inclusive of stain, varnish and linoleum, whereas the equivalent figure for the closed coach was £67. In defence of his loading gauge principles, Heywood stated that a visitor 6 FT. 3½ IN. tall was

CHAPTER 5

PASSENGER CARRIAGE TO SEAT SIXTEEN
DUFFIELD BANK RAILWAY

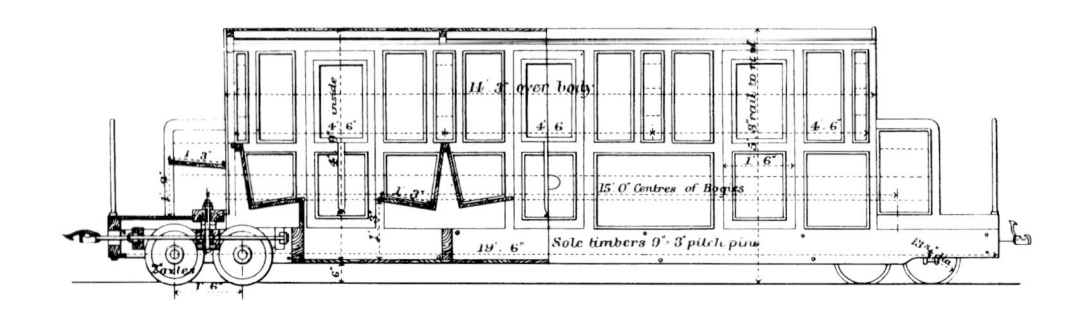

Figure 18. The sixteen seat closed bogie carriage as used on the Duffield Bank Railway and illustrated in 'Minimum Gauge Railways' and 'Engineering' in 1881. The handrails at the extreme ends and the adjacent open seats were distinctive features of many Heywood vehicles, but the design owes much to the principles illustrated in the previous figure. The headstocks at this stage were merely slotted in order to allow the couplings to pass through but it became standard practice on subsequent Heywood bogie vehicles for a bottomless recess to be cut into these components.
By the time it reached Ravenglass, the 1881 carriage had had its headstocks modified to conform with the later vehicles.

able to sit in the closed carriage with ample space for his tall hat.

In addition to the normal closed carriage, Heywood constructed two further bogie closed passenger vehicles for the Duffield Bank Railway which perhaps owed more to Victorian eccentricity than to any serious practical application. These vehicles were a dining car and a sleeping car and both were completed in time for the second 'Open Session' in 1894. The basic principles of construction were similar to the closed carriage save that the bogie frames were of cast iron rather than elm and that the sleeping car did not possess any end balconies. The maximum height of both these vehicles was 6 FT.

The dining car seated eight persons and was fitted with a kitchen compartment equipped with two folding tables, shelving for plates and a Rippingille oil stove. Unlike the normal closed coach, it was not fitted with side doors and entry to both kitchen and passenger compartments was

The Dining Car as photographed in 1894 by Lt. Galloway R.E. Unlike the 1881 closed carriage, this vehicle was not fitted with end seats (Minimum Gauge Railways Plate XVI).

44

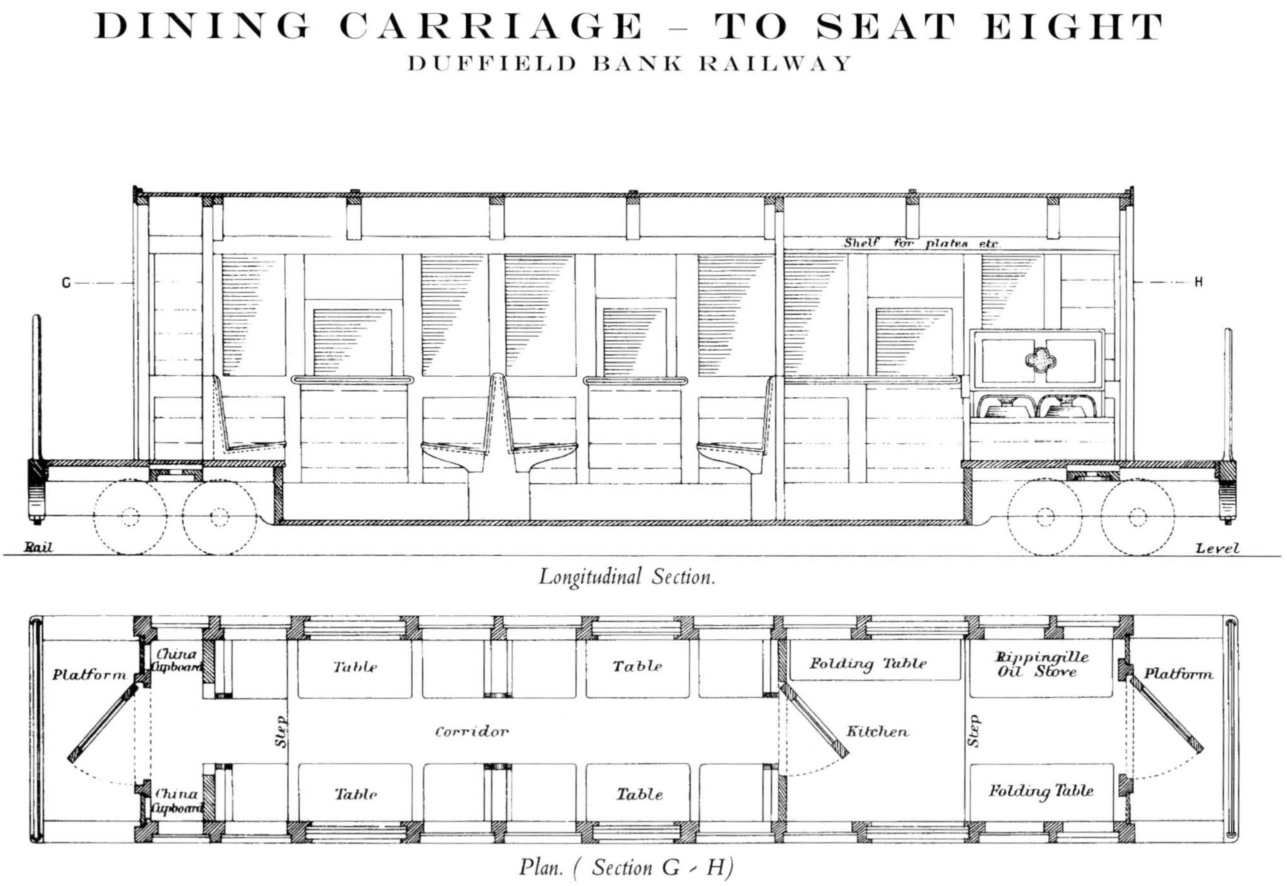

DINING CARRIAGE – TO SEAT EIGHT
DUFFIELD BANK RAILWAY

Longitudinal Section.

Plan. (Section G – H)

Figure 19. The Dining Car constructed for use on the Duffield Bank Railway. As with the ordinary closed car design, Spooner's design principles were closely followed on this vehicle, even to the extent of using end balconies. Entry to this vehicle was by means of centrally positioned end doors on the body rather than the usual side doors and the original passenger capacity was eight persons. (Minimum Gauge Railways).

effected by means of central end doors.

The sleeping car was constructed to accommodate four berths and it was also equipped with a dressing table, coat pegs and a folding washbasin. This vehicle was sometimes used as an overflow bedroom for the Heywood children when the house at Duffield Bank was full of guests, during the many social occasions which took place at Duffield Bank in the two decades from 1894.

A closed luggage van, with entry via central sliding doors, had also been constructed by 1894 and this was used primarily for the conveyance of luncheons and teas to Tennis Ground Station when refreshments were being served there. This vehicle was fitted with a brake (presumably of the same type used on the open coaches) and was sometimes used as a brake van.

There is known to have been at least one further non-Eaton Railway Heywood pattern bogie wagon from the fact that such a vehicle subsequently saw use on the Ravenglass and Eskdale Railway. Photographs of this three ton capacity open vehicle show it to have had full length dropsides and a well frame of similar pattern to the closed luggage van. After much usage during the early days of 15 IN. gauge operation on the R.&E.R. the wagon came to rest in an inverted position, sans bogies, at Irton Road during the mid 1920's. It was scrapped shortly afterwards.

Miscellaneous Vehicles

The bogie vehicles which have just been referred to were adequate for the Duffield Bank Railway's own needs until the line's closure in 1916, although further vehicles were to be constructed using similar principles for the Eaton Railway with one closed carriage, probably intended for this destination, being uncompleted at the date of the auction of Duffield Bank Railway equipment after the line's closure.

CHAPTER 5

SLEEPING CARRIAGE WITH FOUR BERTHS
DUFFIELD BANK RAILWAY

Figure 20. Heywood's Sleeping Car for the Duffield Bank Railway. Unlike most other Heywood bogie passenger stock, end balconies were not provided. (Minimum Gauge Railways).

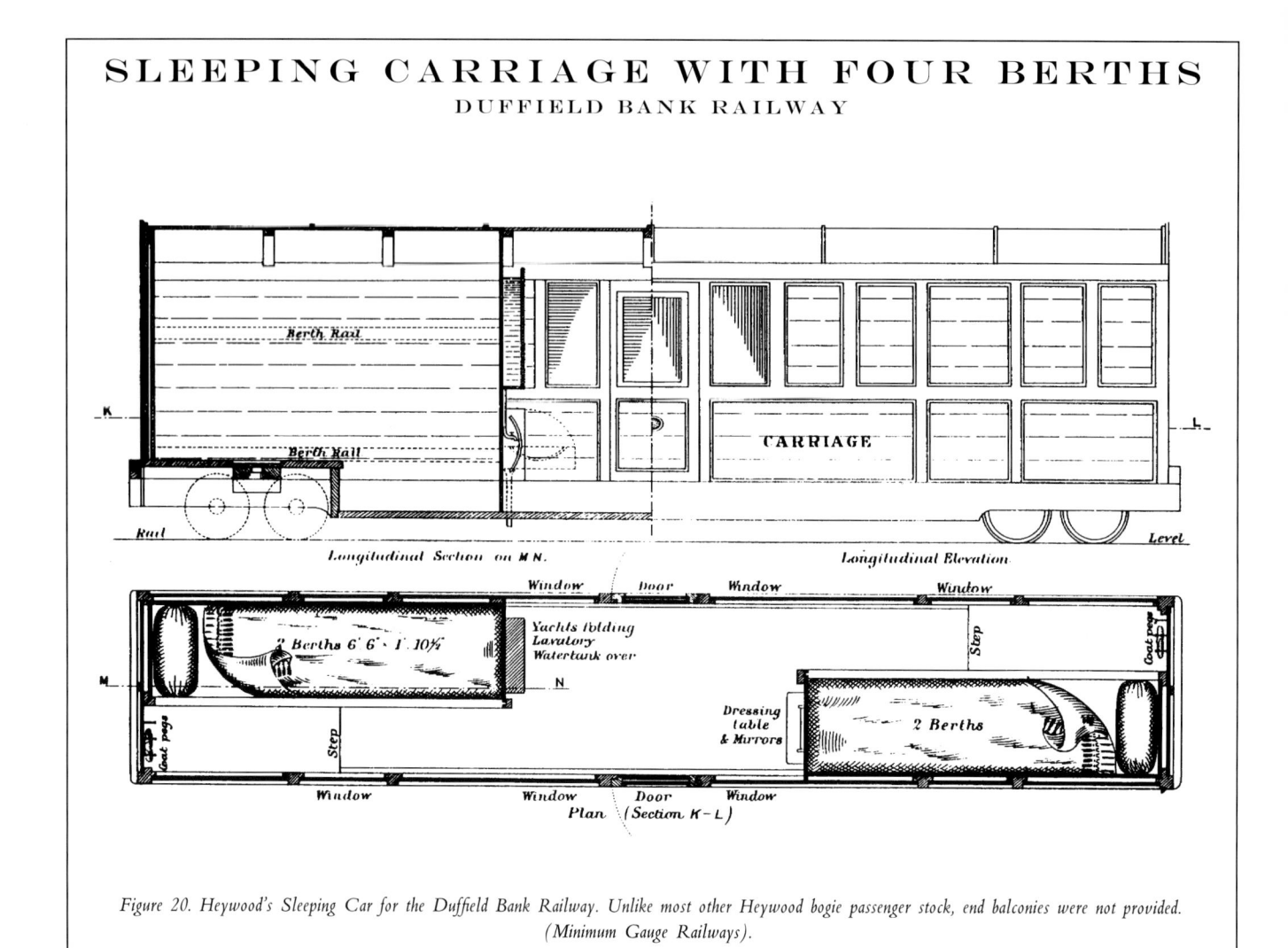

There were, however, some interesting miscellaneous four-wheeled vehicles on the Duffield Bank Railway and these included a dynamometer car with instruments for recording speed, distance travelled and tractive effort, some parts of which currently survive in the possession of the Ravenglass and Eskdale Railway. This latter vehicle certainly existed at the time of Lt. Galloway's visit to Duffield Bank in 1894 although it was not in use on this occasion.

The standard Heywood four wheeled flat or box wagon was adapted in at least two instances to form a workman's car for the conveyance of platelayers' equipment. This was effected by means of the fitting of a superstructure equipped with a seat and a hinged top tool box and, on at least one specimen, a brake (probably of the hand operated type with the sector guide for the handle attached to the superstructure). One of these wagons can be seen accompanying EFFIE in an accompanying Plate, whilst another can be seen in the view of the 'Dove Bank Railway'. This latter photograph also shows the 'children's pedal propelled trolley' described in the 1916 Auction Catalogue which must soon have returned to Duffield Bank after its period of usage at Doveleys. The pedal trolley was of the direct-action variety, worked in similar fashion to a small child's tricycle, rather than being chain driven.

In addition to the four wheeled 'workman's cars' there were a few assorted specialised wagons on the Duffield Bank Railway, some of which have been mentioned in connection with the line's construction. Most of these were associated with permanent way maintenance work.

Figure 21. FACING PAGE. Side elevation, longitudinal section and transverse sectional views of the cast iron bogie design utilised on the Heywood dining and sleeping carriages. The rubber block suspension can be seen clearly in these views, as can the bolt securing the hornblock. (Royal Engineers Journal).

DUFFIELD BANK EXPERIMENTAL RAILWAY
STANDARD BOGIE

Longitudinal Section

Half Section through Axle   *Half Transverse Section through Centre Pin*

Dotted Surfaces Denote India Rubber

Side Elevation

CHAPTER SIX
THE COMMERCIAL IMPACT OF HEYWOOD'S EARLY WORK

EVENTS PRIOR TO 1881 – Arthur Percival Heywood's experimentation in the field of small gauge locomotive worked railways was contemporaneous with the work of the Leeds concern, John Fowler & Co. in this field. As a major world supplier of agricultural equipment, Fowlers were keen by 1877 to expand their product range to include railway equipment suitable particularly for overseas plantations. To this end the Leeds firm initially marketed, and then developed, the Decauville portable railway system for use on overseas agricultural railways of 400, 500 and 600 MM. gauge.

The Royal Agricultural Society's Annual Show was held at Kilburn in 1879 and Fowlers took the opportunity to demonstrate their portable railway (as patented by Alfred Greig) by laying down such a line from one end of the showground to the other. The line was described in 'The Engineer' for JULY 11TH 1879 and consisted of the normal Fowler pattern portable track of 500 MM. (approximately 20 IN.) gauge with 18 LB./YD. rail, assorted rolling stock (including open bogie cars with back-to-back seating) and two locomotives. These were described as: 'slightly differing in pattern, the one with outside and the other with inside valve gear, the cylinders in both cases being outside and horizontal... both the engines were fitted with six wheels each, one pair being put in a bogie, while the other two pairs were coupled'. Elsewhere in the feature the engines were described as the first built by Fowlers for a portable 20 IN. gauge line.

This last-mentioned assertion on the part of 'The Engineer' does not square with other surviving evidence relating to activities at the Steam Plough Works at this time. An October 1878 Fowler catalogue stated that: 'a steam locomotive is now being constructed for 16 and 20 IN. gauges which will weigh about 30 CWT. empty and 36 CWT. with water and coal'. This clearly suggests that Heywood was attempting to persuade Fowler to build locomotives to 16 IN. gauge, although the earliest photograph to show a locomotive on their portable track (probably taken in late 1878) shows a 20 IN. gauge 2-4-0ST with no works no. and named HERCULES. The two locomotives used at the Kilburn Show appear in reality to be the second and third 20 IN. gauge locomotives produced by Fowler. The engine with the inside eccentrics was maker's no. 3688 of 1879, whilst that with the outside eccentrics was effectively a class prototype and bore no Works No. Both these locomotives were of the 0-4-2T configuration.

Although the use of unpowered pony or trailing trucks was praised by 'The Engineer' on account of improving an engine's riding characteristics, the practice was, not surprisingly, condemned in Heywood's letter a fortnight later: '...while agreeing with you that an even grip of the rail is a most desirable thing, I am convinced that this must not be gained at the loss of adhesion... therefore I think Messrs. Fowler's engines, with bogies in front, no matter how little weight the bogies carry, are not the most suitable engines for narrow gauge traffic'. Heywood went on to advocate a simple 0-4-0 for most applications (a view which he was destined to retract nearly twenty years later!) and, after advocating the cylindrical firebox boiler on the ground of its non-interference with the spacing of the axles he further stated: 'Messrs. Fowler's representative, who consulted me on the subject, adopted this boiler, but, against my advice, adopted a two wheel bogie which I think unnecessary...'

Close examination of the earliest Fowler 20 IN. gauge engine, HERCULES reveals it to have had inside mainframes, disc wheels, single slide bars, outside cylinders and steam chests, inside link motion actuating the valves through rocker shafts, and, most significantly, a cylindrical firebox boiler. This engine was obviously the result of the aforementioned consultation between Heywood and Alfred Greig, or one of the latter's subordinates (a view further reinforced by Heywood's reference, erroneous in the context of the Kilburn engines, to the fact that the unpowered truck was 'in front'). Works No. 3688 retained the EFFIE-pattern inside eccentrics (the cylinders were slightly inclined, rather than being 'horizontal' as suggested in 'The Engineer') and other Heywood features whilst the other 0-4-2T retained Heywood's preferred pattern of boiler but in this instance outside Stephenson/Howe link motion was employed. The drawback of this arrangement was excessive side overhang of the rods, a problem which would have been aggravated with an engine incorporating outside mainframes. Witnessing the 0-4-2T in action is what may therefore have prompted Heywood to adopt a different form of valve gear on the embryonic ELLA.

Sir Thomas Percival Heywood's connections with the Royal Agricultural Society would have given his son early and easy access to Fowler representatives, who would have regarded the Society's members as important customers. It would therefore have seemed a logical course of action for Arthur to have approached a firm whose markets consisted mainly of agricultural concerns in an attempt to promote his 'minimum gauge' railway equipment. From the information given in the 1879 letter, it seems certain that he was present at the Kilburn show and as further evidence of the existence of contact with Fowlers two early (circa 1879) D.B.R. wagons survived at Doveleys into the 1960's before acquisition by

THE COMMERCIAL IMPACT OF HEYWOOD'S EARLY WORK

This view shows HERCULES, the 500 mm gauge 2-4-0 saddle tank constructed by John Fowler & Co. circa 1878. This locomotive was constructed by the Leeds firm as part of its first attempt to adapt Paul Decauville's original portable track principles to suit mechanised haulage. As mentioned in the text, the engine exhibits many features shared with EFFIE, although the use of a leading pony truck was contrary to Heywood practice. A feature of significance is the pin and retaining collar for the front coupling rod bearing as fastenings of this type survive today on the valve motion of the R.&E.R.'s RIVER IRT. The engine is shown standing on a stretch of Greig's Patent portable track. (Museum of English Rural Life, Reading).

Mr. Michel Jacot and these are known to have possessed Fowler wheels and axles.

Arthur Heywood was critical of portable railways even in his 1879 letter, pointing out that the little engines on the line at Kilburn should have been able to haul a net weight of 8-9 TONS up the 1-IN-57 incline there with a good road, when in fact they managed about half this amount. He nonetheless praised Grieg's corrugated sleeper pointing out that it retained packing ballast more successfully than the flat-bottomed type. Despite the disappointment of seeing Fowlers build several narrow gauge locomotives incorporating unpowered carrying wheels, it appears that Heywood did not give up trying to persuade the Leeds concern to adopt more of the practices of Duffield Bank Works. The fact that Heywood remained in touch with developments at the Steam Plough Works during the 1879-81 period is evidenced by the fact that at least one of the 500 MM. gauge Fowler 0-4-2T engines of 1879, LITTLE BEAUTY, possessed long tank/bunker assemblies similar to those later used on ELLA, and that ELLA when new possessed circular balanced slide valves, obviously derived from the Church's patent design of 1872 which were used on several Fowler traction and portable engines. The photograph in

CHAPTER 6

This 500 mm gauge Fowler 0-4-2T LITTLE BEAUTY with 4½ in. by 8 in. cylinders was supplied in 1879 to a Mr. E. Cespedes for export. Whilst the chassis with its outside link motion was clearly influenced by continental practice, the engine's superstructure shows much in common with Heywood's ELLA as completed two years later.

This is evident from the design of the boiler, particularly in the fact that once again the cylindrical firebox was used. To all intents and purposes LITTLE BEAUTY'S boiler was a commercial version of that later to be used on ELLA, even to the fitting of three cock water gauges and the use of backhead water feed, although the safety valves were mounted over the firebox rather than on the dome. The side tanks were also of similar, but relatively higher, pattern to those later to be used on ELLA. The mounting of the smokebox door hinge on the right hand side of the engine, contrary to normal railway locomotive practice, was a feature shared with all of the 15 in. gauge Heywood locomotives. The weatherboard, with its window aperture of a more respectable size than on Heywood's engines, was a more practicable commercial proposition than those on the latter and Sir Arthur would certainly not have approved of the roof!

(Museum of English Rural Life, Reading).

'Minimum Gauge Railways' (Plate XIII in that work) shows the firehole door on the engine when new to have been of the conventional lever operated type, similar to LITTLE BEAUTY, but with the rodding hung below, rather than above, the doors.

The Period After ELLA'S Completion

An interesting development in Fowlers' narrow gauge locomotive building policy from the 1880's onwards was the construction of 18 IN. gauge locomotives for War Department and Admiralty use and also for export to the Kimberley Diamond mines in South Africa.

In considering events during the period from 1885 to 1895, the question arises as to whether there is sufficient evidence to show that Heywood made any attempt to persuade John Fowler & Co. Ltd (as the firm became in 1886) to build locomotives based on ELLA's specification with the intention of proving to the military authorities that a commercial manufacturer was willing to undertake the construction of such locomotives. In attempting to answer this question one must first consider the extent of Heywood's contact with Fowlers during this period. An important aspect of the locomotive MURIEL's construction is highlighted by Heywood's statement in 'Minimum Gauge Railways' that: '(the locomotive boilers) have been chiefly supplied to me... by Messrs Abbott & Co. of Newark'. The word 'chiefly' is crucial in this context as an entry exists in the surviving Fowler records showing the supply of a boiler (Works No. 7006) on JUNE 30TH 1893 to A. P. Heywood for fitting to a small locomotive. Since ELLA was probably rebiolered in 1889 and the Eaton Railway was not envisaged at this stage, it must be assumed that the 1893 Fowler boiler was for use on MURIEL.

The decision to use a Fowler boiler on a Heywood locomotive in the early 1890's must be viewed in the light of the 1889 Manual of Military Railways which was still in force at this time. The 18 IN. gauge locomotive worked trench supply railway had impressed the War Department (but not certain influential R.E. personnel!) sufficiently during the Suakin Expedition of 1885 to ensure that the use of such systems continued to be envisaged at the time of the 1889 Manual of Military Railways. Seven 18 IN. gauge 0-4-2T locomotives, delivered to the Royal Arsenal but clearly originally intended for use in the construction of the abortive Suakin-Berber Railway, had been supplied to the War Department by Fowlers in 1885. The possibility therefore arises that by giving work to Fowlers, Heywood may have hoped to have gained greater influence upon the company's narrow gauge product policy. Shortly before the ordering of MURIEL's boiler, as will be discussed in a subsequent chapter, an experiment was performed with ELLA in the presence of two representatives of a locomotive building concern. Unfortunately, the relevant entry in 'Minimum Gauge Railways' does not say which company had sent the representatives. Circumstantial evidence, at least, points very much in the direction of John Fowler & Co. Ltd., although, as we shall see, the Stafford concern W. G. Bagnall Ltd. is another, more remote, possibility.

Whatever may have been the extent of Heywood's dealings with John Fowler & Co. Ltd., any thoughts which may have existed of the adoption of fully adhesive Heywood-style locomotives as part of the latter concern's product policy were destined to be abortive. By the 1890's the market for functional steam locomotives of less than 2 FT. gauge outside of the military and military service spheres was extremely small, largely as a result of the much greater popularity of lines of nominal 2 FT. gauge at home and overseas. The last purely functional 18 IN. gauge steam locomotives constructed in Britain were built by Fowlers (Works No's. 17149-52) for export in 1927, by which time Sir Arthur Heywood's influence had long been forgotten at the Steam Plough Works. In being consulted prior to the construction of any sub – 3 FT. 6 IN. gauge steam locomotives by Fowlers, however, Heywood must have had a great bearing upon the Leeds concern's decision to enter the small gauge steam locomotive market. Viewed in the context of true commercial applications for his early efforts, this was probably his greatest achievement.

Contemporary Products of W. G. Bagnall Ltd.

In closing this chapter, another sphere of possible Heywood influence must be briefly considered. The one major British manufacturer to use the cylindrical firebox boiler as an important part of its product policy was W. G. Bagnall Ltd. of Stafford from 1892 until 1953. The type of boiler used, commonly known as the 'Bullhead', was radically different from that used on the Heywood locomotives in that an enlarged outer wrapper was used in order to increase the inner firebox: boiler diameter ratio, a modification from which Heywood's engines would certainly have benefited. The basic idea could be traced back at least as far as Daniel Adamson's Patent No. 1377 of 1869.

A forerunner of the 'Bullhead' boiler had actually been used on the first of the Fowler Greig and Beadon patent jackshaft drive locomotives constructed as a 'test bed' (see Patent Specification 402 of 1880). This boiler, which had obviously been developed at the Steam Plough Works to mitigate some of the limitations of the boilers used on HERCULES and LITTLE BEAUTY (and whose development indicated a measure of early Fowler disillusionment with Heywood's views on boilers), differed from the Bagnall type in two respects. Firstly the firebox wrapper was concentric with the boiler barrel, and secondly the ashpan and damper depended from the wrapper. An oval cross section shaft passed through the wrapper and lower inner firebox so as to allow communication with the grate.

The extent to which any consultation between Bagnalls' Ernest Baguley and Sir Arthur Heywood occurred is unclear, particularly as Bagnalls were another portable railway manufacturer in direct competition with Fowlers, but their willingness to produce a simple 0-4-0 with cylinders as small as 4 IN. by 7 IN. to a gauge as low as 18 IN. appeared to pay some heed to the views expressed by Heywood, particularly during the pre-1894 period. Unlike EFFIE, however, the small standard Bagnall 0-4-0 saddle tanks did not possess equal front and rear overhangs.

In view of the lack of documentary evidence of an exchange of ideas between Heywood and Bagnalls (one detects a certain stubborn streak in the former's character in refusing to adopt the 'Bullhead' boiler after 1892), any views regarding a possible connection can only be speculation, but there is one particularly interesting passage in Heywood's second letter of 1896 to 'The Times' from this point of view. This stated: 'a quarry owner of my acquaintance is at the present time conveying some 30,000 TONs of stone annually by means of traction engines from his works to the railway along 2½ MILES of highway… the proprietor of the quarry would at once set about making a narrow gauge line… could he only obtain some guarantee that the permission to cross, and in some parts run alongside the road… would not suddenly be revoked at a future date'.

The 'quarry owner of my acquaintance' appears to have been Mr. J. Rupert Fitzmaurice, who had acquired the Cliffe Hill Granite Quarry (near Markfield in Leicestershire) from his father in 1891. According to 'Cliffe Hill Mineral Railway' by Maurice H. Billington (1973), this quarry had been worked in the 1870's and 1880's by a partnership under the name of Jones & Fitzmaurice, which had transported its stone by road to 'Cliffhill Sidings' at Beveridge Lane on the adjacent Midland Railway system. Heywood's 1879 letter to 'The Engineer' referred to: 'a landed proprietor in my neighbourhood…' with '…an annual traffic of 20,000 TONs of stone, which has for some years rendered the roads on his property well-nigh impassable'. It would seem that the 'landed proprietor' was probably Mr. Fitzmaurice senior. The 30,000 TON figure quoted for 1896 has been described as excessive for the Cliffe Hill Quarry, but this may have been a projected figure of the period.

During this latter year the original survey for the 1 FT. 11½ IN. gauge Cliffe Hill Granite Co. Ltd's system was under-taken. This envisaged 1-IN-20 gradients and sharp curves and tender documents for locomotives specified cylindrical fire-boxes. In the event, the curves and gradients were eased before construction commenced and the first two locomotives supplied were of the Bagnall 'Bullhead' boiler type.

The question therefore arises whether Heywood influenced, or even prepared the original survey or tender documents. Such influence, if it existed, would certainly have favoured Bagnalls in the tendering for the Cliffe Hill locomotive contracts as against their Leeds-based competitors. The tenders of two Leeds companies to build the first Cliffe Hill locomotives were rejected because the Cliffe Hill Company wanted these to have cylindrical firebox boilers, which neither Manning Wardle nor Hunslet were prepared to manufacture.

As further evidence of the Stafford company benefiting intentionally or unintentionally from Heywood's efforts, an extract from a report in the 'Isle of Man Times' concerning the 1896 opening of the Groudle Glen Railway (2 FT. gauge) is of interest. This reads: 'the proprietor set to work to find a builder who would make the kind of engine to suit the work; and after a great deal of trouble he found that Mr. Bagnall would undertake to build a small engine on the same lines as those used on the main railway lines. The engine is very small indeed, but powerful and well made, with a telescope tubular boiler, constructed with a firebox or furnace which does not depend below the barrel – a great advantage on a line of this sort where the curves are numerous and the gradients heavy, as the overhang is equalised at each end – and consequently the whole weight is utilised for adhesion…'.

Although the engine in question, the still extant 2-4-0T SEA LION (Maker's No. 1484/1896), did not have a fully adhesive wheel arrangement, it can be seen that the reporter's last sentence in the quote contains Heywood-inspired observations. The suggestion to be made is that R.M. Broadbent, the line's substantive proprietor, was previously acquainted with Heywood and the Duffield Bank Railway. He would thus have been impressed with the value of such a line as a possible tourist attraction, but not with the gauge of 15 IN. Taking this proposition into account, Mr. Broadbent may have laid down a locomotive specification based on 'Minimum Gauge Railways', only to find (as may have been the case at Cliffe Hill) that Bagnalls were to offer the closest commercial match to his requirements. In the event, the original requirement for a fully adhesive wheelbase was sacrificed before SEA LION was completed.

CHAPTER SEVEN
THE HEYWOOD FAMILY 1872-1897

THROUGHOUT THE LAST THREE DECADES of his life, Sir Thomas Percival Heywood suffered greatly from the effects of ill health and these were aggravated by the loss of an eye following a shooting accident in 1871 and the breaking of a thigh bone in a riding accident in 1885. During this time he continued to spend most of his life at Doveleys and his failing health did not prevent him from participating in Church affairs and coming to the defence of the Reverend Sidney F. Green, whom, as Patron, he had appointed to the position of Rector of St. John's Church, Miles Platting in 1869. Although a detailed consideration of this incident is outside the scope of this volume, some discussion of it is necessary in order to appreciate one of the factors which contributed to the deterioration in the condition of Sir Thomas during his final years.

The facts of the Miles Platting affair were briefly that the Reverend Green was prosecuted under the Public Worship Regulation Act as a result of the efforts of a Mr. George McDonagh, a local Orangeman, regarding the former's conduct of church services. Despite being popular with his congregation, the Reverend Green was condemned by the

The Heywood family group circa 1910 at Doveleys.
(Courtesy the late Sir Oliver Heywood).

KEY

Sir Arthur's three sons all saw front line action in the Great War. They were, in order of age: Sir Graham Percival Heywood, 4th Bart. and Lt.-Colonel in the Staffordshire Yeomanry (1878-1946); Cecil Percival, Major-General in the Coldstream Guards, (1880-1936), and Arthur George Percival, Major 6th Battalion Manchester Regiment (1885-1918; died of wounds received in action). His daughters were: Muriel Annette Margaret (1873-1924); Ella Mary Effie (1874-1953); Dorothy Alice (1877-1957); Evelyn Mary (1883-1970); Margaret Sophia (1884-1940); Guendolen Constance (died in infancy, 1888) and Isabel Effie (1890-1975).

CHAPTER 7

court of Lord Penzance and for continuing with his services in the prohibited manner he was imprisoned for contempt of court in Lancaster Castle in 1881. Sir Thomas made considerable efforts to secure the release of Mr. Green, an event finally facilitated only by the latter's resignation from the Miles Platting rectorship in 1882. He also attempted to appoint a successor of his own choosing, which was blocked by the efforts of the Bishop of Manchester in the court of Lord Penzance in January 1884. The affair caused much bitterness in Miles Platting and alienated many of the congregation who had attended the Reverend Green's services. It was only in 1890, when the position of Rector once again became vacant, that Sir Thomas was once again free to exercise his powers as patron and appoint a successor, the Reverend Arthur Anderton. The Reverend Green himself returned to preach at St. John's on JULY 10TH 1892, as if to show that history had ultimately come down on the side of the Church's patron, but the acrimony caused by the affair must have taken a considerable toll upon the health of Sir Thomas Heywood.

On JANUARY 30TH 1894 Lady Margaret Heywood died and this bereavement, together with the deaths of other family members during the 1890's, further aggravated the condition of Sir Thomas' failing health. He eventually died at Doveleys on OCTOBER 26TH 1897. On MAY 3RD during the last year of his life he had, however, been able to pay a visit to the Eaton Railway in company with other members of the Heywood family.

During the years following his marriage, Arthur Heywood had interested himself not only in his experimental railway but also in Church bell-ringing, even to the extent of producing several books on the subject, rejoicing in such titles as 'Towers

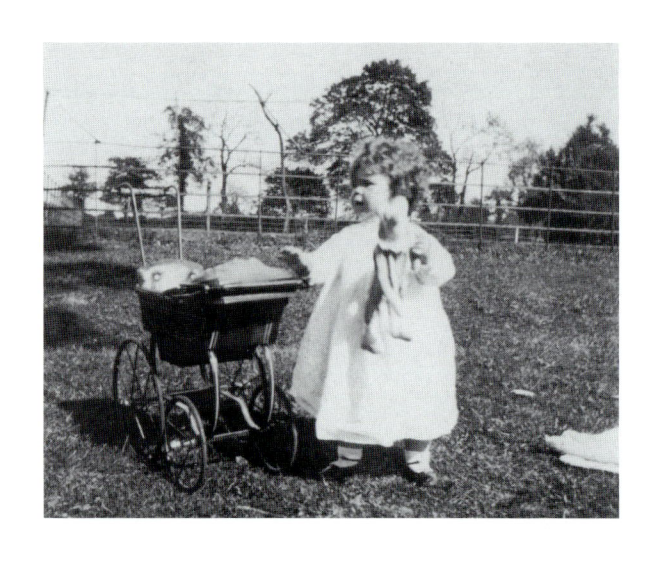

A selection of photographs from the Heywood family album.

Top left: Ella, Betty & Cicely.

Top right: Cicely - aged 14 months.

Lower left: Cicely & Betty.

Lower right: Cicely - May 20th.

All: Courtesy the late Sir Oliver Heywood.

and Bell Hanging' and 'A Treatise on Duffield, a Musical Method for Eight, Ten and Twelve Bells'. He was instrumental in the foundation of the Central Council of Church Bell-Ringers in 1891, holding the post of President of this organisation from its foundation until his death. The influence of his father could also be seen in his involvement in charitable projects, such as the funding of local hospitals, and in his holding of the post of Justice of the Peace from 1872 and, eventually, High Sheriff of Derby in 1899. During the period of eighteen years following his marriage, the future Third Baronet and Lady Heywood had ten children, nine of whom survived infancy.

A fact of significance referred to by Sir Arthur in the Memoir is that his father possessed a talent for estimating the cost of building or earthwork (which would have been put to good use during the additions made to Doveleys in 1856-7 and again during rebuilding after extensive fire damage in 1874). This desire to produce accurate costings was also clearly evident in Arthur Heywood's writings on the subject of the Duffield Bank and Eaton Railways.

The immediate consequence of the death of Sir Thomas Percival Heywood was that his eldest son succeeded to the Baronetcy, and that Doveleys became Sir Arthur's main residence. Duffield Bank was retained until Sir Arthur's death, however, and was used for many social occasions and at least two railway 'open sessions' following his succession to the Baronetcy. Sir Arthur also continued with his bell-ringing activities on many Sundays at St Alkmund's Church at Duffield Bank where a memorial to him can be seen today.

CHAPTER EIGHT
THE EATON HALL RAILWAY

ONSTRUCTION AND ROUTE – although the Duffield Bank Railway had received coverage in both of the major professional engineering journals in 1881 and in the Royal Engineers' own journal some thirteen years later, there seemed to be no apparent wish at that stage on the part of the British railway engineering fraternity to adopt unadulterated Heywood principles in the design and construction of narrow gauge railways. Much has been made by previous commentators of the close proximity of Duffield Bank to the Midland Railway's works at Derby and it may be that a 15 IN. gauge handworked line, probably dating from the 1880-1895 period, constructed at the Midland Railway's sheet stores at Old Sawley was constructed as a result of Heywood's influence. This can, however, only be a matter for conjecture in the absence of more substantive evidence.

In 1894 during the exhibition of the Duffield Bank Railway to interested parties after the construction of MURIEL, a visit was made by the Hon. Cecil Parker who was the agent to the Duke of Westminster. The Duke wished to lay a light railway from his country residence, Eaton Hall, to a transhipment point with the Great Western Railway's Chester-Wrexham main line at Balderton some three miles distant. The estimated traffic requirements of 5,000-6,000 TONS, comprised of building materials and coal for domestic heating and power generation purposes, were felt to be an ideal test for a 15 IN. gauge line and it was further desired that the line should be unobtrusive and of a permanent nature yet moderate in cost. Initial estimates by Heywood put the cost of such a line at around £6,000 exclusive of buildings and he was concerned at that stage as to whether time could be found to construct the line and equipment on his own account. Cost estimates provided by commercial concerns eventually persuaded him that extensive sub-contracting would be prohibitive and he decided to take a free hand in the design and construction of a line on basic Duffield Bank principles and to charge only the basic cost price, without allowing for his own time.

At this point, it is interesting to speculate as to which

THE EATON HALL RAILWAY

PLAN & SECTION OF EATON RAILWAY

Branch to Cuckoo's Nest.

Balderton to Eaton Hall.

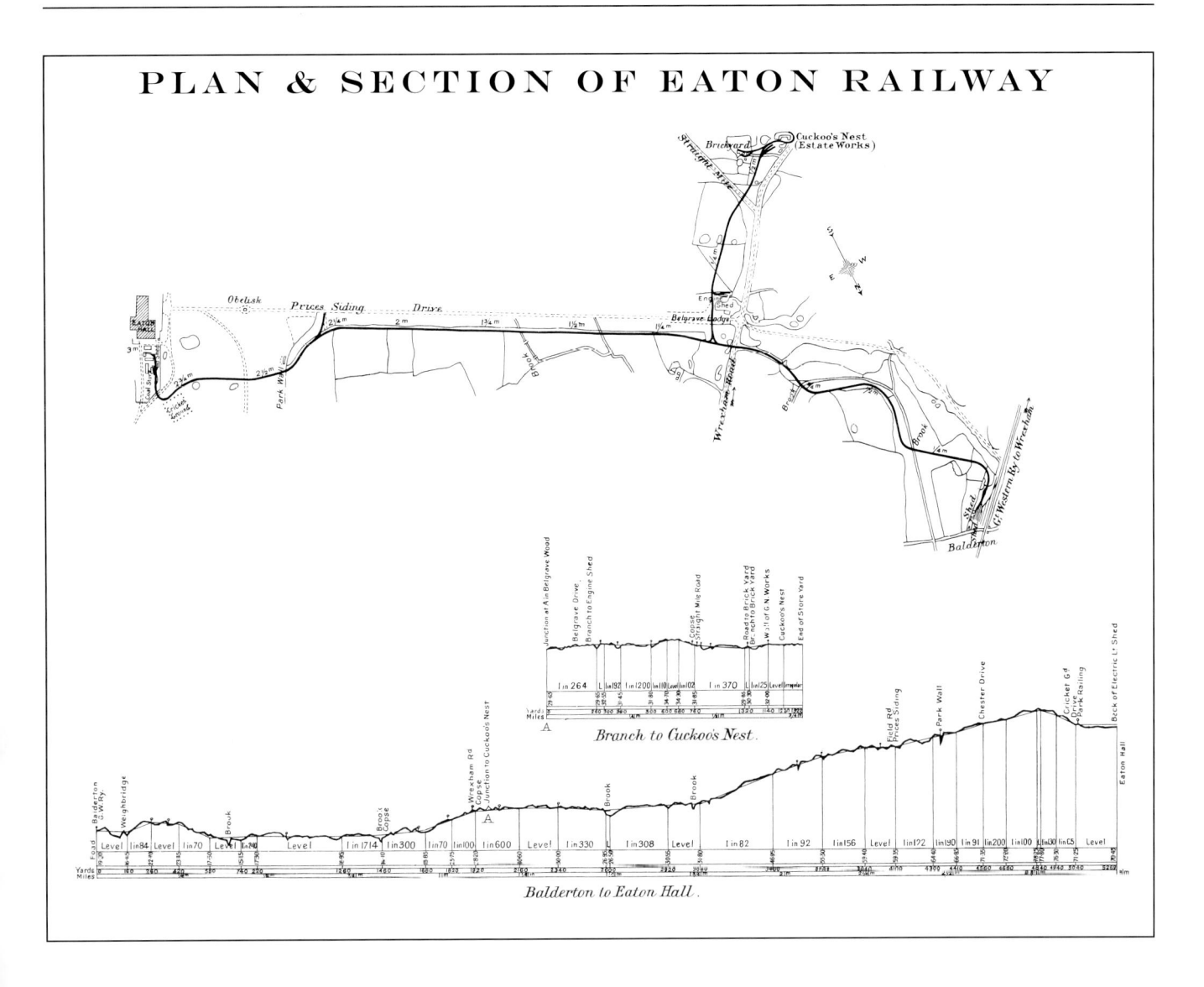

'commercial concerns' were approached with a view to constructing the Eaton Railway. In the light of what has been said previously, Fowler, Bagnall, and (possibly) Kerr Stuart may have been candidates for this task. It seems unlikely that any of these firms would have been particularly enthusiastic about 15 IN. gauge by this time, and Kerr, Stuart in particular would not have been keen on the prospect of building locomotives with cylindrical fireboxes (Fowler too had learned important lessons about cylindrical fireboxes and narrow gauge locomotives during 1879 and 1880).

Construction of the Eaton line commenced in 1895 and the earthworks were well advanced by August of that year when the laying of the rails commenced. At this stage, ELLA was sent over from Duffield Bank, being transhipped by means of the six ton capacity crane at the rail head there, in a specially constructed wooden packing case with a lead covered top. ELLA remained at Eaton Hall for the succceding thirteen months, being used in the movement of materials necessary in the construction process. By Christmas 1895 the 'Main Line' from Balderton to Eaton Hall was completed and by MAY 1896 most of the work on the branch lines had been finished. At the time of its completion, the Eaton Hall Railway was described in a short feature in 'Engineering' magazine.

The total track length of the Eaton Hall Railway was 4½ MILES and this was comprised of the 3 MILE 'Main Line', a branch of ¾ MILES to the 'Cuckoo's Nest' estate works near Pulford and the remainder being made up of sundry small branches. The traffic consisted chiefly of coal, road metal and building materials although there were to be passenger workings during shooting parties and other social occasions when the line saw visits from several important personages of the late nineteenth and early twentieth centuries, amongst them Winston Churchill and King Edward VII.

Owing to the large amount of game present on the estate, Heywood did not consider it prudent to employ a contractor, especially as he felt that men with expert knowledge of platelaying for lines of this gauge were not easy to come by. During the first fortnight of platelaying, Heywood worked by

CROSS SECTIONS OF THE EATON RAILWAY

A { Section on grass plats, to bring top of rails level with surface of roads

Section in parts where desired to avoid prominence } B

Width between turf edges, in **A & B** 4ft.
" " " " **C** 7ft. 6in.
" " " " **D** 6ft.

C { Section in cuttings, giving side drainage

Section on flat or on Embankments } D

When sods and earth are well set, a ditch may be dug in this hollow as shewn by dotted line

8ft. wide formation in cuttings

6ft. wide formation on banks

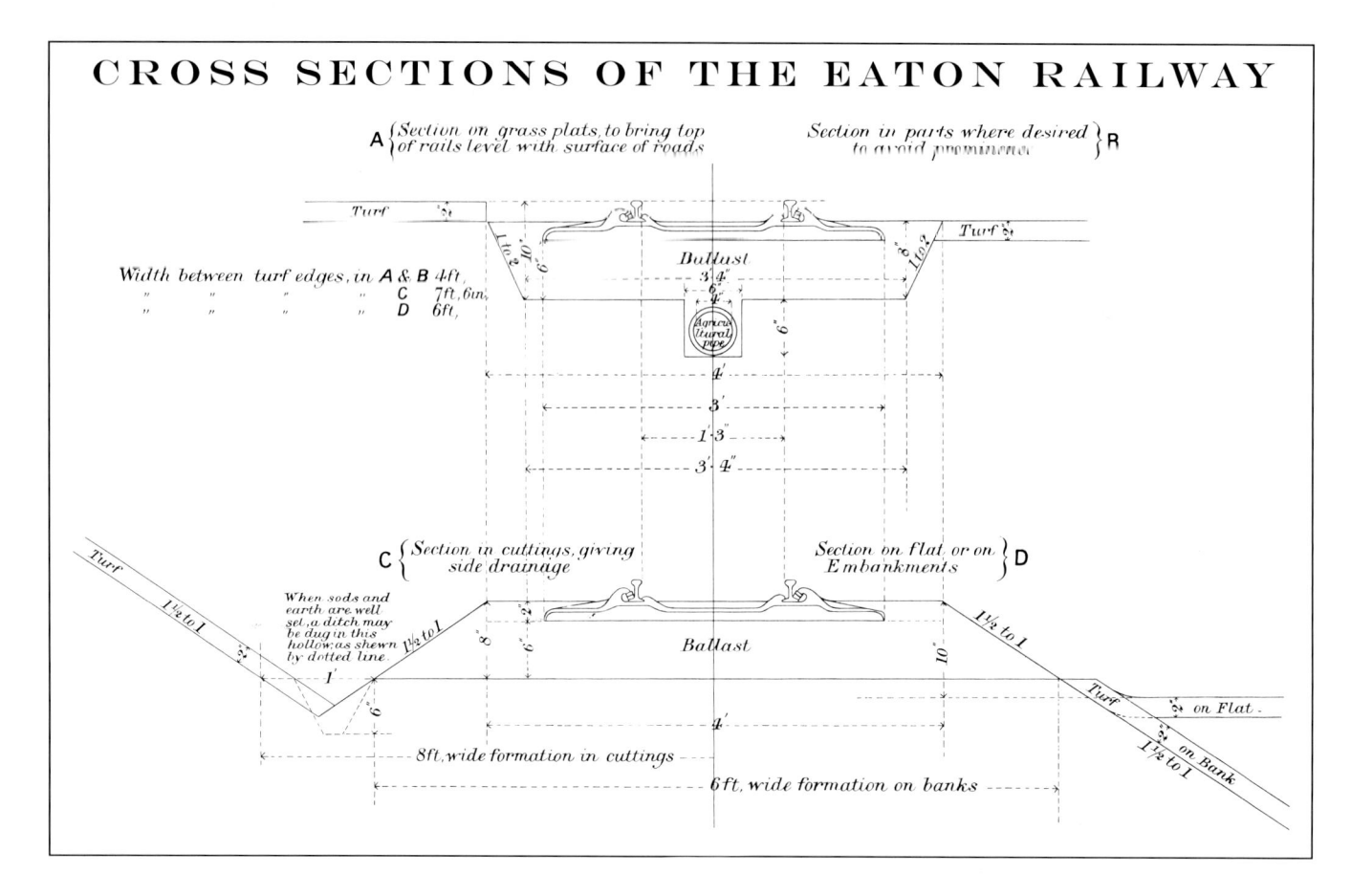

himself with beater, rammer and crowbar until he had managed to demonstrate the principles of platelaying to a sufficiently large proportion of his staff of sixteen. Amongst his staff was an assistant (resident) engineer whose identity was revealed in an advertisement placed in 'The Engineer' for MARCH 13TH 1896 which read:

'Light Railways. Mr. G. D. Scott, at present engaged in constructing a narrow gauge railway for His Grace the Duke of Westminster on Mr. Heywood's system, will shortly be disengaged owing to completion of the work, and is prepared to undertake the survey plans and supervision during construction of other railways of this class. Address – Duffield, Nr. Derby'.

In order to act as an incentive, a bonus was paid to the staff for every rail length completed in excess of one quarter of a mile per week. Heywood's close following of events concerning 18 IN. gauge lines constructed by the Royal Engineers is again revealed by the fact that he felt that the track laying performance at Eaton Hall did not compare well at first glance with the 18 IN. gauge lines constructed by the Royal Engineers in the Sudan during the Suakin Expedition of 1885. The relatively slow track laying at Eaton Hall was explained by the fact that not only had the sleepers and rails to be brought from the base, but also the ballast. In addition, it was stated, that earthworks (which would have been extremely rudimentary at Suakin) needed to be covered with soil and turf to minimise damage to the environment in the vicinity of the railway, and that road crossings needed to be laid in concrete and asphalt and provided with check-rails and special sleepers to carry these rails. The extra work in relation to that carried out in the Sudan also included the making good of field crossings for carts and the provision of girder bridges and cattle stops.

The base for construction work on the Eaton Hall line was the interchange with the Great Western Railway at Balderton where constructional materials were off-loaded. At the point of construction, four 15 FT. lengths of 9 IN. deep timber framing would be laid on the bare formation. A train was then backed up with eight wagons of ballast and four lengths of rail laid on top of the wagons. These rails were already keyed to the sleepers, a practice which owed much to the principles laid down for the construction of military trench railways. The rail lengths were lifted off and placed alongside the formation. The tops of the wagons were then removed and the ballast shovelled off on either side. At this point the construction train would return to Balderton to fetch more materials and the newly unloaded ballast would be shovelled into the space bounded by the framing. The framing was then relocated, section by section, on the next portion of the formation and the newly-laid ballast was shaped and rammed solid by four men with shovels and four with rammers, with care being taken at this stage to ensure that the formation was true. The

Balderton Junction – engine and wagon sheds, Eaton Railway. (Minimum Gauge Railways Plate VII).

rails and sleepers were then lifted into place and the fish-plates affixed. Temporary packing was applied at this stage to the sleepers adjacent to the joints to allow the next train load of ballast and rails to pass over the newly laid track for the process to be repeated. In this manner, some 60 FT. of track could be laid in about forty minutes utilising a staff of ten men at the construction site, a driver and a boy with the train, six men loading ballast, three men straightening and bending rails (it would appear that the Duffield Bank vehicles for this latter purpose were used at Eaton Hall) and three men fixing rails to sleepers. The work rate given by Sir Arthur included delays for field crossings and cattle stops although it apparently excluded packing and finishing work necessary a day or two after initial laying of the track.

The permanent way on the Eaton Hall line consisted of flat-bottomed rails which were of 16½ LB./YD. calibre and these were carried, as per the usual Heywood practice, on cast-iron sleepers. The 'standard' Eaton Hall sleeper was 28 LB. in weight and was 3 FT. long and 6½ IN. wide. The rails were secured in jaws cast into the sleepers by means of steel spring keys bearing against the outward facing webs of the rail. This last-mentioned feature of the design was contrary to normal practice on the Duffield Bank Railway where the keys bore against the inward facing rail webs. The normal spacing of the sleepers on the Eaton Hall line was 2 FT. 3 IN. between centres and this was reduced to 1 FT. 4 IN. between centres at the joints between the rails.

The points were supplied in a ready assembled form from Duffield Bank workshops and consisted of rails rivetted directly to seven flat-topped cast iron sleepers and the other necessary components such as lever, counterweight, base plate and rodding. The switches were planed out of solid and the crossings were of cast steel. One complete point assembly weighed 4 CWT. and cost £7.15s. (£7.75) at 1896 prices.

Special sleepers were employed on girder bridges and these consisted of a basic cast-iron portion in the form of a bar with

CHAPTER 8

an additional cross piece below. This piece was secured to the main portion by two bolts and was designed so as to be able to grip the inner flange of each girder in a manner which could allow for a small degree of radial displacement. The reason for employing this method of sleeper construction on bridges was to allow the track to be set to a moderate curve on a bridge of a linear configuration.

On road crossings a short but very strong sleeper was used and, as has already been stated, these were designed to take check-rails. The length of this type of sleeper was 2 FT. and they were laid on a concrete foundation with tarred macadam upper packing. The road would then be finished to rail level with tar, pitch and screenings with a flange width clearance of 1½ IN. being left free as a groove. Field crossings were also provided with check-rails, but here the sleepers were of the standard length and the packing consisted of ordinary ballast. The ballast used on the Eaton Hall line consisted of red furnace cinder laid to a depth of 5-6 IN. below the level of the sleeper. The surface width was approximately 4 FT. and much of the line was engineered so that the top of the rail was level with the surrounding turf, drainage being effected via a low set centrally positioned pipe of 4 IN. diameter.

The railway was unfenced throughout its length with the exception of Eaton Hall terminus itself, and it crossed from one field to another on short open girders placed over dykes so as to prevent the straying of cattle. The route of the line did not incorporate the spectacular gradients encountered at Duffield Bank and the steepest officially recorded stretch was 1-IN-65 near to the Cricket Ground. This gradient was fortunately in such a direction as to assist the passage of loaded trains and the steepest gradient against the load was a 1-IN-70 stretch about a mile from the Balderton interchange. The highest point on the railway was 63 FT. above the lowest and Eaton Terminus was 51 FT. above Balderton sidings. Another important contrast with the Duffield Bank railway was apparent in the nature of the curves on the 'Main Line' which were of not less than 300 FT. radius, with more severe curves at the termini and on the sundry branches tending to be in the region of 60 FT. radius.

With one exception, road crossings presented no legal difficulties as the land over which the railway operated was, for the most part, the property of the Grosvenor Estate. At one point, however, it was necessary to cross the main Wrexham road and this crossing was sited approximately one mile and 200 YDS. from Balderton sidings. The potential difficulty arose out of the fact that any agreement with the local authority regarding the crossing would not be binding upon successors in office. This situation was not remedied in favour of private railways of this type by the Light Railways Act passed in the same year that the Eaton line was completed (for Heywood's views on this subject and the compromise reached with the local authority in an attempt the circumvent the problem, see Appendix Two). Whatever may have been the legal position, the crossing remained in use for over half a

KATIE with open coach and four wheel brake van circa 1899 at Balderton. The tarpaulins on the brake van are once again much in evidence.
(Courtesy F. Wilde Collection).

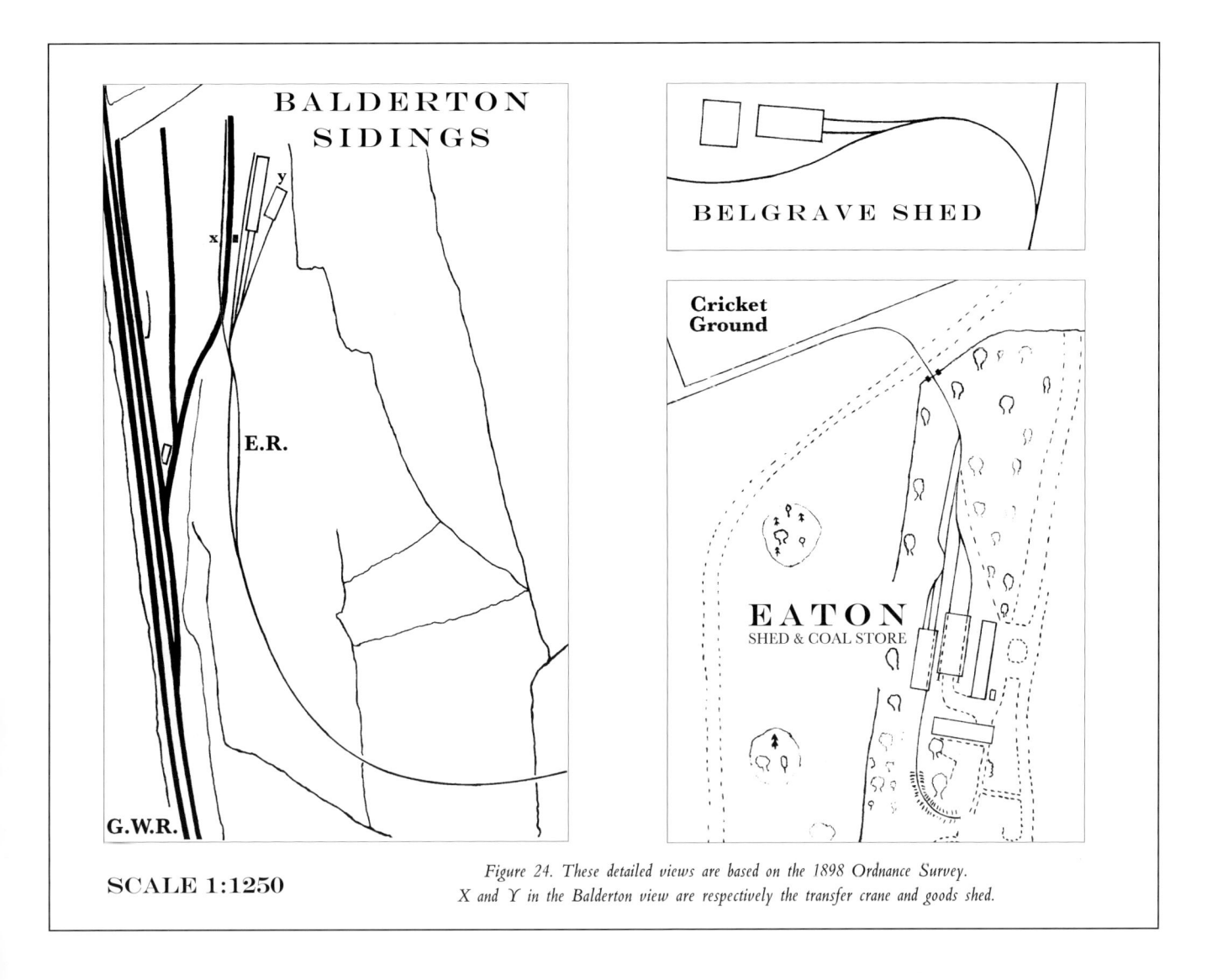

Figure 24. These detailed views are based on the 1898 Ordnance Survey. X and Y in the Balderton view are respectively the transfer crane and goods shed.

century until the ultimate closure of the main part of the Eaton Railway system in 1947.

The facilities at the Eaton Terminus consisted of a three road shed intended primarily for the carriages and bogie wagons. This was of a rather peculiar construction in which the upper walled portions of the ends were finished in a 'Mock Tudor' style. The two outer roads of the shed were covered by awning portions whilst the centre formation was walled on both sides. Adjacent to the carriage and bogie wagon shed was a coal store and transhipment facility. Underneath its canopy, two lines ran in on each side and these flanked a recess which was approached by a downward sloping road ramp. The horse drawn cart supplying coal to the cellars beneath the Hall would be driven empty down the ramp into the recess. Here, coal would be offloaded from a train on one of the flanking lines into the cart. The cart would then ascend the ramp and return fully laden to the Hall.

The fencing surrounding the Eaton Terminus is shown in outline in the plan view of the line in an accompanying figure and in order to reach the terminus from the 'Main Line', a gate was provided for the trains to pass through, this being kept closed when passage was not required.

The Belgrave locomotive sheds consisted of a substantial two road brick structure located at the end of a branch which originated about 200 YDS. along the Estate works line from the junction with the 'Main Line' (which was of a formation so as to permit approach from either the Balderton or Eaton end). The decision to provide a two road shed from the outset suggests that the intention even at this stage was to provide two locomotives, with one being maintained as a spare.

At Balderton the facilities consisted of a transhipment crane and two sheds intended principally for the storage of four wheeled wagons. At one point it was necessary for the Eaton and Great Western sidings to intersect and this is shown in an accompanying figure. As an additional safety measure, gates were provided at Balderton which closed off the standard gauge G.W.R. transhipment siding when the transfer of goods was in progress. These are the gates referred

CHAPTER 8

Eaton terminus – coal store and carriage shed. (Minimum Gauge Railways, Plate IX).

to in Appendix Three (Rule 50).

Unlike the Duffield Bank system, the line at Eaton Hall was not equipped with semaphore signalling equipment and working appears to have been largely on the 'one locomotive in use' principle throughout its existence. The smooth running of an extensive 18 IN. gauge functional railway system largely without the use of Semaphore signalling had previously been shown to be feasible at Woolwich Arsenal and therefore, despite its use at Duffield Bank, there was no surprise in its non-adoption at Eaton Hall. The detailed signalling regulations in force on the Eaton Railway in 1898 are reproduced in Appendix Three.

Steam Locomotives used at Eaton Hall

The locomotive practice of the Eaton Hall line followed the lead set by the Heywood locomotives ELLA and MURIEL although the first locomotive was of the four-coupled variety, in accordance with Heywood's views expressed in 1881 regarding non-military narrow gauge railways. This locomotive was completed in 1896 and bore the name KATIE, after Katherine, the wife of the first Duke of Westminster, Hugh Lupus Grosvenor (1827-1899). KATIE possessed all of the features which were to be associated with standard Heywood practice, with the exception of the flexible wheelbase system which could not be used on a four-coupled locomotive.

Some surviving evidence suggests that KATIE was originally intended to have been fitted with Stephenson/Howe link motion, rather than the Brown/Heywood gear eventually fitted. If the link motion had been used in conjunction with the normal Heywood pattern of cylinder/valve chest arrangement, it would seem certain that an EFFIE pattern rocker shaft valve drive was also envisaged. One essential difference between KATIE and the other Heywood locomotives completed during or after 1881 was that KATIE's steam brake control valve was mounted forward of the combined reversing rod/brake control pedestal and was actuated via an intermediate connecting rod. This was necessitated by the position of the mounting for the upper anchor link pin on the valve gear.

The dimensions of the locomotive are shown in the reproduced table and although Heywood was satisfied with the performance and reliability of the engine, he was not satisfied with its effects on the permanent way. He stated in 'Minimum Gauge Railways' (3RD Edition) that he would not have recommended a four coupled locomotive again except for very short distances and low speeds and that nothing but the experience which he had had with this locomotive could have impressed on him so forcibly the advantages of the radial axle system in the negotiation of sharp curves without flange squeal. When one considers the comparative rarity of sharp curves at Eaton Hall when compared with Duffield Bank, and the abundance of curves of approximately 25 FT. radius on 18 IN. gauge lines at Woolwich Arsenal and Chatham Dockyard where locomotives with a rigid coupled wheelbase 3 IN. greater than that of KATIE operated successfully for many years, it appears rather illogical that Heywood should have blamed any difficulties with KATIE at Eaton Hall on the lack of a flexible wheelbase. A far more likely source of difficulties was inherent in the use of ash ballast at Eaton Hall (particularly when one considers that KATIE's axle loading was approximately 1.63 TONS, as against 1.25 TONS for ELLA, after the 1897-1900 rebuilding, and for MURIEL). A possible motivation for recommending Heywood-style flexible wheelbases for estate railway use in 1898 was inherent in the fact that by this time, there was no real prospect of a British military application for such a system.

Examination of KATIE's surviving mainframes shows that the engine had one set of clasp brakes and that these were pivoted adjacent to the leading axle. As with ELLA and MURIEL, the brake piston moved towards the rear of the engine to actuate the brake, but KATIE was unique amongst the four later Heywood locomotives (and ELLA after 1898) in another important respect. On all of these locomotives, the steam brake cylinder was attached to the rear bufferbeam casting. From the positions of the holes for the transverse slide shaft (later the linear linkage shaft) and the transverse handbrake shaft in the mainframes, it is clear that the brake cylinder could not have been mounted in this manner on KATIE. Four holes on each side frame forming a rectangle between the two sets of horn cheeks indicate the former presence of a single cast intermediate frame stretcher. The bulk and position of this stretcher suggest that: (1) it formed the mounting for the steam brake cylinder, which was located beneath the firebox, with the piston rod gland being at the rear, and; (2) the 'blow-

KATIE simmers in front of the brick kilns at the Estate Works, circa 1898. Harry Wilde has dismounted from the footplate and is holding onto the engine's handrail. (Courtesy F. Wilde Collection).

CHAPTER 8

A head-on view of KATIE when new. Note that unlike the later 0-6-0T's for the Eaton Railway, the transverse rod for the front pair of cylinder drain cocks passed in front of, rather than through, the mainframes. (Courtesy F. Wilde Collection).

off flange' (steam manifold) was located slightly forward of the stretcher. This latter assertion is also supported by attempts to locate the manifold by applying the principles evident from the surviving Abbott Heywood boiler drawings.

In SEPTEMBER 1896, a series of trials was undertaken with KATIE at Eaton Hall with the weights being accurately tested on the weighbridge. The weight of the engine with two men on the footplate was 3 TONS 5 CWT.; the weight of the brakevan was 14 CWT. inclusive of two men and a boy; the boiler pressure was maintained between 155 and 165 P.S.I. whilst the ruling gradient was 1-IN-65.

The first trip from Balderton to Eaton was made up of a gross load of 16 TONS 3 CWT. consisting of thirteen wagons with a total tare of 4 TONS 18 CWT. 1 QTR. loaded with 10 TONS 10 CWT. 3 QTR. of coal and the brakevan as described above. From start to stop the trip took 17 minutes at an average speed of between 10 and 11 M.P.H. including a stop prior to crossing the main Wrexham road. The coal was then emptied and the second return trip made to Balderton in a time of 12 minutes at an average speed of 15 M.P.H.

The third trip, from Balderton to Eaton, was undertaken to assess the maximum speed of working for an average size of train. The gross load, exclusive of engine, was 14 TONS and the trip was accomplished in 15 MINUTES at an average speed of 12 M.P.H. The fourth (return) trip successfully verified the ability of the locomotive to haul a 33 vehicle 14 TON train round the 60 FT. radius curve, and attendant 1-IN-65 nominal upgrade, which took the line out of Eaton.

The fifth trip, from Balderton to Eaton, was to test the maximum capacity of the locomotive and the gross load, exclusive of engine, consisted of a total of 22 TONS 13 CWT. 2 QTR. made up of twenty loaded coal wagons and the brakevan. The total time for this trip was 21½ MINUTES at an average speed of a little under 8½ M.P.H. The long gradient up to Eaton (including a stretch of 1-IN-82) was run at just under 10 M.P.H. with the steam blowing off freely, injectors full on and the damper three quarters closed for the last mile and a half.

For the last of the trial trips, KATIE must have returned to Balderton with the van only. Here, the open bogie passenger carriage was added to form a light load and the train then returned in the Eaton direction with timings being taken on the stretch between the 1¼ and 2¼ MILE posts (which included an upgrade of 1-IN-80). The purpose of this run was to test the maximum running speed of the engine with light loads. The time by stop-watch for the part of the run between the '1½' and '2' mileposts was 1½ minutes, giving an average speed for this portion of 20 M.P.H.

Although a detailed analysis of the test results with KATIE is not possible because of the test data being incomplete (there were, for instance no indicator diagrams taken), certain observations may be made about the engine's tractive effort and power output. If the performance in Test Five of taking a train of 22.68 TONS up an incline of 1-IN-82 at an approximate speed of 10 M.P.H. is considered, and (according to experimental data given by Heywood), a resistance of 10 LB. for each ton of the 22.68 TON rolling stock weight is assumed, then the drawbar horse power at this speed would have been approximately 25, with the tractive effort being 934 LB. If, again using Heywood's own data, the journal friction on the 3.25 TON locomotive is assumed as being 10 LB. per ton, and the other internal resistances 60 LB. per ton, then the indicated horse power can be estimated as approximately 31 and the mean effective pressure as 116 P.S.I.

On NOVEMBER 4TH 1896, Heywood is recorded as visiting the Eaton Railway in company with some Officers from the War Department in London. Having failed to make a lasting impression upon the Royal Engineers Committee at Chatham, it appears that he was trying to extol the virtues of his 15 IN. gauge railway system to the higher authority.

By the turn of the century, KATIE was apparently suffering from some mechanical problems and Driver Wilde's notebook

Figure 25. A reconstructed General Arrangement drawing of KATIE as built at Duffield Bank in 1896. This drawing has been compiled from information in 'The Engineer', 'The Royal Engineers Journal' and 'Minimum Gauge Railways' along with further assistance from measurements taken from the surviving mainframe components and other photographic evidence. The position of the dome in relation to the firebox tubeplate is assumed to be the same as for SHELAGH (Abbott drawing 187D). (Author).

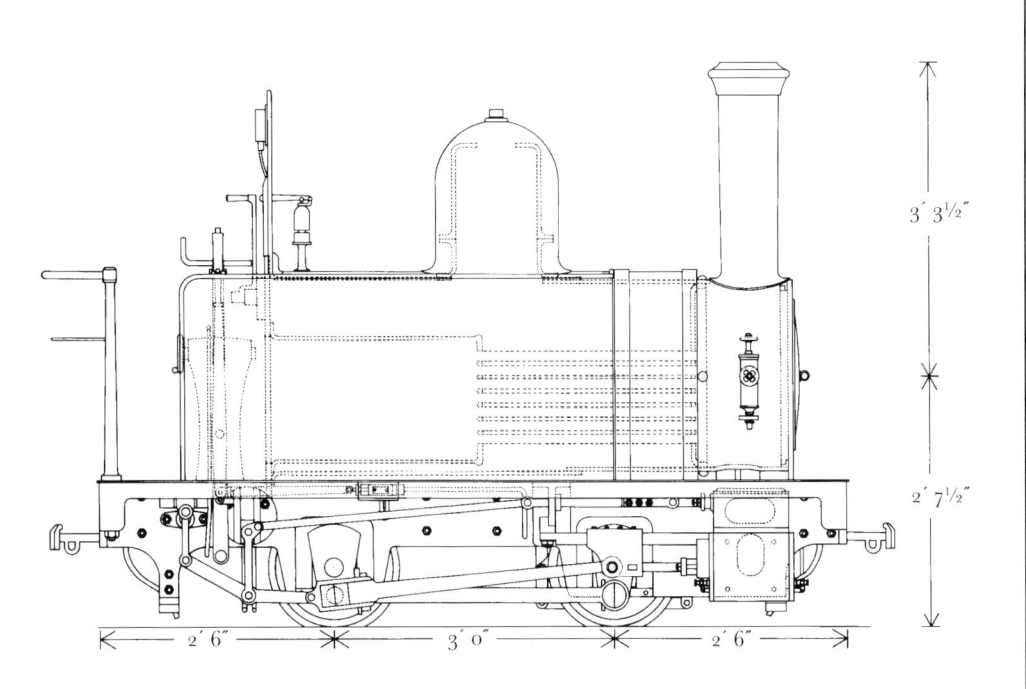

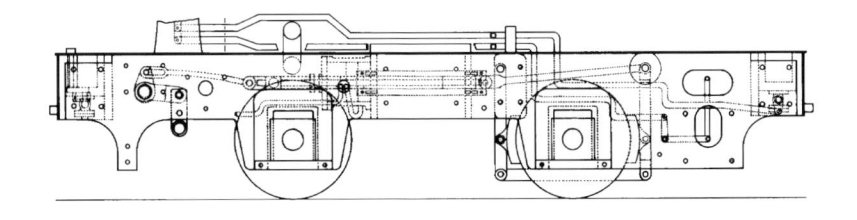

KATIE

SCALE 1:24
© MARK SMITHERS 6.93

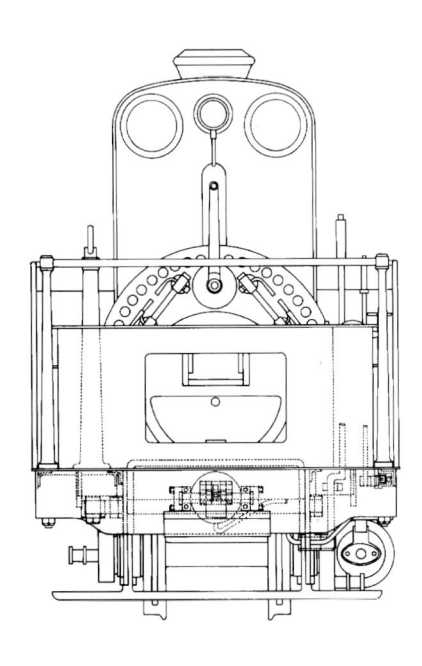

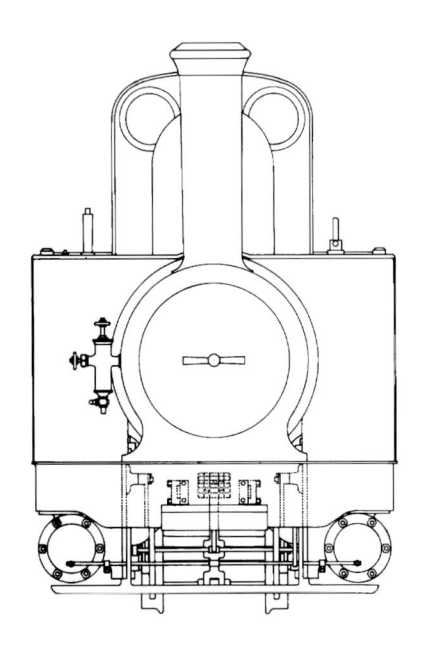

CHAPTER 8

indicates that MURIEL came to Eaton Hall (accompanied by Sir Arthur) on JANUARY 12TH 1900. The choice of this locomotive from the two available at Duffield Bank appears to have been motivated by two considerations. The first of these would have been that ELLA would still have been undergoing the rebuild mentioned by Heywood in 1898; and the second was that Heywood may have wished to demonstrate the advantages of a locomotive incorporating the dual advantages of greater power and lower axle loading so as to 'sell' his final design to the Eaton Railway (another objective envisaged in 1898). KATIE was back in sole charge before AUGUST 1903 as MURIEL had returned to Duffield Bank by this time. Visits to Eaton Hall by Sir Arthur Heywood on JUNE 19TH 1902, and by William Midgley on SEPTEMBER 29TH during the same year suggest these as possible return dates for MURIEL to Duffield Bank.

The pressure of work at Duffield Bank at the turn of the century (and possibly the uncertainty surrounding the railway at Doveleys) was of such a magnitude as to delay completion of the fifth Heywood locomotive until 1904. Five years earlier, the second Duke of Westminster, Hugh Richard Arthur Grosvenor (1879-1953) had succeeded to the title and the engine entered service at Eaton Hall with the name SHELAGH, after the popular name for Lady Edwina Cornwallis-West who married the second Duke in 1901 (it is an interesting coincidence that the Cornwallis-West family is mentioned in the 1899 Memoir of Sir Thomas Percival Heywood). The dimensions of the locomotive were larger in most instances than D.B.R. ELLA, as can be seen by an examination of the accompanying table although its appearance was very similar. The use of a five foot wheelbase on this new six wheeled design ensured that, as with MURIEL, the one inch sideplay used on the middle sleeved axle on ELLA was inadequate and it is suggested that the corresponding dimension on the new design was 1½ IN. From photographs taken of the Eaton Railway 0-6-0 tank locomotives undergoing scrapping, it is evident that the design of intermediate linkage for the sleeved axles was altered once again from the configuration adopted on ELLA. The injectors on the two E.R. 0-6-0T's (and also probably those on all of the Heywood locomotives surviving in 1916) were both mounted on the left hand side of the engine in order to clear the piping for the steam brake. SHELAGH was

The Eaton Hall Railway 0-4-0T KATIE when new in 1896. The constructional features of this engine largely followed those of MURIEL with the exception of the fact that sleeved axle articulation could not be used. (Minimum Gauge Railways Plate XV).

THE EATON HALL RAILWAY

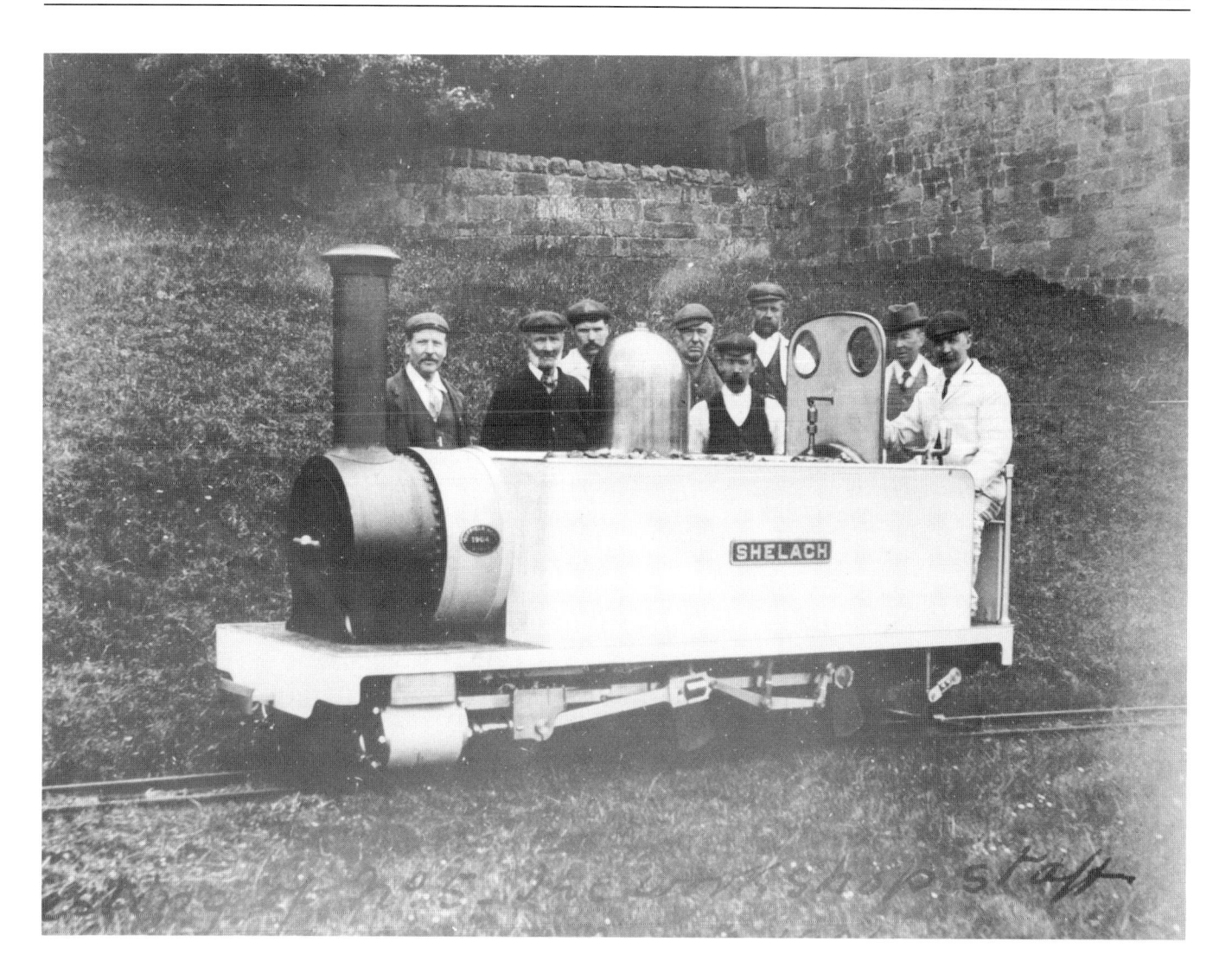

Above: A 'works grey' photograph of SHELAGH taken at Duffield Bank in June 1904 with Sir Arthur (second from right) and the workshop staff. This photograph was taken on the stretch of line linking the six ton crane to the workshops. (Courtesy F. Wilde Collection).

A good view of SHELAGH at the Estate Works circa 1910. Many constructional features of the locomotive can be seen to good advantage in this particular view, and a feature of particular interest is the straight intermediate valve rod, a feature of all of the Heywood locomotives with the exception of MURIEL. (Courtesy The Grosvenor Estate).

probably delivered to Balderton on AUGUST 29TH 1904, a day upon which it is recorded that Sir Arthur Heywood and William Midgely were visitors to the Eaton Railway system. Unlike the three preceding Heywood 15 IN. gauge designs, SHELAGH possessed linear linkage valve gear when new.

SHELAGH was featured in 'The Model Engineer and Electrician' for FEBRUARY 23RD 1905. This feature described tests carried out after delivery. It was shown that SHELAGH could take a gross load of 33½ TONS from Balderton to Eaton in 27 minutes, inclusive of a minute's halt at the main level crossing. With a gross load of 19 TONS (fifteen loaded wagons and one van) a total time, including a stop, of 16 minutes was taken giving an average speed of 11¼ M.P.H. With a light load and a 30 second stop at the main level crossing, the total journey time was 10 MIN. 30 SEC. giving an average speed, inclusive of stop, of 17.1 M.P.H.

In the figures for drawbar and indicated horsepower for KATIE and for the Bassett-Lowke 4-6-2 JOHN ANTHONY quoted elsewhere, since these were derived from data obtained whilst traversing a straight incline in the course of normal running, only 10 LB. per ton is allowed for journal friction and nothing for tyre friction. An allowance of 60 LB. per ton is made for internal locomotive friction. Using the same assumptions, tests carried out with SHELAGH at Eaton Hall in 1905 which involved the engine surmounting the 1-IN-82 gradient at 10 M.P.H. with a gross load of 33 TONS 10 CWT. would yield an approximate drawbar horsepower of 36 and an approximate indicated horsepower of 44 (other assumptions must have been used in the 1905 'Model Engineer' feature, which quotes the indicated horsepower as 60!).

SHELAGH apparently gave satisfactory service until 1914 when the engine was returned to Duffield Bank for reboilering. During the period from 1914-16, the four coupled KATIE was once again the sole source of motive power for normal E.R. traffic.

Abbott drawing No. 408D of JULY 27TH 1914 shows two boilers of similar pattern to the one delivered in 1903 under drawing 187D for SHELAGH. The main differences were that the later boilers had fireboxes 3 FT. 3 IN. long (rather than 3 FT.) and steel tubes instead of brass. A significant omission from the later boilers were the copper stays used on the 1903 one as an attempt to counteract the effects of differential expansion

SHELAGH with the closed bogie coach and the bogie brake van at Eaton Hall Terminus circa 1906. The carriage shed is visible in the background. (Courtesy F. Wilde Collection).

THE EATON HALL RAILWAY

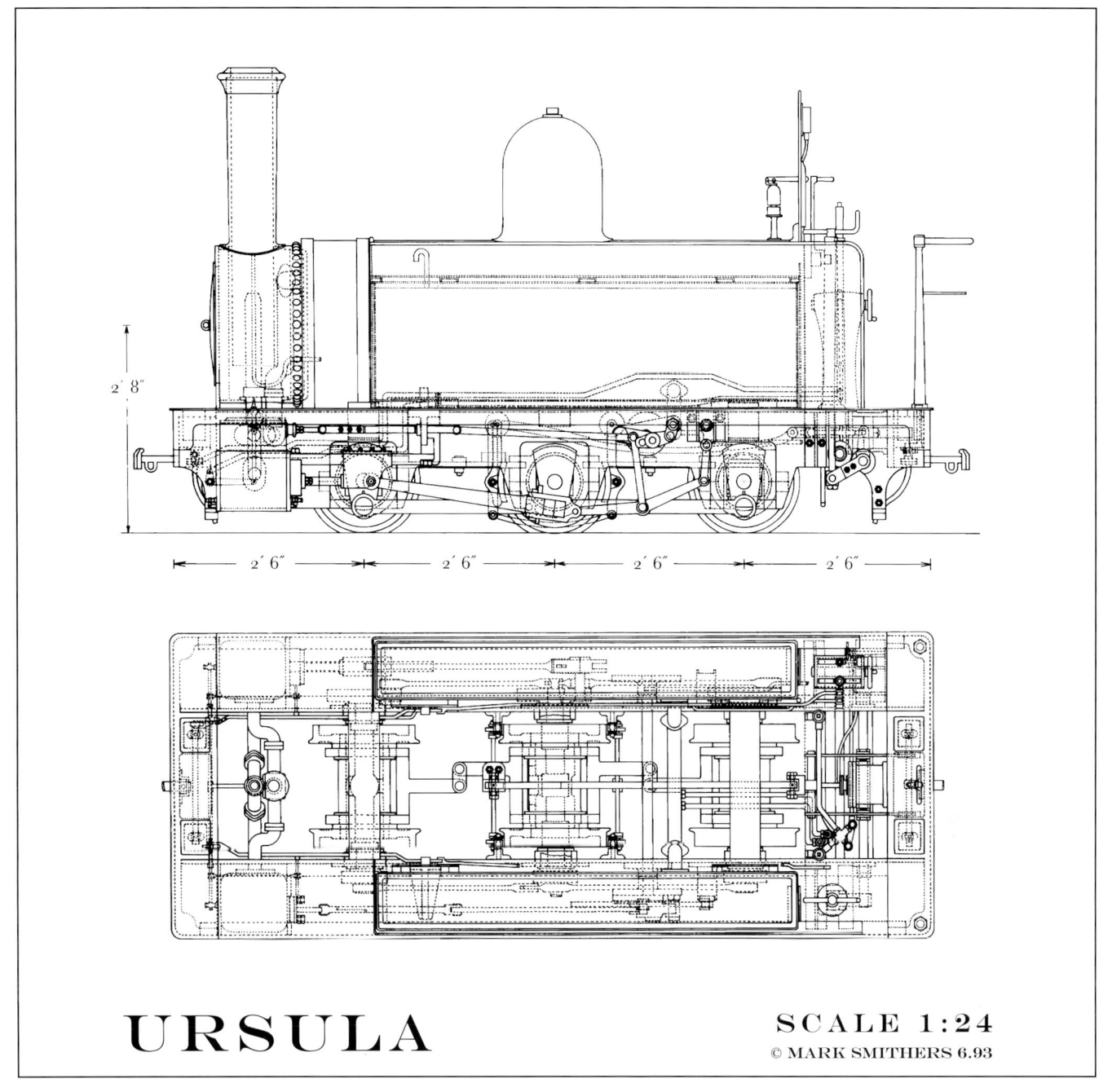

URSULA

SCALE 1:24
© MARK SMITHERS 6.93

Figure 26. Above and pages 70 & 71. A reconstructed General Arrangement drawing of Eaton Railway 0-6-0T URSULA, the locomotive completed at Duffield Bank Works in 1916. This drawing has been compiled from photographic evidence and known technical data. The reasoning behind the significant assumptions is shown under the various component headings below. (Author).

Boiler... The basic boiler dimensions have been taken from Abbott drawing No.408D. As the full tube arrangement is not shown on this drawing, it has been necessary to infer this from the position of the two tubes shown on the Abbott drawing and the photographic evidence from the scrapping of the engine at Balderton in 1942. The height of the spectacle plate has been scaled from the drawing of MURIEL (as EFFIE) in 'The Royal Engineers Journal' for October 1894, whilst the design of the regulator and water gauges have been inferred from photographic evidence. The chimney height is calculated from known dimensions of the components shown on Abbott drawing No.408D and from the chimney cap proportions shown on the schematic drawing of MURIEL in 'The Royal Engineers Journal'. The pitch of the boiler rivets, quoted on drawing 408D as being 1¾ in., has received slight adjustment in relation to circular rivet arrangements in order to ensure an even pitch in these localities. One constructional feature about which little is known is the brass valence on the rear portion of the boiler cladding. For the purpose of compilation of this and the preceding two drawings, it has been assumed that the original mounting bolts for the spectacle plate were concealed beneath the valence.

Side Tanks... The basic dimensions of these components have largely been inferred from measuring MURIEL'S surviving side tanks at Ravenglass. Heywood appears to have been slightly optimistic in calculating tank capacities, even when the capacity of the equalisation pipe is taken into account, or he may have allowed for permissible water level fluctuations in the boiler.

Continued over...

CHAPTER 8

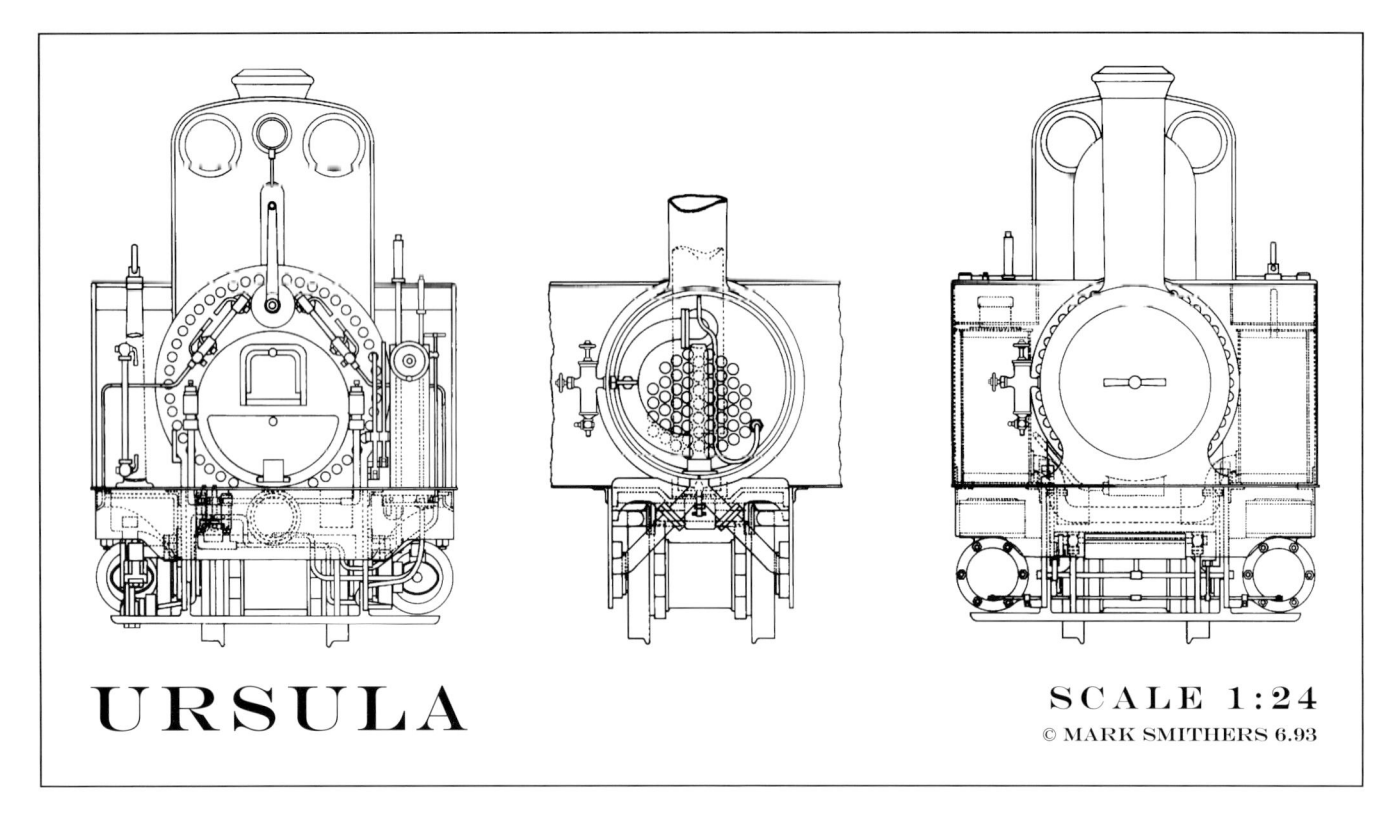

URSULA

SCALE 1:24
© MARK SMITHERS 6.93

Bufferbeams ... These are assumed to be sheeting faced iron castings incorporating sandboxes mounted between the mainframes. It is known from both surviving photographs and from the drawings in 'The Royal Engineers Journal' that the smokebox front sheet made contact with the rear of the forward bufferbeam casting and this fact, together with the assumption that the longitudinal mid-points of the dome and the wheelbase coincide (as with ELLA), has made it possible to calculate the dimensions of the bufferbeam/ sandbox castings.

Mainframes... The height of the top of the mainframes from rail level has been scaled from published drawings of ELLA and MURIEL and this appears to be 1 ft. 7 in. Using this figure and the known information from Abbott drawing No.187D, it has been possible to scale the boiler pitch of URSULA as 2 ft. 8 in. It would appear that the thickness of the mainframes was ⅝ in. by reason of the notches shown in the front plate of the smokebox in Abbott drawing No's. 187D & 408D.

Cylinders and Valve Gear... The assumption made in ascertaining the proportions of these locomotives is that the steam chests, valves, and all valve gear components with the exception of the intermediate valve rods are standard with MURIEL as rebuilt during 1907-11. The connecting and coupling rod thicknesses and bearing proportions have been taken from MURIEL and the other dimensions of the rods have been derived from the wheelbase and cylinder position. The crossheads, slide bars, motion brackets and crank webs are assumed to be similar to MURIEL but the external circular parts of the cylinder casting have been reduced in diameter by ¾ in. from the dimensions quoted for MURIEL to take into account the difference in the quoted cylinder bores for the two designs.

Injectors... The basic design of the injectors can be inferred from the 1888 feature in 'Iron' magazine as amended by information derived from the 1942 scrapping photographs. The injector design used on the locomotive differed from that shown in 'Iron' on that water, delivery and overflow ports all faced in the same direction. The two injectors on the locomotive (according to photographic evidence) were bound together by a manifold which combined the two delivery flows before they were divided once again to feed each of the 'clack' valves.

Radial Axles and Intermediate Linkages... The dimensions of the radial axle components are mostly taken from the published drawings of ELLA and MURIEL as built and adapted to suit URSULA (dimensions such as the ball joint measurements and the diameters of core and sleeved axles appear to have been common to all of the Heywood articulated locomotives). The design of the intermediate linkages has been inferred from photographic evidence. A consequence of using a six wheeled chassis in conjunction with the longer wheelbase, as referred to in the main text, is that the side play for the middle sleeve has been widened to 1 ½ in. from ELLA'S side play of 1 in.

Steam brake and Control Valve... A light helical spring (surrounding the brake piston rod) was fitted within the brake cylinder on the remote side of the piston from the pipe to the control valve. For clarity reasons, this has been omitted from the drawing. The steam supply to the injectors was also taken from the brake valve control manifold, via a cock worked by the handle mounted on the right hand face of the reversing pedestal.

Intermediate brake linkage... Examination of the 'scrapping' photographs shows that URSULA'S brake linkage worked on the normal floating clasp principle. Calculations have shown that the suggestion in the photographs of articulation of the brake hangers being effected by means of universal joints at their upper pivots is perfectly feasible in the light of the fact that a 1½ in. sideways swing at the brake blocks would push these items up only just over ⅛ in. in relation to the axle centreline. It seems certain, therefore, that articulation of the linkage was effected in this manner, with the necessary tolerances being incorporated into the bearings of joints which were affected by the swinging action. The relevant passage from 'Minimum Gauge Railways' reads: "... and the rigging is arranged to swing with the wheels..."

URSULA

SCALE 1:24

© MARK SMITHERS 6.93

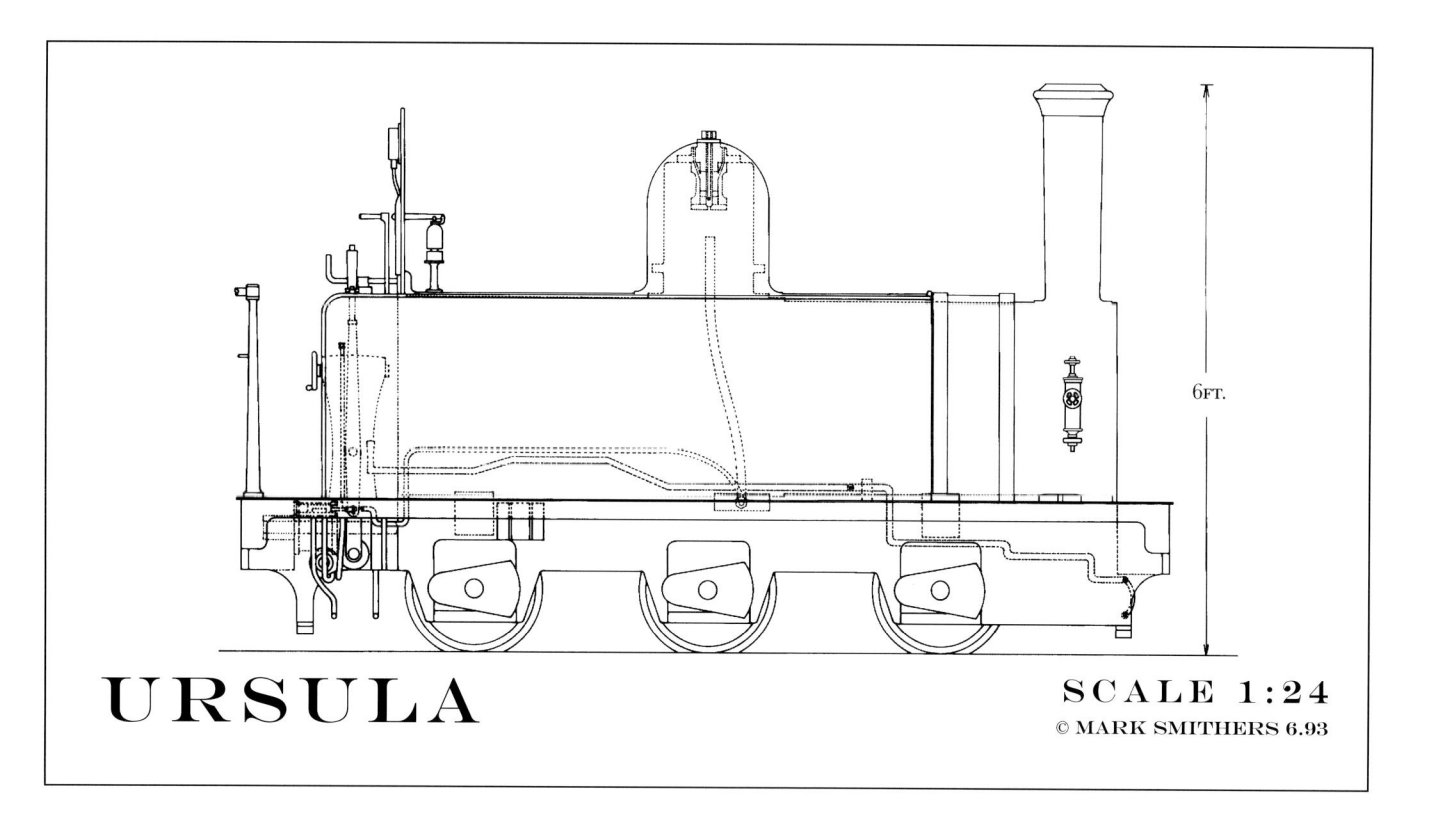

6FT.

Figure 27. This drawing is a reconstruction of the working principle of the smokebox door hinge used on the post-1881 Heywood locomotives. The drawing uses as its basis Abbott drawings 187D and 408D, together with photographs showing KATIE (nee SHELAGH) in 1940 and again during scrapping. Owing to the internal mounting of the door hinge pin, it was necessary for the door to be able to slide laterally and, within the space bounded by the two discs of the door, forwards and backwards in relation to the hinge during opening or closing. As the door was hinged on the left hand side of the locomotive, it would appear that opening would have been accomplished by rotating the handle 90 degrees in an anti-clockwise direction (i.e. an 'upper quadrant' movement). Although workable, if a little complex, in theory, this type of hinge would have been particularly vulnerable to corrosion damage in service and photographs of ELLA and MURIEL during their last days at Ravenglass show that the hinges on these locomotives had been removed by that stage. (Author).

POST-1881 SMOKEBOX DOOR

SCALE 1:8

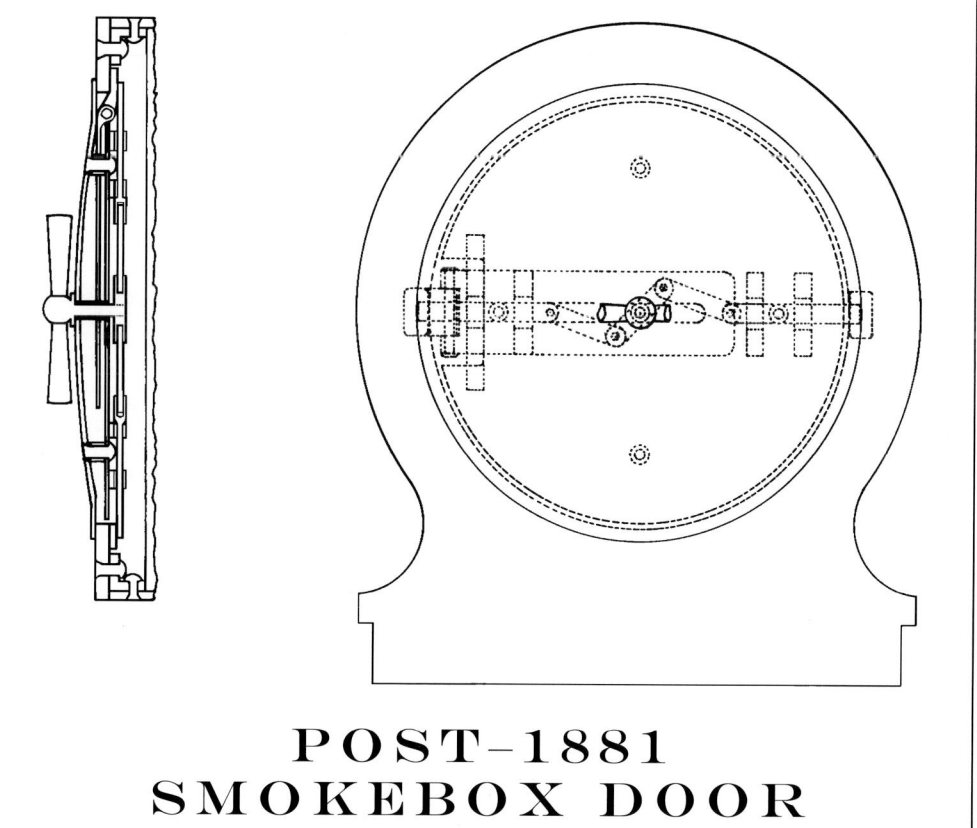

© MARK SMITHERS

CHAPTER 8

This view shows URSULA when new at Eaton in 1916. The rear footplating has been removed and the steam brake cylinder is visible. (Courtesy F. Wilde Collection).

in the firebox (owing to the cold air in the lower portion) upon the rear tubeplate and fire tubes. One of the 408D boilers was delivered to Duffield Bank on Christmas Eve 1914, the other on 21st January 1915. As will be discussed later, the reason for the ordering of two boilers to drawing 408D specification in July 1914 is unclear.

The early months of 1916 saw the completion of URSULA, the second locomotive of the enlarged six coupled design whose chassis had been noted under construction in 1903. The engine was named after one of the Duke's daughters and utilised one of the new Abbott boilers. URSULA appeared rather archaic for 1916, particularly as even at this late stage Sir Arthur clung to the belief that a stout Mackintosh was a better and safer precaution against the elements for the drivers of his engines than a cab.

The second Abbott boiler was apparently utilised in the rebuild of SHELAGH undertaken whilst URSULA was under construction. The second Duke of Westminster's 1900 marriage was ended by separation in 1913 and divorce in 1919. The erstwhile SHELAGH therefore returned to service in late 1915 or early 1916 with new KATIE nameplates. The four-coupled KATIE was thus rendered surplus to requirements at Eaton Hall, and this engine's later career will be considered in subsequent chapters. So far as is known, this locomotive never received the linear linkage arrangement of valve gear.

Rolling Stock at Eaton Hall

The rolling stock supplied from Duffield Bank Works for the opening of the Eaton Railway was of typical Heywood pattern and consisted of an open sixteen seat bogie carriage of similar design to the type used on the D.B.R. and several wagons. The most numerous design of wagon was the standard four

KATIE at Eaton terminus with a train consisting of six standard four wheeled wagons and (one from the rear) one of the six tipper wagons constructed for the Eaton Railway. One of these latter wagons also appeared in a photograph taken at the time of the 1905 LITTLE GIANT trials.
(Courtesy F. Wilde Collection).

wheeled variety with the usual pattern of removable 'top' and facility for the fitting of a cradle for the carriage of long loads between two wagons. There were initially thirty of these wagons, which could hold 16-17 CWTS. of coal or 20-22 CWTS. of bricks or road metal. In addition, six wagons were constructed so as to be able to carry a load of 1½ TONS and a further pair to carry 2 TONS.

The bogie carriage was 20 FT. long and 3 FT. 6 IN. wide and weighed 23 CWT. Two bogie vans with sliding doors were also supplied and both of these were constructed on the well frame principle. One of the bogie vans was a brakevan of similar pattern to its D.B.R. counterpart but fitted with door and sliding end windows and a roof reaching 6 FT. above rail level. The brake was worked by means of a vertical column (which passed through one of the end seats) with a handle reached by opening a sliding window. The other bogie vehicle was a parcels van and was constructed as with the D.B.R. sleeping car, without end balconies or brakes. This could carry approximately two tons. A four wheeled brake van with a canopy and screw operated brakes, as opposed to the open footbrake vehicle found in some of the early Duffield Bank Railway illustrations, was also supplied for use on the Eaton Railway from its opening.

Sir Arthur disliked the use of tipper wagons on two grounds. These were their relatively high initial cost and the fact that the proportion of payload to tare weight was lower, he felt, than normal open box wagons. He also felt, however, that the relative ease of unloading of such wagons merited experimentation with a batch of six on the Eaton Railway soon after the 1896 opening. These wagons consisted of 'V'-section steel tubs hung at each end on two trunnions riding in cast iron pedestals with these latter components being bolted

CHAPTER 8

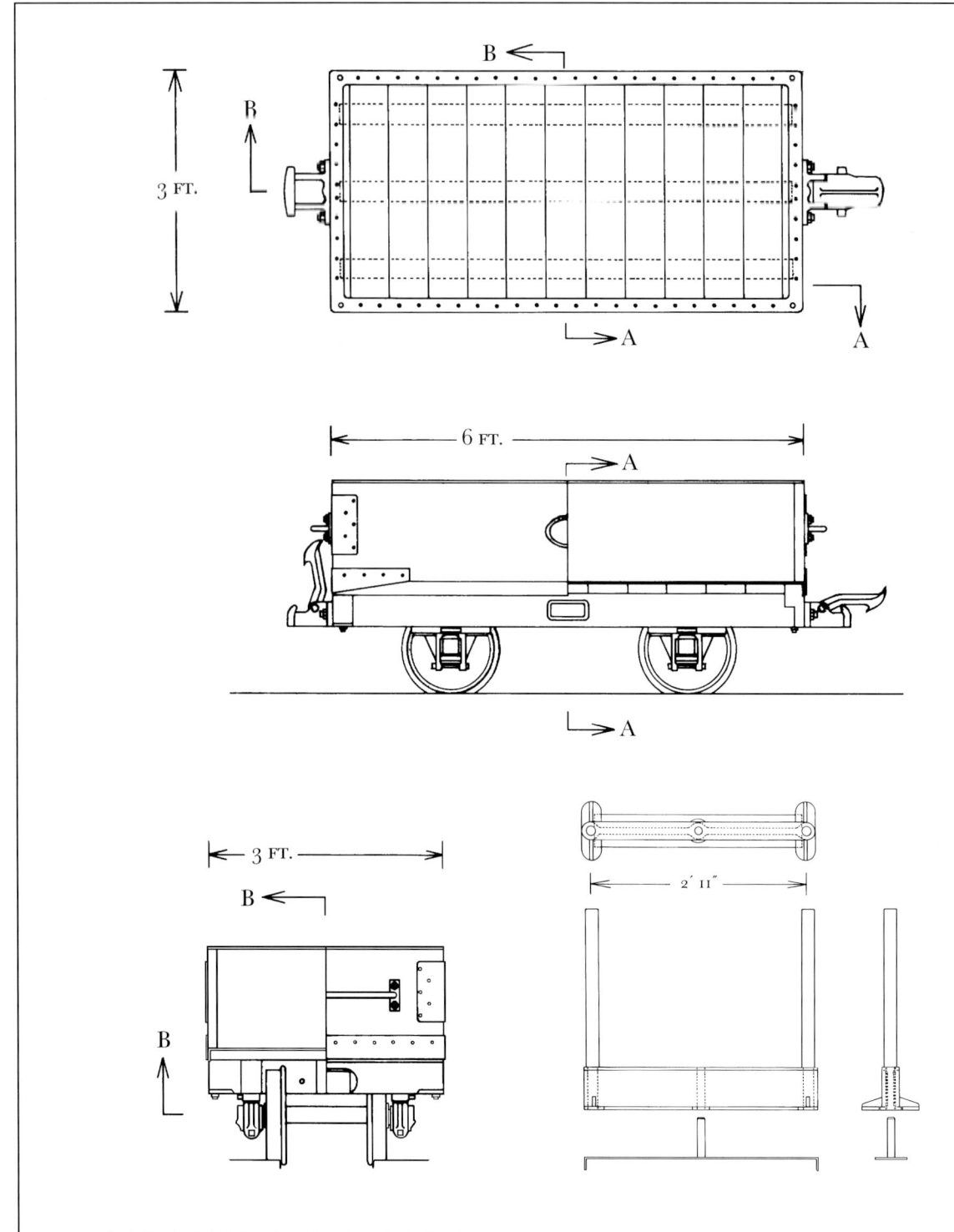

STANDARD FOUR WHEEL 'TOP' WAGON & BOLSTER

SCALE 1:24   © MARK SMITHERS

Figure 28. These views show the standard four wheeled 'top' wagon used at Eaton Hall, together with a cast iron bolster used on Heywood wagons at Ravenglass. Sadly for present day historians, it appears that only some of these wagons appear to have been adapted to carry bolsters, none of which apparently survive today. As a consequence it has not been possible to provide details of how the bolsters were anchored to the wagon frames. (Author).

THE EATON HALL RAILWAY

Above Left: A Heywood axlebox of 1895 on a later 'top' wagon preserved at Ravenglass. This wagon was one of the original batch supplied to the Eaton Railway. The track on which the wagon is standing is ex-Eaton Railway permanent way with cast iron sleepers, provided by the R.H.&D.R. (Author).
Above Right: The standard Heywood dual purpose buffer/coupling used on his rolling stock and which could be utilised for 'fly shunting'. This example, which is to be found on the ex-Eaton Railway four wheeled brakevan at New Romney, has lost its hook. (Author).

Below: The passenger carriage which was supplied for use with SHELAGH at Eaton Hall. According to an insert in 'The Royal Engineers Journal' for August 1st 1903 this vehicle was in the course of construction at the time of the 1903 Open Session, as were SHELAGH and URSULA. This view was taken at Duffield Bank and the carriage still exists today, having been cut down to a loading gauge of 5 ft. 3 in. at New Romney. (Courtesy F. Wilde Collection).

CHAPTER 8

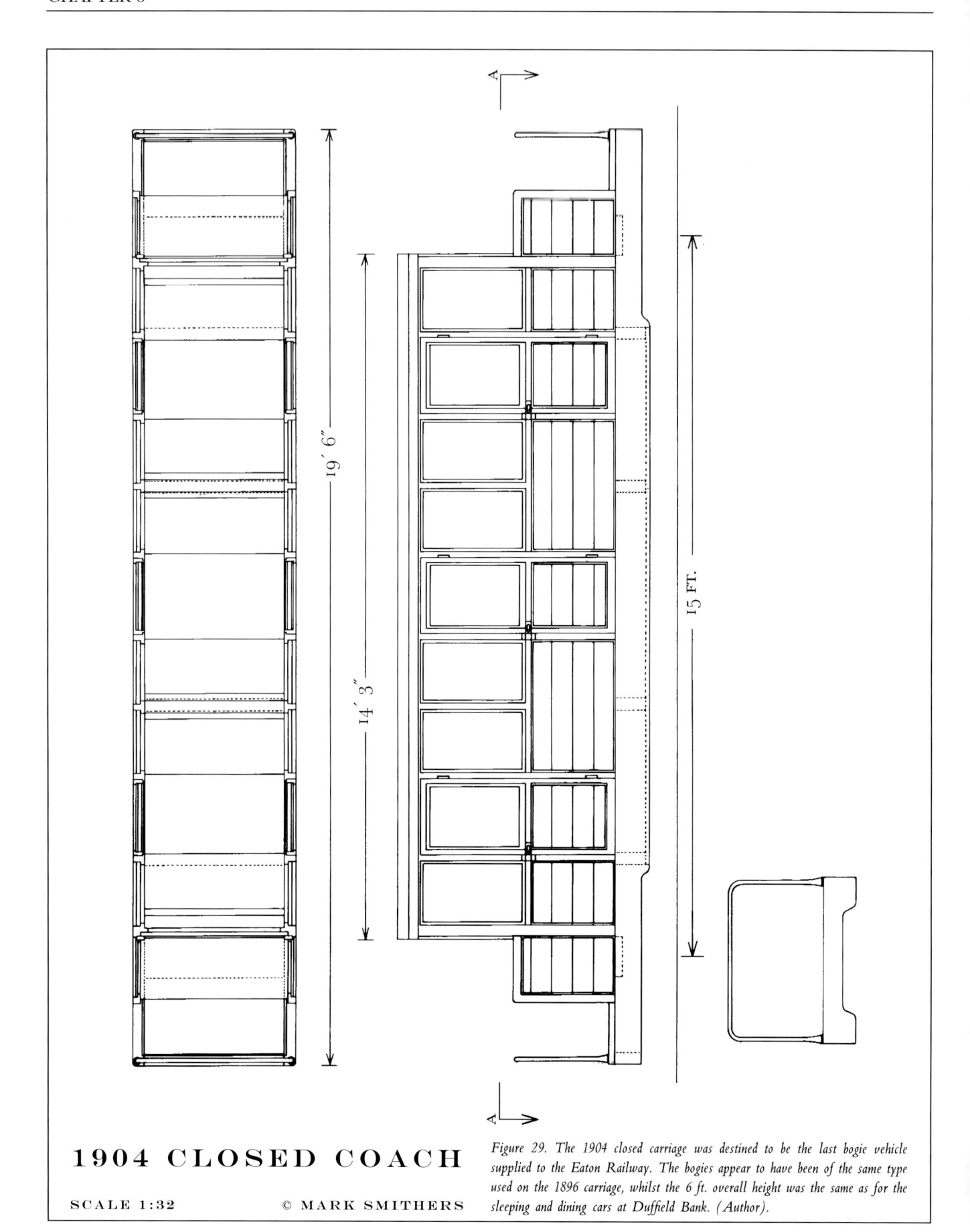

1904 CLOSED COACH

SCALE 1:32   © MARK SMITHERS

Figure 29. The 1904 closed carriage was destined to be the last bogie vehicle supplied to the Eaton Railway. The bogies appear to have been of the same type used on the 1896 carriage, whilst the 6 ft. overall height was the same as for the sleeping and dining cars at Duffield Bank. (Author).

THE EATON HALL RAILWAY

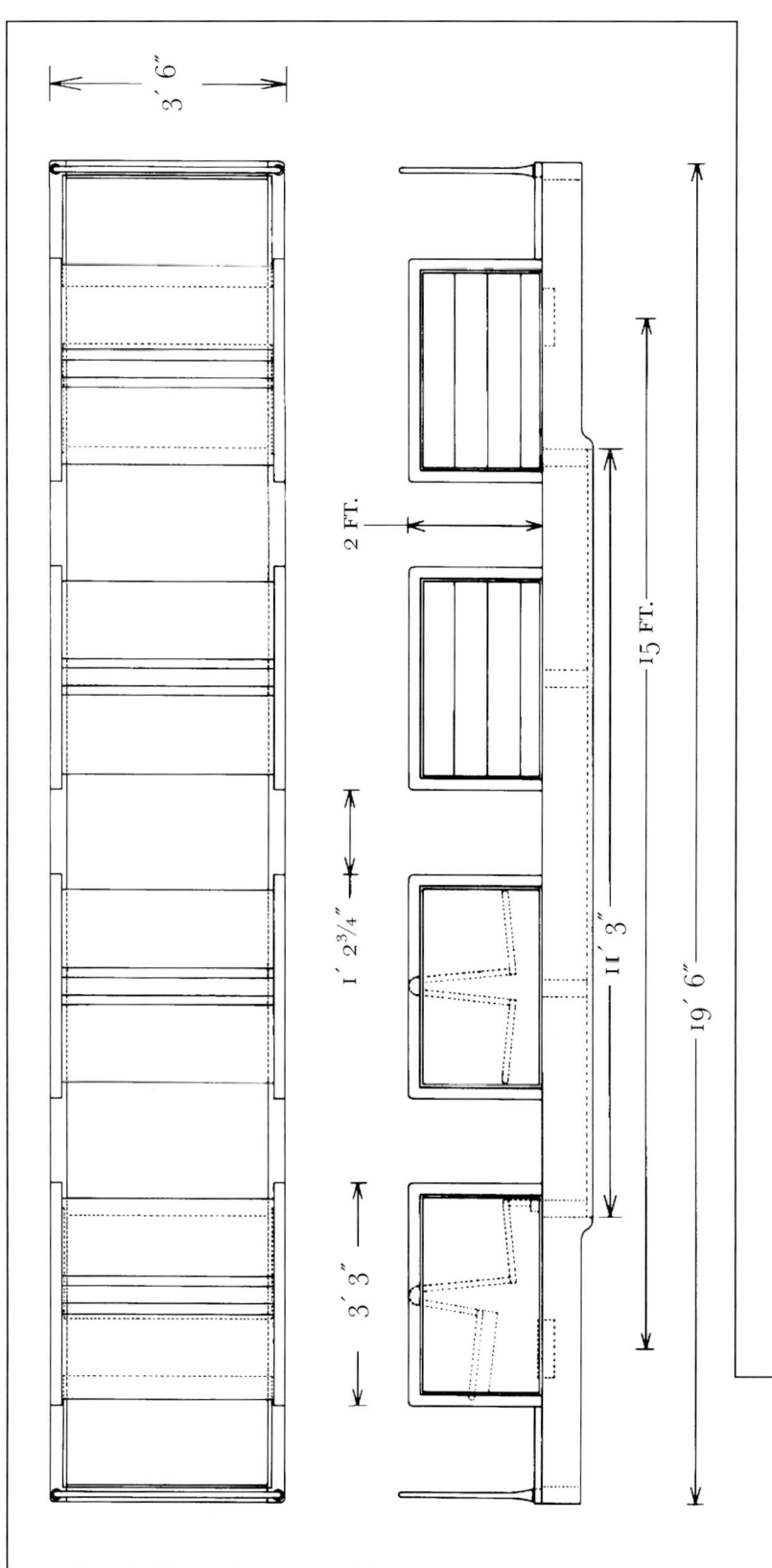

to an underframe with sides of channel section steel and ends of cast iron. These frame ends were secured to the sides by means of rivets and each end carried a drawbar with rubber cushions which was attached to the buffer/coupler assembly. The tare weight of these wagons was 11½ CWT. and their coal capacity was approximately 12 CWT. Their cost was given as £20 each as opposed to £12 for each of the ordinary four wheeled wagons with a removable box top, which had a tare weight of 7½ CWT. For the same total weight, therefore, the ordinary box wagon could carry four units of payload for every three carried by the tipper wagon and so, it was argued, tipper wagons would only be justified where distances travelled were relatively short and loading time was long in relation to journey time. In the event, four of the tipper wagons were quickly withdrawn and replaced by examples of the normal pattern of Heywood four-wheeled top wagon.

With the increasing use of the Eaton Railway for social occasions during the years following the turn of the century, the need was felt for a closed bogie carriage and one was supplied in 1904 along with SHELAGH. Its design followed that of the D.B.R. sixteen seat closed vehicle of 1881 but it was constructed to a loading gauge of six feet and with a different design of end panelling for the enclosed part of the superstructure. A further vehicle of this design was under construction at Duffield Bank in 1916, but it is not clear whether this was intended to accompany URSULA, or was to stay at Duffield Bank as a replacement for the recently sold 1881 coach. Events were to take a different course, however, and the uncompleted vehicle was destined to pass to the Ravenglass and Eskdale Railway.

An item of rolling stock referred to in Appendix Three, and which is shown in at least one surviving photograph, was a four wheeled permanent way trolley. This could be padlocked to the rails when not in use and it could also carry a snowplough when required.

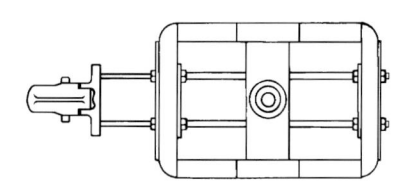

Figure 30. The general arrangement of the superstructure, solebars and bogie frames for the Eaton Railway open carriage is shown here. Unlike the open 'sixteen seaters' used at Duffield Bank, no footbrake appears to have been fitted.

OPEN BOGIE COACH

SCALE 1:32   © MARK SMITHERS

CHAPTER 8

Figure 31. This drawing shows the 1896 bogie brake van used at Eaton Hall. The vehicle in present condition does not fully reveal how the brake linkage worked and this has had to be inferred from photographic evidence and general principles. This drawing consists of a part sectional side elevation view (with some brake details omitted for clarity); a half plan view on A-A; a full section view on B-B (with accompanying plan view of the primary brake lever); a scrap view showing the location at one end of the bearing for the longitudinal brake transmission rod, together with one of its two bellcranks; a sectional view of the secondary brake lever at C-C and its associated plan view.

1896 BOGIE BRAKE VAN

SCALE – 1:32   © MARK SMITHERS

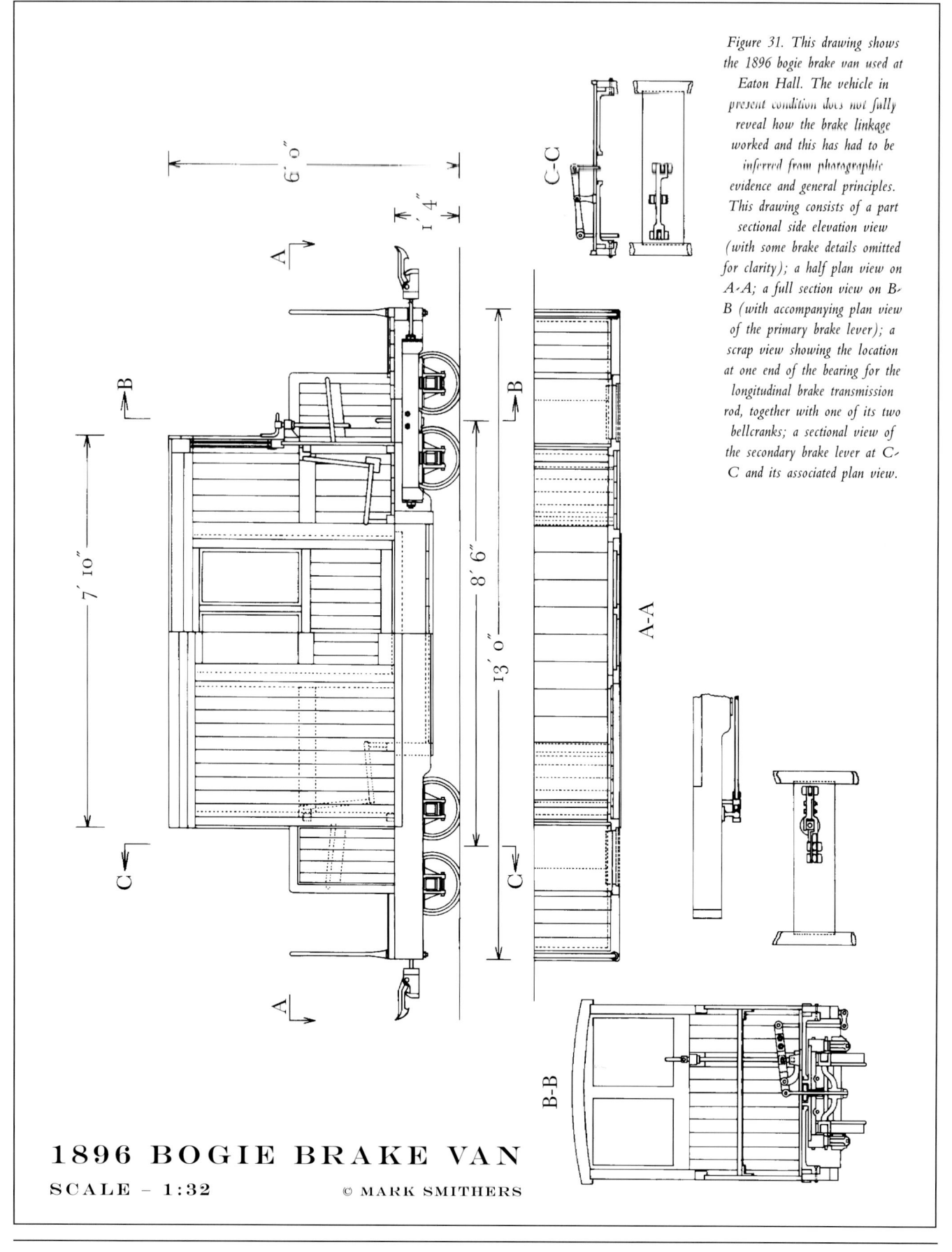

THE EATON HALL RAILWAY

SHELAGH with the closed bogie coach and the bogie brake van at Eaton Hall Terminus circa 1906. The carriage shed is visible in the background. (Courtesy F. Wilde Collection).

Figure 32. The total cost breakdown for the Eaton Hall Railway. These costs did not include the coal store and shed at Eaton, the engine shed at Belgrave Lodge or the sheds at Balderton.

ITEM	£.	s.	d.	The cost of stock was as follows…	£.	s.	d.
Earthwork to formation level	923	18	0				
Drain pipes	33	2	1	1 four wheel locomotive,			
Rails, sleepers, and fastenings	1814	15	1	4⅝ in. by 7 in. cylinders, 15 in. wheels	400	0	0
Girders and fittings for four bridges				Covered bogie parcel van	50	0	0
and 19 cattle stops	143	5	9	Open bogie passenger car (16 seats)	40	0	0
Foremen, trainmen & platelayers	563	5	8	Covered brake van (4 seats)	250	0	0
Ballast (red furnace cinder)	337	10	4	Wagons (load 1 ton)	336	0	0
Road metal, cement & asphalt	39	1	7	Special wagons (load 2 tons)	29	0	0
Fencing at cattle stops	42	10	2	Rail bending wagon with press and drill	32	0	0
Sodding in park & finishing banks	224	5	5	Platelayer's trolley and tool chest	9	2	0
Locomotive coal, oil, etc.	17	3	11	Sets timber carriers and sundries	43	17	8
Laying water-supply, Balderton, Belgrave and Eaton	90	8	6				
Weighbridge at Balderton	22	18	2	Total cost of stock	964	19	8
Tools, huts, carriage of goods, repairs etc.	248	13	4				
Resident Engineer	427	5	3	Add construction	4928	3	3
Total cost of construction	£4928	3	3	**TOTAL COST OF RAILWAY**	£5893	2	11

79

Figure 33. Sir Arthur Heywood's estimate of the annual capital and working expenses for the Eaton Railway.

Item	**£.**	**s.**	**d.**	**Working expenses...**	**£.**	**s.**	**d.**
				Driver	91	0	0
Interest at 4% on gross expenditure	235	0	0	Brakesman (boy)	26	0	0
				Two platelayers	99	0	0
Renewal of permanent way				Coal and oil	39	0	0
@ 25 years life (4% on £2,000)	80	0	0				
					255	0	0
Renewal of rolling stock							
@ 12.5 years life (8% on £900)	72	0	0	Brought Forward	387	0	0
	387	0	0	Estimated Annual Expenses	642	0	0

Figure 34. Operational data for the first two years of operation of the Eaton Railway. At this stage, the cost of locomotive coal, of the best Welsh smokeless variety, was approximately £1 per ton.

Item	**£.**	**s.**	**d.**	**Item**	**£.**	**s.**	**d.**
Wages (driver and boy)	115	3	4	Wages (driver and boy)	115	12	0
Wages (platelayers)	145	8	8	Wages (platelayers)	94	15	8
Locomotive coal	19	15	0	Locomotive coal	19	17	7
Oil, stores and sundries	8	1	10	Oil, stores and sundries	9	7	1
Working Expenses for 1896	288	8	10	Working Expenses for 1897	239	12	4

1896		**1897**	
Tons of material hauled	6067	Tons of material hauled	5986
No. of days in steam	225	No. of days in steam	207
Tons of material hauled per day in steam	27	Tons of material hauled per day in steam	29

Eaton Light Railway, Balderton.

No. Railway Truck

No. L. R. Truck Date__________ 191

Description__________

Where from__________

Where to__________

	Tons.	Cwts.	Qrs.
Gross			
Tare			

Weighed by__________

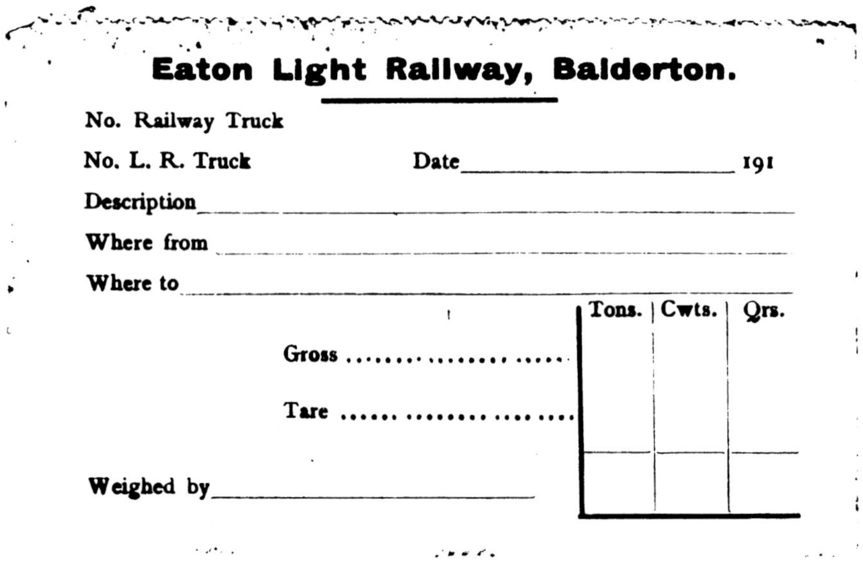

Figure 35. A waybill from the Eaton Railway of a pattern issued for the decade 1910-1919. (Collection W. J. Milner).

CHAPTER NINE
THE RAILWAYS AT DOVELEYS

THE NINE INCH GAUGE – both 'The Engineer' in 1881 and 'Minimum Gauge Railways' refer to the construction of a 9 IN. gauge Railway by Sir Arthur Heywood, in the former case 'for some friends as a toy' and in the latter instance 'for my younger brothers'. The latter reference would suggest that this railway was situated at Doveleys. No documentation of the course of this line appears to have survived to the present day but circumstantial evidence suggests that part of its course ran very close to the River Dove. A candidate for the status of a relic of this railway is a tunnel situated on the riverbank almost due east of the house. This tunnel, which is unlined, is approximately 13 FT. 6 IN. long and has portals 5 FT. high at the sides and 5 FT. 9 IN. in the centre. The width of the portals, as built, was 4 FT. 7 IN. The cross-sectional dimensions would have been appropriate for a 9 IN. gauge line but certainly not for Eaton Hall and later Duffield Bank equipment. It may be, however, that the tunnel was merely a folly and was not intended for railway usage. Of Sir Arthur's brothers who survived the age of 11, Bertram Charles Percival was born in 1864 and Gerald Graham Percival in 1867 and therefore it would appear that the 9 IN. gauge line was built in the late 1870's. 'The Engineer' certainly implies that it was constructed after work began on the Duffield Bank Railway.

Early Fifteen Inch Gauge

From a surviving photograph in an album containing pictures from the 1888-90 period, it can be seen that there was definitely a stretch of 15 IN. gauge line at Doveleys during this period. This is believed to have skirted the cricket ground to the south of the house so as to meet the woodland overlooking the riverbank. At the woodland end was a station complete with nameboard, printed timetable, platforms, a siding and a Semaphore signal post. The timetable which appears in the 'Dove Bank Railway' photograph clearly indicates that passenger working took place over this stretch of line, although the only form of 15 IN. gauge motive power shown in the photograph was the pedal trolley previously referred to in the chapter devoted to Duffield Bank rolling stock. The suggestion that the 15 IN. gauge 'Dove Bank Railway' was constructed during the early 1880's is given further weight by the fact that a Heywood rail-bending wagon, of a rather simpler design than the one described in 'Minimum Gauge Railways', appeared at a farm sale near Uttoxeter in 1982.

This view shows the woodland terminus of the 15 in. gauge Dove Bank Railway circa 1889 with a train consisting of the pedal trolley, a single seat 'workman's car' (adapted from an early 4 ft. by 2 ft. 'top' wagon) and a 'top' wagon with an improvised plank seat. Arthur Percival Heywood is providing the motive power on this occasion, whilst the scene is completed by the provision of a platform, station nameboard and signal post. Recollections of a former butler to the Heywood household suggest that a steam locomotive ran on this line and if so, this would probably have been EFFIE. Today, a building survives to the south of the house (see later plates) which appears to have been a shed for railway equipment. (Courtesy Sir Oliver Heywood).

CHAPTER 9

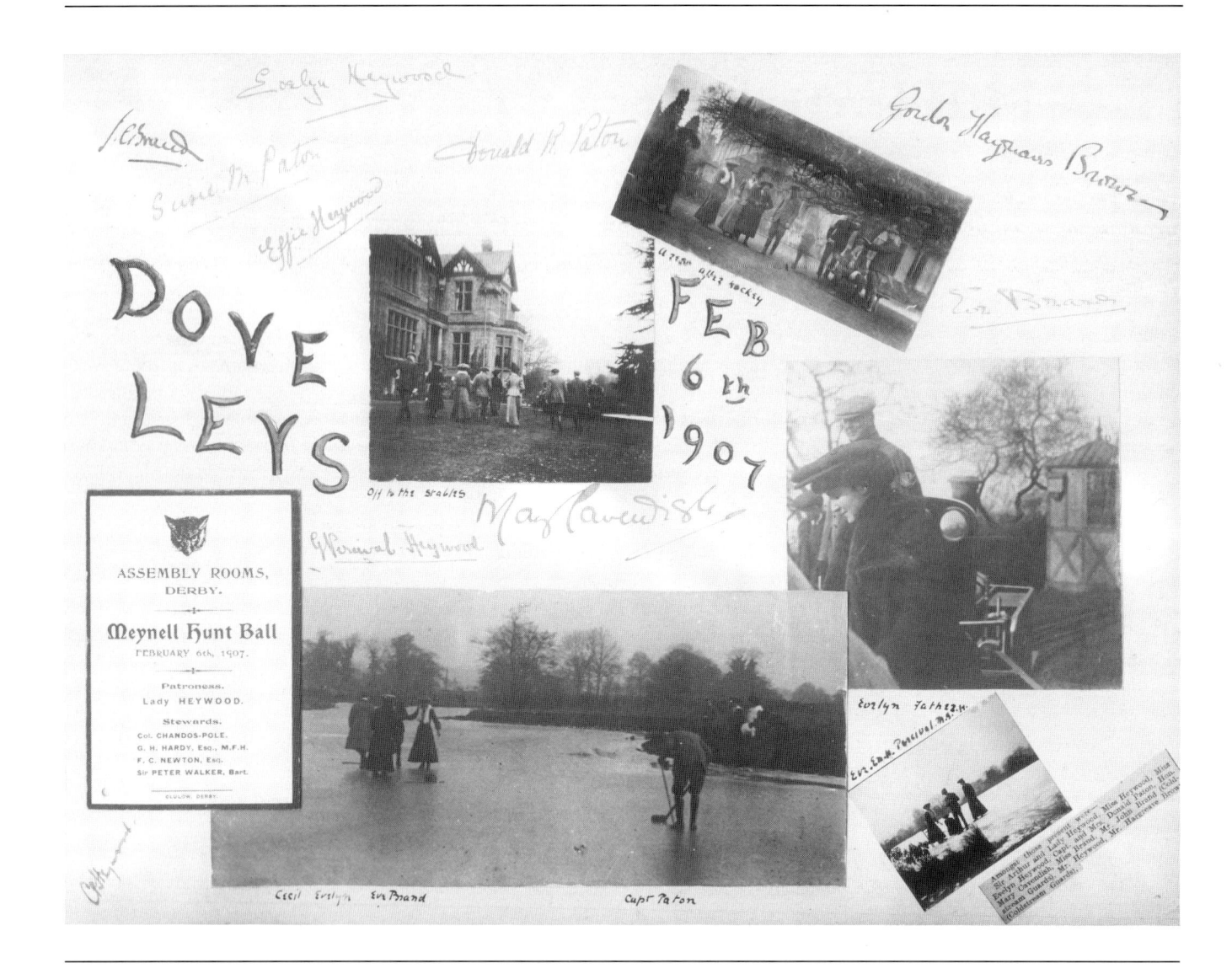

This vehicle bears the relief legend 'D.B.R. 1883' on one wheelset and both couplings (the common initials with the Duffield Bank Railway may be significant here). The rolling stock appears to have been housed in a shed (to the south of the main house) which was constructed in a style rather similar to the covered signal boxes on the Duffield Bank Railway. This little railway, like the 9 IN. gauge line referred to previously, was intended purely for the amusement of Heywood family members and does not appear to have fulfilled any experimental or estate function.

Turn of the Century Schemes

Although neither the First nor the Second Edition Ordnance Survey Maps showing Doveleys (surveyed circa 1879 and 1896 respectively) acknowledges the presence of a small gauge railway, it would appear that the 15 IN. gauge railway continued to operate on occasions during the 1890's decade. The appearance of a green painted steam locomotive on the 15 IN. gauge line at Doveleys was recalled by an ex-butler of the Heywood household during research carried out by Mr. Michel Jacot during the 1960's and although the butler would appear to have been recalling the Edwardian era, the possibility remains that EFFIE was transferred to Doveleys around 1894.

In contrast to the efforts made to promote the Duffield Bank Railway, there appears to have been no desire on the part of Arthur Percival Heywood to publicise the whereabouts of the 15 IN. gauge line at Doveleys. During the 1880's and early 1890's this would have been understandable as the estate still belonged to his father, Sir Thomas. According to a letter written by Miss Isabel Effie Heywood to Mr. B. G. Markham in JANUARY 1974 the railway which existed during her lifetime never extended to more than a tramway between outbuildings with hand pushed wagons for moving coal, wood and other stores. Miss Heywood was also keen to point out that no locomotive ever ran at Doveleys, a view which appears to conflict with the aforementioned butler's recollections.

The 1960's conversations with the ex-butler revealed that

This building in the grounds of Doveleys appears to have been the shed for 15 in. gauge railway equipment, and probably would have been the shed for one of the later Heywood 0-6-0T's had either of these locomotives reached Doveleys. The general style of construction is of interest as it greatly resembles the signalboxes at Duffield Bank and the portion of the shed represented by the forward side panel is a later addition. (Author).

upon inheriting Doveleys in 1897, Sir Arthur planned to create an estate railway there. In conjunction with this view, it has also been suggested that the larger 0-6-0T design (eventually built as SHELAGH and URSULA for Eaton Hall) first referred to in the 1898 edition of 'Minimum Gauge Railways' was originally intended for use at Doveleys.

Support for the view that one of the two later Heywood 0-6-0 tank locomotives was intended for use at Doveleys can be derived from an entry in the AUGUST 1903 edition of 'The Royal Engineers Journal'. Here it was revealed that during the 20TH-22ND of that month, Heywood held yet another 'open session' for the Duffield Bank Railway where both ELLA and MURIEL could be seen in steam. The entry went on to record: 'The workshops can be inspected; in these there are now under construction two six coupled flexible wheelbase locomotives and a bogie carriage; the latter and one of the engines being for the Eaton Hall Railway'. Whilst not conclusive in itself, this entry is strongly suggestive of an intention to send one of the embryonic locomotives to Doveleys bearing in mind the fact that neither ran, apart from for testing purposes, at Duffield Bank. The other relevant piece of circumstantial evidence is the fact that the Duffield Bank style shed previously referred to has clearly been extended at its forward end in a manner similar to its original style of construction. This extension was probably carried out during the Edwardian period when many alterations to the main house were undertaken.

According to the ex-butler, Sir Arthur planned to extend the reincarnated 'Dove Bank Railway' to one of the two adjacent stations on the North Staffordshire Railway's Uttoxeter-Ashbourne branch in order to provide an interchange of the type which had been created at Balderton siding on the then new Eaton Railway. In both instances his ambitions were to be blocked by unsympathetic neighbouring landowners: in the case of Norbury station to the north this was Col. Clowes and in the case of Rocester station to the south this was Col. Dawson. The route to Norbury station would have involved crossing the River Dove and there are no tangible remains today to suggest that construction of the necessary formation or bridge ever commenced. As regards a possible route to Rocester station, the position is rather different as we shall see.

From the lie of the land on the Doveleys estate it is evident that the course of the proposed southerly extension of the 15 IN. gauge line could not have been on the immediate riverbank but instead would have passed at higher level through the overlooking woodland. There are no tangible remains here but immediately to the south one comes upon the formation for an incline which leads to a little ravine. At the bottom of this ravine on each side are concrete abutments which formed, or were intended to form, the base of a viaduct. Further south there are more earthworks which appear to have been intended to create a formation on the hillside but there are 'gaps' in the remains of these today.

CHAPTER 9

The Heywood rail bending and tool wagon acquired by Mr. Alan Headech for the princely sum of £10 at a farm sale in Uttoxeter in 1982. It is tempting, in view of the wagon's age to suggest that it was used in the construction of the line featured in the 'Dove Bank Railway' photograph. This photograph was taken on March 3rd 1992 and shows the wagon undergoing extensive restoration. It has since changed hands again and is now part of a 15 in. gauge collection at Southport. (Author).

There is certainly sufficient evidence to suggest that construction of the earthworks for the Rocester extension commenced but the missing sections in the formation show that there could have been no working railway between Doveleys house and the Estate's home farm situated to the south of the surviving earthworks. To this extent Miss Isabel Effie Heywood's claims about the nature of the railway at Doveleys were valid. In view of what has been said earlier regarding 'The Royal Engineers Journal', it would appear that Sir Arthur's dreams of an estate railway on the Eaton pattern at Doveleys would probably have been frustrated during the 1909-15 period. Evidence for this proposition derives from the fact that one of the workshop buildings at Doveleys bears the inscription 'A.P.H. 1909'.

The decision by Sir Arthur to order two new Abbott boilers to drawing 408 specification in 1914 is an enigmatic one: did he still harbour dreams of using the then uncompleted 0-6-0T at Doveleys? There was no question at this early stage of Narrow Gauge Railways Ltd. buying the Eaton Railway's 0-4-0T KATIE for use at Ravenglass, and the alternative suggestion can only be that the Eaton Railway had decided to dispose of this locomotive come what may.

If either Doveleys extension proposal had come to fruition, it would have incorporated very heavy gradients against the prevailing inward loads, thereby imposing severe restrictions upon the payload which could be handled by one train.

The Last Remnants

During the last three decades of Heywood family ownership the only working rail-borne vehicles on the Doveleys estate were those associated with the hand worked tramway between outbuildings referred to in the letter by Miss Isabel Effie Heywood.

One of the most significant of the outbuildings was referred to as 'The Engine Houses'. This housed a steam engine which was used to supply power to a bank of storage batteries which in turn supplied the 16V. D.C. lighting system used in the house. This engine is today preserved at Shugborough Hall Museum. Doveleys also enjoyed its own water supply in the form of a well and attendant pumping station. There were also a variety of workshops mostly constructed during the Edwardian period whose construction, one suspects, helped to seal the fate of Duffield Bank as a workshop for supplying domestic equipment to Doveleys and other Heywood family properties.

Doveleys passed out of the Heywood family's ownership in 1946 upon the death of the fourth Baronet. The 'Uttoxeter Advertiser' for OCTOBER 16TH 1946 carried an advertisement on behalf of Messrs. Bagshaw & Sons (Auctioneers) describing an auction of effects at Doveleys which was to take place from OCTOBER 28TH until NOVEMBER 2ND in that year. Under the heading 'Outside Effects' were listed 'Four 15 IN. Railway Trucks'. Whether any of these wagons were actually sold at this time is debatable.

Doveleys subsequently passed into local authority ownership and during this time, some wagons still remained on the site. Two of these were salvaged by Mr. Michel Jacot during the 1960's and, as has been discussed in Chapter Six, probably dated from the late 1870's. A third, known as a 'tool chest on wheels', is thought to have remained on site until circa 1980, and this is the rail bending wagon referred to earlier in this chapter. This wagon is currently undergoing a complete renewal of timbers with a view to putting on public display.

Doveleys is once again in private ownership, having been sold by the local authority in 1989. The house has recently undergone renovation under the direction of Mr. and Mrs. H. Pilkington who kindly allowed the author to photograph important parts of the site. Sadly, owing to the present economic climate, the future of the 'Riverside Doveleys' development (as the project is known) is uncertain.

CHAPTER TEN
THE ROLE OF THE MINIMUM GAUGE RAILWAY

GENERAL CONSIDERATIONS – the chief ends involved in the construction of the Duffield Bank Railway were summarised in an article by a Mr. Harold F. Piper in 'The Windsor Magazine' in 1895. These he divided under three heads:

1) *The application of such lines to agricultural and commercial purposes, and;*
2) *To the requirements of military transport in countries devoid of roads; also*
3) *To learn something more definite about adhesion and friction on light railways.*

This summary of the objectives of the Duffield Bank Railway was probably the best expressed contemporary analysis of this type and forms an excellent background to the subjects considered in this chapter.

Nineteenth Century Experiments

The experimental nature of the Duffield Bank Railway was evident not only from attempts by Heywood to promote his work in military and engineering circles, but also from his letters to the editors of 'The Engineer' (SEPTEMBER 2ND 1881) and 'Engineering' (2ND AUGUST 1883) which discussed, amongst other considerations, the effects of braking and locomotive reversal in relation to train control on an incline. The results of one experiment carried out in connection with these observations were presented before a meeting of the British Association at Sheffield. In this experiment, it was found that when the wheels of a locomotive were spinning in a reverse direction upon descending an incline, the locomotive showed a greater descent acceleration than when the wheels were simply locked. This experiment was clearly intended to show the inadequacy of reliance upon the reverser to control a locomotive which was slipping down an incline, and the advantages for train control of keeping slip between the tyre and the rail to a minimum. The locomotive used in the experiment was ETTIE and the experiment was carried out before 1881.

Another (later) experiment was carried out in the presence of two representatives of a firm of locomotive builders when, according to Heywood, it was under consideration to build some locomotives of ELLA's basic type for military purposes. At this stage, it must be observed that Major Hogg in the R.E. Professional Papers in 1883 had merely stated that once satisfaction had not been achieved with the Handyside 18 IN. gauge locomotives: 'attention was directed towards the flexible wheelbase system as applied by Mr. Percival Heywood … to an experimental engine of 15 IN. gauge and 3 TONS in weight. Some account of this engine was published in the issue of 'The Engineer' for JULY 15TH 1881'. Major Hogg went on to mention the fact that ELLA had been shown to be able to haul a load equal to its own weight up an incline of 1-IN-10, even when the rails were hardly dry. He went on to say; 'The opinions of the system which have been expressed by eminent authorities upon locomotive structure lead only to the conclusion that its non-application, as yet, is mainly due to the small demand that has existed for engines of less than metre gauge'. This experiment therefore appears to have been a subsequent attempt by Heywood to find a commercial builder prepared to manufacture locomotives based on ELLA, presumably of 18 or 30 IN. gauge, in sufficient quantities to enable consideration by the Royal Engineers of their adoption for field usage.

In the experiment for the two representatives of the locomotive building firm, which was probably carried out circa 1892, an attempt was made to determine the coefficient of adhesion (maximum tractive effort: locomotive weight ratio) for ELLA. It was found that the maximum gross load which the locomotive could hold on a 1 IN 10 gradient was approximately four tons. Adding this to the engine weight (3.1 TONS when loaded with sufficient coal and water for the experiment), the total train weight was 7.1 TONS which meant that the tractive effort sufficient to hold this weight on a 1-IN-10 gradient was 0.71 TONS. Heywood then made an error in calculating the engine's weight available on the incline for adhesion as he took this to be the total engine weight minus a tenth for the gravity component. In reality this would have been the engine weight multiplied by the cosine of the inclination (approximately 5.73 DEGREES to the horizontal). When this correction is applied, the coefficient of adhesion from the experiment works out at 1 : 4.28, or 0.23, rather than the figure of 1 : 3.9, or 0.26, calculated by Heywood.

Sir Arthur also outlined the basis of calculation used in ascertaining the net loads which his locomotives would haul on the level and on various gradients. The train resistance on the level, he divided under three heads: journal friction, tyre friction and locomotive internal friction. Journal friction, he felt, could be covered by an allowance of 10 LB. per ton. Tyre friction was virtually nil on the straight and 10 LB. per ton on curves. To these figures he added a further 20 LB. per ton to allow for losses in starting on inclines and curves in normal railway operation. Internal locomotive friction was determined experimentally by Heywood (by unspecified means) as being between 60 and 80 LB. per ton.

Applications For Small Gauge Railways

In addition to giving details of the Eaton Railway's construction in the 1898 Edition of 'Minimum Gauge Railways', Sir Arthur went on to discuss the application at home and abroad of small railways of 2 FT. gauge and under as a replacement for horses and carts. This he had done much earlier in 1881 but the subject was especially relevant in 1898 as railways of this type were discussed by the Institution of Mechanical Engineers during the same year. Heywood declined to discuss military railways in detail, merely pointing out the fact that other countries were ahead of Britain in this field (he was presumably referring to the use by the French and German authorities of 600 MM. gauge military railway equipment) and classified the civilian usage where railways of 2 FT. gauge and under could be profitably employed under two heads.

The first of these was concerned with the situation where, in a country possessing ports or a main line railway network (such as the United Kingdom or India), large establishments, whether public or private sector, could be connected with an adjacent port or main line rail head so as to reduce the transportation costs below the level inherent in the use of animal power on roads. The second head concerned the situation, often prevalent in remote parts of what were then colonies of the British Empire, where no roads were present and the choice was between a narrow gauge railway and nothing. In both instances Heywood felt that the governing factor for success of such a railway was the level of traffic between two or more points on the line.

With regard to the argument that the use of narrow gauge railways increased transhipment costs, Sir Arthur pointed out that in reckoning up the cost of transhipment from small wagons onto a main line system, one could not lose sight of the fact that large wagons could not often be got to the point where their cargo lay and that additional conveyance by means of horses and carts was usually necessary. With narrow gauge wagons it was often possible (and the 18 IN. gauge system at the Royal Arsenal at Woolwich was a good example in this connection) to load cargo directly so that these could perform the same function as road carts. It was further pointed out that transhipment was also necessary within the standard gauge network in the interests of economic expediency and that this was not related to any break in gauge.

Further arguments in favour of narrow gauge railways of 2 FT. gauge and less were advanced and these included their increased ability (as against their standard gauge counterparts) to negotiate tight curves and severe gradients, and their less obtrusive appearance.

Figure 36. Costings for a mile of 15 in. gauge railway drawn up by Heywood in 1881 and 1898.

	1881 £	1898 £		1881 £	1898 £
2,000 yards permanent way (to allow for points, sidings and earthwork)	1000	1100	Interest on above capitals (1881:5%) (1898:4%)	76	72
One 4½ in. cylinder locomotive	250	400	Driver and boy/ line maintenance	30	100
12 wagons, each 1 cub. yard	100	144	Fuel, oil, stores and sundries	26	25
Extras	150	156	Renewal of line and stock at 15 years life. Capital values: 1881…£900, 1898…£1200	60	80
Total cost of a mile of line	£1500	£1800			
N.B. In the 1898 costing, cast iron sleepers are substituted for timber.			Total cost of moving 6,000 tons one mile with twice weekly working.	192	277
			Approximate cost per ton	7¾d.	11d.
			Cart haulage costs over same distance per ton (approximate)	1s.	1s. 3d.
			Approximate saving from use of railway	4¼ d.	4 d.

N.B. These figures are taken from 'The Engineer' and 'Minimum Gauge Railways'. The 1881 costing has been adjusted for twice weekly working from the original, which allowed for weekly working and 3,000 tons per annum capacity.

This view shows KATIE with Harry Wilde circa 1897 with a train of eleven empty four wheelers, the open bogie coach and the closed bogie 'game' wagon. The caption in 'The Car' magazine in 1903 suggested that this was the crossing point over the main Chester-Wrexham road. The number of rolling vehicles (13) is the same as specified for the August 1897 'working day' tests, although there is a passenger coach in the train rather than just a van. Could there have been an error in the 'Minimum Gauge Railways' text regarding these tests? (Minimum Gauge Railways Plate VIII).

In laying out narrow gauge railways, Heywood suggested that gradients steeper than 1-IN-40 were inadvisable as wet weather would cause difficulties. The speed of operation was not material on most railways of this type owing to their usually moderate length but it was suggested that passenger trains should run at as many miles an hour as there were inches in the gauge and goods trains at half this speed (a suggestion possibly influenced by the Fell railway trials at Aldershot in 1872).

Sir Arthur was, as has been mentioned, no advocate of portable railways for locomotive usage as he felt that locomotives required a solid and clean road to work to advantage. The difficulty inherent in this line of argument was that some railway applications simply did not afford the luxury of a solid and clean road. Examples would include the logging railways of the U.S.A. or New Zealand (which gave rise to their own types of flexible fully adhesive locomotive designs in the form of the Shays, Climaxes, Heislers and their derivatives), and, critically for Heywood, the 'front line' portions of the 60 centimetre gauge railways of the Western Front. Another characteristic of the W.D.L.R.'s, and of some contractors' and agricultural lines was that they could not by definition be 'permanent' in nature. This latter observation accounts for the success over many decades, despite Heywood's assertions, of locomotive-worked portable lines, albeit in many instances using internal combustion power.

Sir Arthur also mentioned a subject which he had already discussed in a letter to 'The Times' in relation to the Eaton Railway during 1896, namely the procurement of way-leaves over land not owned by the railway's proprietor. This, it was felt, could normally be accomplished by the payment of an annual acknowledgement of 3d. to 6d. per yard run.

Sir Arthur went on to compare the cost of transportation using a mile of 15 IN. gauge railway, and allowing 2,000 YDS. to include sidings, with the cost of the equivalent amount of horse and cart haulage. The detailed costings for 1898 are reproduced in an accompanying Figure, alongside the 1881 estimates as adjusted for the volume of traffic envisaged in the 1898 calculations. According to the 1898 costings the initial cost of a mile of line, fully equipped, was estimated at £1800 (£1700 with pitch pine sleepers at the expense of higher renewal costs) and this included a locomotive capable of taking a gross load of 12 TONS up a ruling gradient of 1-IN-50. Such a loading would include an average paying load of about 8 TONS and if an average daily workload of one trip per hour were assumed, this would equate to about 60 TONS per day. If the line were worked approximately two days per week or 100 days per annum 6,000 TON-MILE's worth of traffic would be conveyed at a working cost, according to Heywood, of £277. This would have resulted in an average transportation cost of approximately 11d. (4.58p) per ton-mile. Commercial rates of haulage by horse and cart at this time were in the region of 1s. 3d. (6.25p) per ton-mile.

Sir Arthur repeated the view which he had expressed in 1881 that a traffic of 5,000 TONS annually over a mile of 15 IN. gauge line would be the minimum level of traffic necessary to repay the construction cost and that where the line was longer, the same annual tonnage would yield a profit. If a mile long line were equipped with a larger engine, capable of handling an annual tonnage of 40,000, then the owning concern would have been able to reduce the freight costs to approximately 6d. (2.5p) per ton mile. The mitigating factor in favour of horse drawn road transportation was that it was not confined, as with a specific permanent railway line, to one particular route.

In detailing his experiences with the Duffield Bank and Eaton Hall Railways in 1898, Heywood stated that on neither line had there been any injuries and that the rolling stock had not suffered anything but the most trivial derailments and damage in use. This he put down the standard of workmanship of the equipment and permanent way used on both systems. The relative lack of interest shown in Britain at large in the adoption of lines on the Duffield Bank model was attributed by Heywood to the innate conservatism (with a small 'c') present in every Englishman which resisted certain innovations.

CHAPTER ELEVEN
DECLINE AND FALL OF THE DUFFIELD BANK RAILWAY

HEYWOOD'S VIEWS IN 1896 – the eventual failure of any attempt at Doveleys to create a steam worked estate railway on the Eaton model has already been noted but Heywood's views on narrow gauge railways generally are of interest, particularly at the time of the passing of the Light Railways Act in 1896. In that year he wrote a letter to the Editor of 'The Times' (reproduced here in Appendix One) which referred to the 1896 Board of Trade Conference on Light Railways which was undertaken in the same year as the passing of the first of the Light Railways Acts. Unfortunately, Heywood was not invited to take part in this conference but his work was considered of sufficient importance to merit inclusion in Mackay's influential treatise on the subject and for the Institution of Mechanical Engineers to pay a visit to the Duffield Bank Railway in 1898 at the time of preparation of Leslie

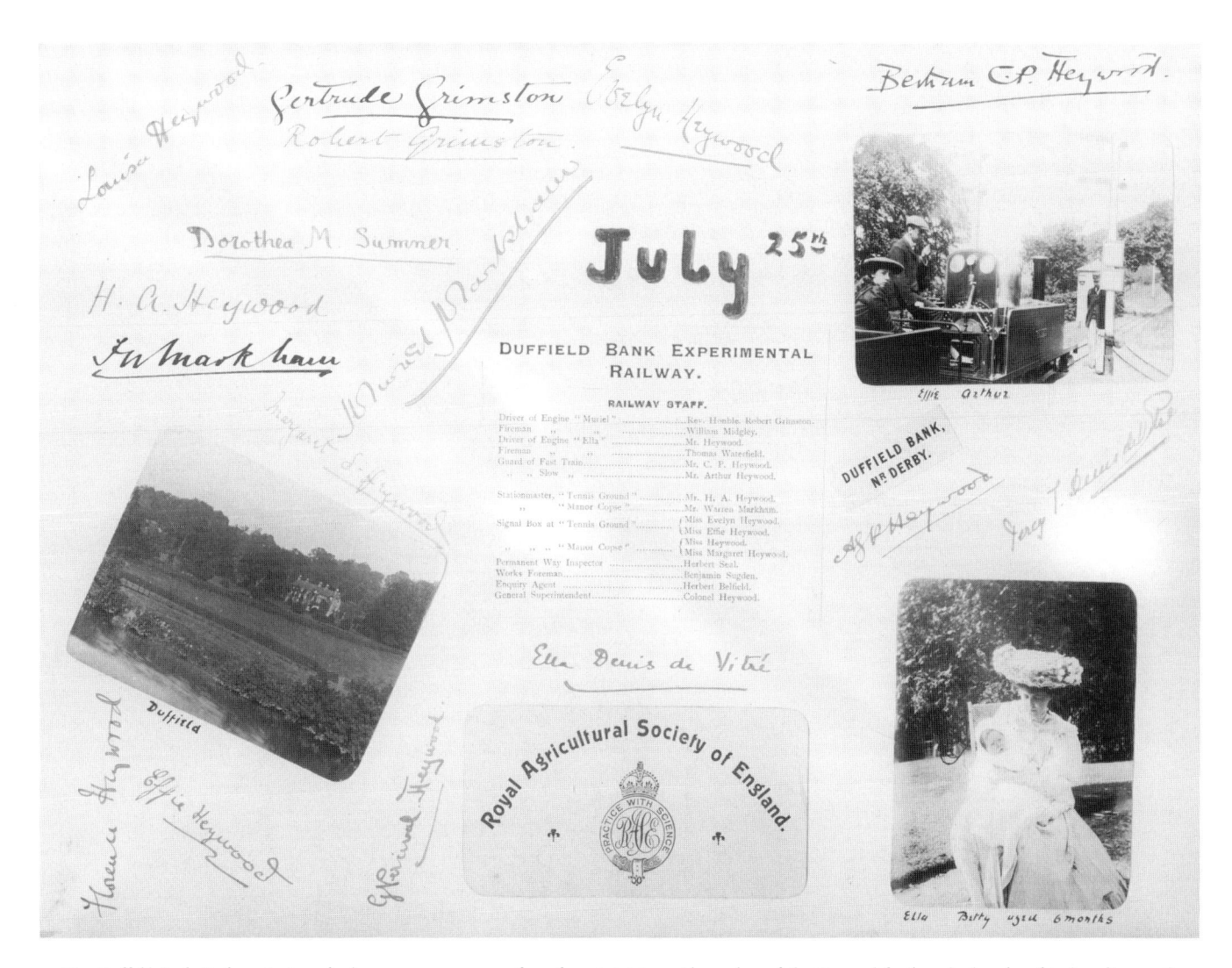

The Duffield Bank Railway in its early days saw some use as a focus for entertaining, with members of the Heywood family and other close friends making up the bulk of the Duffield Bank Railway 'Staff'. The line was used almost exclusively in this capacity after the 1903 'Open Session'. This cutting shows the Duffield Bank Railway staff as at July 25th 1907 and it is interesting to note that the line is still billed as the 'Duffield Bank Experimental Railway' despite the fact that its days as a basis for serious experimentation were over by this time.

PARCELS & TELEGRAMS TO DUFFIELD, DERBY.

DUFFIELD BANK,
Nr DERBY.

Ap 29. 99

Dear Charlie –

2' 6" gauge

[sketch of track cross-section with dimensions: 5' 6", 2' 6", 2', 2', formation wid'th 10", width between centres of fences 18" on level ground, width between outer edges of ditches in cuttings 14']

Where the line is on a bank or in a cutting, the fences will be wider apart, according to the difference between the top of formation & natural level of ground. The *above are* ample for a light line.

Yours very truly

A. P. Heywood –

P.S. I think I understated the width to you on Wed'y — Of course where the formation rises more than 1ft above the natural ground level, no ditches are required –

Robertson's paper 'Narrow Gauge Railways Two Feet and Under'. The subsequent history of the Light Railways Acts has not followed Heywood's distinction between light and narrow gauge railways and Light Railway Orders have been obtained for lines of both standard and narrow gauge. Another point of interest inherent in the letter to 'The Times' in Appendix One was that Heywood clearly envisaged connected 2 FT. gauge systems in North Wales and it his suggested here that he was referring to the possibility of linking what was then the North Wales Narrow Gauge Railway with the Festiniog Railway, thereby linking Blaenau Festiniog with Dinas Junction on the then L.N.W.R. Afon Wen-Carnarvon line, via Beddgelert. By the time this was eventually accomplished by means of the Welsh Highland system, opened in 1923, economic circumstances had changed and the venture proved to be a short-lived commercial disaster.

Narrow Gauge Military Railways
In considering the viability, or otherwise, of a military application for 15 IN. gauge railways of the Heywood pattern, even assuming that this was Sir Arthur's intention, the significant factor which should be noted is that even by the early 1880's there was a considerable body of opinion within the Royal Engineers which opposed the use of a gauge as low as 18 IN. for narrow gauge field (as opposed to service) railways and instead favoured 2 FT. 6 IN. gauge. The influence of this lobby grew over the succeeding years, although the (at least partially) successful use of 18 IN. gauge at Suakin in 1885 and the 1889 Manual of Military Railways helped to delay the inevitable for over a decade. Quoting Heywood's views in 'The Windsor Magazine', Mr. Piper remarked that the matter of light railways for war purposes had been allowed to drop in England since the Egyptian war (more specifically the Suakin campaign). The matter was reconsidered in 1896 however, when the Royal Engineers recommended that provision for locomotive usage on 18 IN. gauge field railways be discontinued and in 1900 this gauge was officially dispensed with as a standard for field railway usage altogether. One of the causes given for the ultimate rejection of 18 IN. gauge was

that the heavier artillery coming into use during the 1890's was too large for the gun trolleys constructed during the previous decade. Against this background, it can be seen that Heywood's 15 IN. gauge stood no realistic chance of adoption for 'front line' field usage. In the letter reproduced in Appendix One, it is interesting to note that 2 FT. 6 IN. is taken as the maximum economically useful gauge for narrow gauge railways. This would appear to stem from from the views of the Royal Engineers' lobby (the 'Major Hogg' school of thought) under whose influence the Chattenden & Upnor system was regauged from standard to 2 FT. 6 IN. gauge in 1885-6. The regauged system was operated by 53RD Railway Company R.E. for nearly two decades prior to its transfer to the Admiralty and Sir Arthur's familiarity with the Chattenden and Upnor line is revealed in 'Minimum Gauge Railways'. Here he stated that he had designed cast steel buffer-couplers of his standard type for use on 'the Royal Engineers' 30 IN. gauge experimental field railway, near Chatham'. These were, according to Heywood, not adopted owing to reasons unconnected with their construction.

Agricultural and Industrial Railways
The general lack of adoption of Heywood style railways for estate and industrial usage was the result of a combination of factors. The 1880's and 1890's decades, which had seen the completion of the locomotives ELLA and MURIEL, also saw a recession in the agricultural industry (partly caused by the growing level of imports of frozen meat from Australia and New Zealand) and the financial position of large estates was certainly not helped by the introduction, in the 1894 Finance Act, of the modern pattern of Estate Duty (now known as Inheritance Tax), partly in order to finance the armaments build up during the period prior to the outbreak of World War One, and partly as a result of misguided political objectives. Heywood's dislike of portable railways also represented, as we have seen, a major misjudgment in relation to the demands of agricultural concerns, particularly those situated overseas.

The general lack of substantive assistance which the passing of the Light Railways Act would bring to alleviate the financial plight of British farmers during the 1890's was recognised by Heywood. In this connection he cited a parody which had appeared in a London evening newspaper in 1896. This is reproduced as Appendix Seven.

By the early 1900's, a mere few years after the production of the last edition of 'Minimum Gauge Railways', developments in transport technology were taking place which were to ensure that Heywood's concept of a 15 IN. gauge steam worked railway for estate or industrial use with locomotives constructed to full loading gauge proportions would never be universally adopted. The internal combustion engine in its various forms was beginning to make is commercial presence felt and with it were to come the motor car and the motor lorry with their ability to facilitate cheap and convenient transportation of passengers and goods to and from destinations

---

Figure 37. OPPOSITE. Although the tide was turning against the widespread adoption of functional railways of less than 2 ft. gauge by the late 1890's, Sir Arthur was still prepared to give advice which was relevant to narrow gauge lines of 2 ft. 6 in. gauge. The Third Edition of 'Minimum Gauge Railways' mentions the fact that he designed a coupling with a view to its use on the Royal Engineers' Chattenden & Upnor Railway (regauged from standard to 2 ft. 6 in in 1885), and this letter, dated April 29th 1899, would appear to relate to the Leek & Manifold Valley Light Railway. The Light Railway Order for this concern had been obtained a month previously and it was destined to be the closest public passenger carrying narrow gauge railway to the Heywood family residence at Doveleys. Sir Arthur's interest in this project can be deduced from his appearance at the 1904 Opening Ceremony.

previously inaccessible by rail. The development of economical internal combustion road transportation was not only to be the single most significant nail in the coffin of Sir Arthur Heywood's railway ambitions, but also for the non-tourist orientated steam railway generally in the developed world. In Sir Arthur's defence here, it can be observed that as early as 1881 in 'The Engineer' he wrote: 'It is often not a question of whether steam is the cheapest form of transport, but whether there is any alternative'. The alternative had simply arrived.

Duffield Bank into the Twentieth Century
During the Edwardian era and in the following years up to the outbreak of World War One, the Duffield Bank Railway was to become merely a focus for social occasions, with Sir Arthur's three sons and six surviving daughters often being involved in the running of the line. Surviving family album pictures, of the type reproduced in accompanying Plates, show the line in use in this capacity and indicate that it was still referred to at this time as the 'Duffield Bank Experimental Railway'. In common with normal railway practice, the Duffield Bank Railway Staff were provided with uniforms, complete with peaked caps bearing the initials 'D.B.R.' throughout the railway's lifetime. The Works at Duffield Bank provided a useful base for the repair of D.B.R. equipment and also that belonging to the Eaton Railway and the expertise of Heywood's assistant, Mr. William Midgley was invaluable. William Midgley acted as Heywood's engineer at Duffield Bank Works from the time when ELLA was new until his death in 1915. He also acted as one of the locomotive footplate staff during 'open sessions' for invited guests. Midgely's widow was destined to attend another funeral in the year following her husband's death, as will be seen shortly.

A Different Direction for 15 in. Gauge
Although Heywood's attempts to gain commercial acceptance for 15 IN. gauge lines of his specification were to end in failure

Prior to its entry into service at Blackpool on Whit Monday 1905, the Bassett-Lowke class 10 Atlantic LITTLE GIANT underwent trials on the Eaton Railway. In this photograph, SHELAGH is shown in the foreground whilst LITTLE GIANT has just been transhipped from the G.W.R. main line in a wooden crate.
(Bassett-Lowke Collection)

during his lifetime, the gauge was taken up as a standard for several of the mainly pleasure-orientated lines which were opened during the present century using steam locomotives which had some pretensions at least to 'scale model' appearance. This trend received an important impetus from the United States at the turn of the century in the form of some miniature 4-4-0 locomotives marketed by the Cagney brothers (trading as the Miniature Railroad Company in New York) and constructed firstly by Peter McGarigle of Niagara Falls and finally by the Herschell Spillman Company of North Tonnawanda. These were all modelled on a single prototype, the record-breaking New York Central and Hudson Railroad 4-4-0 No. 999. In 1901 a 15 IN. gauge example operated at the Glasgow International Festival under the auspices of Captain Boyton and two years later the eclipse of the Heywood style locomotive in its own natural 'territory', the 15 IN. gauge estate railway, was beginning as Charles Bartholomew, the owner of Blakesley Hall, decided initially on the use of Cagney 4-4-0 locomotives on the Blakesley Hall Railway (linking Blakesley Hall with its adjacent station on the East & West Junction Railway, later the Stratford-upon-Avon and Midland Junction Railway), rather than using steam locomotives of a purely functional narrow gauge design.

In 1904 the design of a new locomotive commenced at the Northampton Works of Bassett-Lowke Ltd to the design of Henry Greenly, which was to be an important landmark in the history of 15 IN. gauge railways in the United Kingdom. This was LITTLE GIANT, a freelance 4-4-2 locomotive of one quarter scale proportions which was ordered by a new miniature railway at Blackpool. This locomotive, together with other examples of the Bassett-Lowke/Greenly 15 IN. gauge school which followed during the years leading up to World War One, was instrumental in advancing the development of the purely pleasure orientated 15 IN. gauge miniature railway using 'scale model' style locomotives. Henry Greenly's views will be considered in greater detail later, but it should be noted that when one also takes into account the 1905 description of the Heywood's Eaton locomotive, SHELAGH in 'The Model Engineer' which states: '…personally, I think the outside appearance might easily have been improved…', it can be seen that the Heywood view of locomotive design was not particularly fashionable during the Edwardian era. Sir Arthur's own views on the subject of 'scale model' locomotives were quoted in 'Meccano Magazine' for JULY 1929. He believed that such locomotives: 'although handsome in appearance would be far too costly to construct, and, when finished, would not fulfil the same duties as an engine of his own design with anything like the same success or economy'.

A 'foreigner' on E.R. metals! With wooden crate removed, LITTLE GIANT poses for the camera in Balderton yard. (Bassett-Lowke Collection).

CHAPTER 11

With safety valves and right hand injector overflow both issuing large jets of steam, LITTLE GIANT is seen in a sylvan setting in the grounds of Eaton Hall. (Bassett-Lowke Collection).

The Bassett-Lowke Locomotive Trials

Construction of LITTLE GIANT was completed in MAY 1905 and, before being put into service at Blackpool on Whit Monday, it was sent to Eaton Hall for a thorough trial. Here was an opportunity to test LITTLE GIANT on a well-maintained track with easy curves and a maximum 1-IN-65 gradient and compare her with the Heywood engines. Three tests were completed before a distinguished gathering of model engineers including Bassett-Lowke, Greenly and Fred Smithies, another pioneer in this field.

Tests showed that LITTLE GIANT could haul a maximum load of 12 TONS from a standing start without slipping, reach a maximum speed of 12.5 M.P.H. with a 5 TON load without slipping, and an absolute maximum of 26.4 M.P.H. over ¼ MILE with a 2½ TON load.

The ultimate development of the LITTLE GIANT concept came in 1914 with the building of a COLOSSUS class 'Pacific', JOHN ANTHONY for a Mr. J. E. P. Howey (of later R.H.&D.R. fame) for his Staughton Manor Railway. This came to Eaton Hall for trials in JULY 1914. Most of these second trials were undertaken between the 1¼ and 2¼ MILE posts where the straight track and steep ascent between 1¾ and 2¼ MILE posts gave a severe test. These trials proved the considerable increase in power of JOHN ANTHONY compared with LITTLE GIANT, 16 TONS 14 CWT. being moved on the level and a maximum speed as high as 34.7 M.P.H. running light. With the outbreak of World War One, JOHN ANTHONY remained immured in a shed at Balderton until purchased by the R.&E.R. with KATIE in 1916.

Disposal of the Duffield Bank Equipment

The outbreak of the First World War ensured that the Heywood family would have rather less need of the 'Experimental Railway' at Duffield Bank than in previous years, but a new 15 IN. gauge line was coming to life on the course of the old 3 FT. gauge Ravenglass and Eskdale Railway to the North of Barrow-in-Furness. The new owners, Narrow Gauge Railways Ltd. (whose directors at this time were Messrs.

DECLINE & FALL OF THE DUFFIELD BANK RAILWAY

LITTLE GIANT passes through the grounds of Eaton Hall with a train of 'top' wagons and the two brake vans. The lack of turntables at Eaton and Balderton ensured that on a return trip between these two termini, the bogie brake van had to make half the trip with the brakesman at the rear end, contrary to the interests of safety. (Bassett-Lowke Collection).

This well-known postcard was produced to record the trials of Bassett-Lowke Pacific JOHN ANTHONY (later COLOSSUS) on the Eaton Railway in July 1914. In addition to the this locomotive and KATIE, the photograph shows (from left to right): Harry Wilde; journalist Cecil J. Allen; the second Duke of Westminster, and Capt. J. E. P. Howey (JOHN ANTHONY'S first owner). Despite the impending situation in Europe, Howey did not see fit to abandon the tests with JOHN ANTHONY at this time, although the engine was destined never to return to Howey's own line at Staughton Manor.
JOHN ANTHONY remained at Eaton Hall until acquisition, along with KATIE, by the R&E.R. in 1916.
The photograph was thus mis-captioned in order to publicise the latter concern.

R. Proctor-Mitchell and W. J. Bassett-Lowke), were in dire need of suitable locomotives and rolling stock to work the line and consequently, approaches were made to Duffield Bank with a view to the purchase of any available equipment.

The result of the approaches was that the closed bogie coach of 1881, the bogie brake van and the D.B.R.'s entire working complement of standard unbraked four wheeled top wagons were sold to Narrow Gauge Railways Ltd. for the opening of the R.&E.R. 'The Locomotive' for SEPTEMBER 15TH 1915 made reference to the fact these items of rolling stock were already in R.&E.R. service, and carried two photographs, both of which showed the 1881 carriage and one of which showed the bogie brake van. It was also stated that another locomotive was being sought for goods traffic, thereby suggesting that negotiations were in hand for the acquisition of one of the Heywood locomotives (the non-'main line' appearance of these engines would not have been seen as a handicap for non-passenger working). This suggestion was also supported by an article about the R.&E.R. in the 'Railway Magazine' during the same year which speculated about the possible acquisition of ELLA or MURIEL as an alternative to another Bassett-Lowke locomotive.

The result of the negotiations was that Narrow Gauge Railways Ltd. were notified of the availability of the four coupled KATIE at Eaton Hall and this engine arrived at Ravenglass in time for the 1916 season. The dining car also passed to Ravenglass around the same time.

The death-knell for the Duffield Bank Railway was sounded on the afternoon of APRIL 19TH 1916 when Sir Arthur Heywood died whilst on a visit to Duffield Bank. His funeral was held at Denstone three days later and those present included the Reverend Grimston, Mrs. Midgley (the widow of William Midgley) and, despite any difficulties which may have arisen earlier relating to plans to extend the Dove Bank Railway, Mrs. Clowes and Mrs. Dawson.

The Auction
Following Sir Arthur Heywood's death the remaining equipment of the Duffield Bank Railway was auctioned by the Manchester concern of F. S. Airey, Entwistle & Co.. The Auction Catalogue, which has already been quoted in earlier chapters, provides an interesting inventory of the Duffield Bank Railway in its final days. The auction began at 11.30 A.M. on MAY 31ST 1916 and most of the railway items were to be found in lots 500-516. These comprised (lot numbers in brackets): the permanent way (500); the signal boxes (501); the long viaduct and small bridges (502-504); the wagon weighbridge (505); MURIEL (506); ELLA (507); the four open passenger cars (508); the sleeping car (509); two wrought iron swivel-tip wagons (510); a wrought iron snowplough (511); the childrens' pedal wagon and box car (512-513); the four wheeled brake van (514); wood and iron patterns (515-516). These lots, together with certain other railway items, such as the dynamometer car and uncompleted bogie carriage were purchased by a Mr. Wilkinson, who spent a total of £808.0s.2d. of which £575 was for lots 500-516. Six standard four wheeled wagons which were also under construction at the time are believed to have passed to Eaton Hall.

Mr. Wilkinson turned out to be a nominee for the Derby concern, Messrs. Hill Bros. who were metal merchants and who probably acquired the railway equipment with a view to its re-sale at a profit to a buyer wishing to use it elsewhere. As was indicated in the catalogue, lots 500-516 were offered en bloc at 2 P.M. : 'to anyone desirous of acquiring same with a view to future use for military purposes, on a private estate, public fair ground, contractor or for some commercial undertaking…'. Despite the stipulation in the catalogue that the railway equipment had to be removed by JUNE 14TH, this deadline passed without any equipment being removed.

A correspondent in the JUNE 24TH 1916 edition of 'The Derbyshire Advertiser' warned of the danger of the railway, which was still then in situ, being dismantled and scrapped. He suggested that the entire Duffield Bank estate, together with the railway, should be purchased by a wealthy philanthropist and dedicated for the benefit of the soldier-servants of the various railway companies of the Kingdom. Sadly, no such philanthropist was forthcoming.

The Duffield Bank Railway was thus allowed to pass into history as an integrated unit during the summer of 1916. ELLA and MURIEL were requisitioned by the Ministry of Munitions, it is believed for construction work on the Munitions Factory at Gretna, which opened during the following year, although sadly no photographic evidence has currently come to light to show them engaged on any duties at this location.

Most of the rolling stock was acquired by Narrow Gauge Railways Ltd. and passed to the Ravenglass and Eskdale Railway where the story of the ex-D.B.R. equipment will be continued in the next chapter.

The site of the Duffield Bank Railway is today in private ownership, but a special visit to the site on MAY 14TH 1994 revealed that certain landmarks, such as the long and short tunnels, the sites of the two smaller viaducts and the embankment formation approaching 'Edgehill' station, have changed comparatively little since 1916. The Southern tunnel is now almost blocked at both ends by soil slippage, although it was just possible to crawl through the clearances which remain in order to walk through the tunnel. As if to confuse modern historians, a pair of rails (without sleepers) have been placed in the short tunnel, whilst the remains of a 60 CM. gauge 'V'-skip wagon now lie on the section of formation which once linked the Southern tunnel with Tennis Ground station.

CHAPTER TWELVE
HEYWOOD EQUIPMENT ON THE R.&E.R.

ELLA AND MURIEL 1916-17 – ELLA's and MURIEL's spell under Ministry ownership lasted for approximately a year. It is fairly certain that they would not have been used for normal traffic at Gretna since the main operating narrow gauge line there was of 2 FT. gauge with special fireless locomotives. The elongated perforated petticoat pipes of the Heywood locomotives would not have given adequate protection as spark arresters for the purposes of a munitions railway of this type. The timing of the engines' disposal by the Ministry appears to fit in with date of delivery of the fireless locomotives from Andrew Barclay & Co. Ltd. to the Gretna factory, and hence the completion of the 2 FT. gauge system at this site.

D.B.R. Rolling Stock at Ravenglass
Following the departure of the locomotives, the Duffield Bank Railway was dismantled. Narrow Gauge Railways Ltd. at last took the opportunity to acquire some more much needed rolling stock for the Ravenglass and Eskdale Railway and by the latter part of 1916, the four ex-D.B.R. sixteen seater 'opens', the partially completed closed carriage for Eaton Hall, the sleeping car, the dynamometer car and various assorted goods vehicles had found their way to Ravenglass. At this stage Messrs. R. Proctor-Mitchell and W. J. Bassett-Lowke must have been sufficiently impressed by the design of the 1881 closed carriage to prepare a design for a slightly modified version. Modifications from the original design included raising the clearance from the rail to the lower edge of the solebar by 2 IN. and the height of the enclosed portion of the superstructure by the same amount, giving a revised overall height of 5 FT. 7 IN. Solid ends to the balconies were also provided in lieu of the bare handrails used on the Heywood originals and the bogies were slightly enlarged. It is thought that three carriages were constructed at Ravenglass to the revised specification, in addition to the completion of the

In its December 1915 issue the 'Railway Magazine' recorded that the 1881 Duffield Bank bogie coach and the 15 ft. brake van of slightly later vintage had already been acquired by Narrow Gauge Railways Ltd. from Sir Arthur Heywood, along with some of the earlier pattern D.B.R. four wheel wagons. This view, apparently dating from April 1916, shows Bassett-Lowke Class 30 Atlantic SANS PAREIL with the two earliest Heywood bogie acquisitions at the then newly-reopened Eskdale Green station. Visible beneath the solebar on the bogie brake van is the longitudinal rod which connected the brake linkages for the two bogies. In the reconstructed drawing of the Eaton Railway bogie brake van, it has been assumed that the brake linkage on that vehicle worked on the same principle.

CHAPTER 12

MURIEL in early 15 in. gauge R.&E.R. days with one of the Narrow Gauge Railways Ltd. 'reproduction' Heywood coaches and at least two Heywood wagons (apparently of differing sizes!) adapted for carrying logs by means of bolsters. (Courtesy P. Van Zeller ex-Mary Fair Collection).

unfinished 'Eaton' design of closed carriage. All of the conventional Heywood pattern bogie open and closed passenger stock on the R.&E.R. had been withdrawn from service by the mid-1930's although some axles and bogies from these vehicles remained in existence at Murthwaite after this period. Some representative fragments survive in the R.&E.R. Museum at Ravenglass.

The sleeping car spent about a decade in use at Irton Road as a stationery storeroom and dormitory until the mid-1920's. In 1925 control of Narrow Gauge Railways Ltd. passed to the shipowners, Sir Aubrey Brocklebank and Henry Lithgow and, under the appointed General Manager William Gillon and Engineer Ted Wright, measures were taken to bring into use any suitable passenger rolling stock on the R.&E.R. The erstwhile sleeping car was therefore converted to a three compartment twelve seat closed carriage. It was withdrawn from ordinary service on the outbreak of war in 1939, thereafter surviving intact for a further decade at Murthwaite before gradual demolition during the post-World War Two period. Today the washbasin survives in the R.&E.R.'s Museum at Ravenglass.

The dining car underwent removal of the kitchen and its attendant partition, and the substitution of four further transverse seats, thereby producing a twelve seater saloon. To the end, it could be distinguished from the other Heywood vehicles by reason of sole access via end doorways and its later career was similar to that of the sleeping car, with final scrapping taking place around the same time after a period of use as a store and mess room at Murthwaite. The bogie brake van was withdrawn in the 1920's and the body ended its days as a shelter at Beckfoot Quarry until it was damaged beyond repair in 1940 by a runaway wagon. The ex-Duffield Bank wagons acquired in 1916, which included the pedal trolley, at least one 'workman's car' and the bogie open wagon, had mostly been scrapped by 1930, after a period in which some of the 'top' wagons were adapted as overflow passenger accommodation by being fitted with slatted seats.

ELLA, MURIEL & KATIE after 1917

During 1917 the Ravenglass and Eskdale's proprietors succeeded in persuading the Ministry of Munitions to part with ELLA and MURIEL and the locomotives were purchased,

Another view from the early days of 15 in. gauge operation on the R.& E.R., with MURIEL in the foreground on a mixed train working and one of the Greenly/Bassett-Lowke designed locomotives (with appropriate coaches) in the background.

arriving at Ravenglass via the Furness Railway's main line. It is believed that the R.&E.R.'s attempts to reopen the ironstone mines at Boot during the same year may have been the deciding factor in facilitating this deal. First ELLA and then MURIEL arrived at Ravenglass on standard gauge railway wagons and their condition suggested that little use had been made of them at Gretna. The survival of some D.B.R. rails and sleepers in the Museum at Ravenglass suggests that some Heywood permanent way was also obtained from Gretna.

At Ravenglass, with a relatively long running line of nearly seven miles, and with less scheduled opportunity for intermittent steam raising than had been the case at Duffield Bank or Eaton Hall, the limitations of the Heywood cylindrical fireboxes became more apparent. Probably as a result of the severe gradients on the Duffield Bank Railway, the firebox diameter found on the Heywood locomotives was smaller in relation to the boiler barrel diameter than had been the case with the Crewe works 18 IN. gauge locomotives. This in turn contributed to the relatively low firebox volume and inadequate steam raising capacity for sustained work on the undulating Eskdale line. The result was that at Ravenglass the Heywood locomotives often used to have to incur unscheduled delays for steam raising en route. In spite of the restricted firebox dimensions, damage to the crown as a result of a low water level in the boiler proved to be a recurring problem with the Heywood locomotives in the years following Sir Arthur's death and incidents of this type with ELLA at Ravenglass and KATIE at Fairbourne are recorded. In 1921 a new firebox was supplied by Abbott of Newark for MURIEL's boiler and in 1924 it was necessary for this exercise to be repeated when this engine was required for the R.&E.R. granite traffic between Beckfoot quarry and Murthwaite crushing plant.

On the Ravenglass and Eskdale, it was also found that the Heywood locomotives were well worn owing to the level of usage they had seen during their early careers. This was particularly true of the 0-4-0T KATIE, which had probably never been reboilered. A feature in 'The Locomotive' for MAY 15TH 1919 described a new 4-6-2 locomotive of 'scale model' appearance, SIR AUBREY BROCKLEBANK and went on to state: 'it is also proposed to rebuild the little four coupled side tank locomotive KATIE… with a new locomotive type boiler instead

CHAPTER 12

GRADIENT PROFILE – ESKDALE RAILWAY
RAVENGLASS TO BOOT

Figure 38. This gradient profile for the R.&E.R. appeared in 'Railway Magazine' for December 1915. The undulating and demanding nature of this line of more than seven miles in length made a sharp contrast with the Duffield Bank Railway 'Main Line' and heavily taxed the cylindrical firebox boilers of the Heywood locomotives. At this time, Boot was used as the inland terminus in preference to Dalegarth, but its remoteness, together with an approach line incorporating a 1 in 46 gradient, ensured that this situation was reversed during the 1920's.

Although plans existed to rebuild the ex-E.R. 0-4-0T KATIE at Ravenglass in 1919, economic circumstances prevailed and the engine was sold instead to Llewelyn's Miniature Railway at Southport. This postcard was printed circa 1920 and shows the engine at this location sans nameplates and in a lighter (apple?) green livery with appropriate lettering. Certain modifications made at Ravenglass, such as the cylinder lubricators and the weatherboard struts, are visible in this view. KATIE'S stay at Southport was a brief one as in 1923 the engine moved to Fairbourne. (Courtesy E. Hughes via S. Townsend).

RAVENGLASS AND ESKDALE RAILWAY.
TIME TABLE, July 11th to September 30th, 1920.

	WEEK-DAYS.							SUNDAYS.			
	a.m.	a.m.*	a.m.*	p.m.*	p.m.*	p.m.	A	a.m.*	a.m.*	p.m.*	p.m.
Ravenglass dep	8 30	11 20	12 10	3 5	4 40	6 15	7 30	9 30	11 20	2 30	7 35
Muncaster	B	...	B	B	B	B	B	B	B	B	B
Irton Road	8 55	...	12 35	3 30	5 5	6 40	7 55	9 55	11 45	2 55	8 0
Eskdale Green	9 0	...	12 40	3 35	5 15	...	8 0	10 0	11 50	3 0	...
Beckfoot	9 15	...	12 55	3 50	5 30	...	8 15	10 15	12 5	3 15	...
Dalegarth arr.	...	12 0	1 0	3 55	5 35	...		10 20	12 10	3 20	...
		*	*	*	*			*	*	*	*
Dalegarth dep.	...	1 25	3 5	4 45	6 15	Sun-		12 15	...	4 45	6 15
Beckfoot	9 40	1 28	3 8	4 48	6 18	days.		12 18	...	4 48	6 18
Eskdale Green	9 50	1 40	3 20	5 0	6 30	...		12 25	...	5 0	6 30
Irton Road	10 0	1 50	3 30	5 10	6 40	...	10 15	12 30	1 30	5 10	6 40
Muncaster	C	C	C	C	C	..	C	...	C	C	C
Ravenglass arr.	10 25	2 15	3 55	5 35	7 5	...	10 40	...	1 55	5 35	7 5

*—These Trains are worked by the Scale Model Type of Locomotives.
B—Calls at Muncaster 5 minutes after leaving Ravenglass to pick up Passengers for Irton Road and beyond only.
C—Stops to set down Passengers on notice being given to the Guard at Irton Road.

This Time Table will not be in operation on Bank Holiday, Monday, Aug. 2nd, or Friday, Sept. 24th.

Narrow Gauge Railways, Limited,
R. PROCTOR MITCHELL, GENERAL MANAGER, RAVENGLASS.

R. BURLINGTON, PRINTER, WHITEHAVEN.

This R.&E.R. timetable from 1920 is an indication of the esteem in which the Heywood locomotives were held on the R.& E.R. where promoting the railway's public image was concerned. All of the peak hour workings were to be handled during this high season period by 'scale model' locomotives, with the Heywoods seeing only mineral and off-peak passenger usage. The four coupled KATIE in particular was not popular during its stay on the R.& E.R. partly because it had not (unlike ELLA and MURIEL) been reboilered during its lifetime (hence the Cauchi reboilering proposal of 1919). KATIE'S firebox in particular was apparently in very poor condition, even by 1916.

---

of the present one which has a circular firebox'. Unfortunately, the then R.&E.R. locomotive superintendent, Mr. William F. Cauchi, had second thoughts on the matter and later in 1919 the engine was sold to the Llewellyn Miniature Railway at Southport. A recently discovered postcard, sent by Mr. G. V. Llewellyn from Southport to Mr. A. Barnes of the Rhyl Miniature Railway on JANUARY 22ND 1921 shows KATIE sans nameplates and bearing the legend 'Llewelyn's Miniature Ry. Ltd.' on the side tanks. The letter on the reverse of the postcard read: 'Dear Mr. Barnes, Is this loco any good to you? Gauge 15 IN. in good order. It's a bit too wide (4 FT.) for my shed. It would do well for your yard or grounds. Price £190. About the price of boiler only. Insured + policy transferred. Yours G. V. Llewelyn'.

KATIE did not go to Rhyl but passed instead to the Fairbourne Miniature Railway near Barmouth (a line which had been owned by Narrow Gauge Railways Ltd. until 1922) and by this stage the engine had definitely seen better days, with the original holly green superstructure livery having been replaced by an unlined lighter shade. The weatherboard had

CHAPTER 12

Above: ELLA on a stone working from Beckfoot Quarry to Murthwaite Crusher circa 1923 with a train consisting of five ex-D.B.R. Heywood wagons and five Theakston wagons built new for the Ravenglass & Eskdale. (Photomatic Ltd.).

Left: By the 1950's, the original KATIE mainframes had ceased to be of further use on the Fairbourne Railway and they eventually came to rest in an upturned position at Fairbourne. During the 1970's they were moved to the Narrow Gauge Railway Museum at Tywyn and again in 1981 to Ravenglass.

ELLA is seen here at Ravenglass in 1924 with Mr. Bert Thompson, the driver of the engine. Externally, the engine had changed little since 1916 although the wheel operated cock (located immediately forward of the reversing pedestal) for shutting off steam to the injectors and steam brake was certainly a post-1916 feature. Immediately to the rear of the backhead is the removable square spanner handle used for operating the water feed to the injectors, whilst to the left of the handle can be seen the positions of the two protruding square shanks. (R.&E.R.).

been strengthened by the addition of a pair of struts at Ravenglass (a modification also made to ELLA and MURIEL) and the dome cover sported a dent on the left hand side.

KATIE soldiered on at Fairbourne through the 1924 operating season as the line's only source of motive power but a change in ownership of the railway during that year allowed the acquisition of a replacement engine, once more of Bassett-Lowke/Greenly parentage and KATIE was withdrawn. After the scrapping of the boiler the engine's chassis was used for several years, firstly as part of a passenger coach and eventually as part of a tool wagon. By the 1950's the frames of KATIE could be found discarded in an upturned position at Fairbourne and they were subsequently rescued with the intention of display at the Narrow Gauge Railway Museum at Tywyn. The decision was eventually taken to move them to Ravenglass as part of the museum collection there, however, and it is at Ravenglass where they currently rest. As will be dealt with shortly, work is now in progress to incorporate these components into a full size working replica of the original engine.

ELLA and MURIEL both survived into the mid-1920's on the Ravenglass and Eskdale in substantially the condition in which they left the Duffield Bank Railway in 1916 although a number of modifications to mechanical details were made to suit the operational requirements of the R.&E.R. The most important of these was the disabling of the 'radiating gear' by the removal of its intermediate linkages on both locomotives during 1921, the year in which Henry Greenly had assumed the position of R.&E.R. Consulting Engineer. The cause of this modification was recalled in a letter from ELLA's driver at this time, Mr. Bert Thompson, to Mr. B. G. Markham that during a light engine working to Boot, ELLA had just left Beckfoot when the front radial axle sleeve refused to function properly. It was found that the engine could be worked in reverse and so it was necessary to return to Ravenglass for attention. The result of the consequent modification was that the only element of wheelbase flexibility subsequently retained by the chassis arrangements of ELLA and MURIEL was inherent in the retention of the sliding intermediate axle sleeves.

In another attempt to improve riding characteristics, ELLA was temporarily fitted with coil springs instead of rubber blocks but these springs were found to have insufficient

CHAPTER 12

Above: Bassett-Lowke class 30 4-4-2 SANS PAREIL keeps MURIEL and ELLA company outside Ravenglass shed in 1925. Within two years, all three had ceased to exist in the forms illustrated. (Real Photographs).

inherent damping and the rubber blocks were soon refitted.

A constructional peculiarity possessed by the five later Heywood locomotives was that the valve gear was not all of the usual construction, where bushes are provided for steel pins, but some components had no bushes and bronze pins. The rationale behind this measure was that the bronze pins would bear the brunt of the wear in use and the steel rods would suffer relatively little wear. Unfortunately, largely owing to the action of dirt particles, the theory did not work too well in practice and the aforementioned valve gear components of ELLA and MURIEL certainly required bushes during the period of Henry Greenly's tenure of office as Consulting Engineer at Ravenglass (1921-1924). Cylinder lubrication proved to be inadequate on the Heywood locomotives for R.&E.R. needs and initially ELLA, MURIEL and KATIE were provided with auxiliary oil cups mounted on the steam chests. As regards the first two of these locomotives, this was to prove only a stop gap measure and both were eventually fitted with mechanical lubricators with supply pipes brazed into the oil cups.

By 1926, MURIEL was in use as a stationary boiler at Beckfoot stone quarry and by the following year the boiler had been removed and mounted on a flat wagon for continued use in this capacity for a few more months. The chassis, however, was basically sound and it was given new bufferbeams and lengthened at the rear end to carry a trailing truck. A new

Page 105 – Upper: A front left hand three quarter view of MURIEL at Ravenglass in 1925. Unlike ELLA, struts are fitted to both sides of the weatherboard. The excess amount of piping visible under the rear part of the footplate suggests that the steam brake control may have been moved latterly to the left hand side of the engine, a proposition supported by a later photograph showing the engine providing steam for drills at Beckfoot Quarry.

Lower: MURIEL seen from the other side, showing the added mechanical lubricator. Supply and waste pipes for an injector can be seen in this view, but not the piping for the steam brake. The damage to the front bufferbeam, caused by a head-on collision with COLOSSUS (the former JOHN ANTHONY) at Eskdale Green in March 1925 is also visible. The nature of the damage suggests that the bufferbeam casting was relatively thin above the drawgear, and that a thin sheet iron or steel facing was in some way attached to this casting. For some unknown reason, a dome cover from one of the 'main line' outline locomotives has been deposited on MURIEL'S right hand side tank.
(Both: Real Photographs).

HEYWOOD EQUIPMENT ON THE R.&E.R.

CHAPTER 12

ELLA outside Ravenglass engine shed in 1925. Close examination of this photograph reveals much detail about the locomotive's construction: the final type of 'linear linkage' valve gear, the rivets securing the footplate valence to the bufferbeam castings, the injector steam supply pipe, and (just visible in front of the lower part of the reversing lever) the pipe leading from the steam brake control valve to the brake cylinder. The location of this pipe, as close as possible to the rear axle can only be consistent with the view that it entered the forward part of the cylinder and that the piston pulled to actuate the brake (see also next caption). One of the flanges joining the sandpipes to their control valves is just visible beneath the bufferbeam. The 'boxed in' coupling rod bearings fitted from new to MURIEL seem never to have been fitted to ELLA. This view also shows certain alterations made at Ravenglass. These include the mechanical lubricator; high wooden partition allowing coal to be carried over the boiler as well as the left hand tank; another partition blanking off the filler cap from stray lumps of coal; a new chimney barrel fabricated in two pieces and a mechanical lubricator. The smokebox door was held in place at this stage by two external catches, the door handle presumably being 'locked' into the position shown. (Real Photographs).

A broadside left hand view of ELLA, possibly taken a year earlier than the previous view. The weatherboard supporting strut fitted during early Ravenglass days has been removed from this side. One of the cast iron intermediate frame stretchers fitted during the 1897-1900 rebuild can be seen above the leading axle. These appear to have been fitted in order to incorporate secondary suspension. (Real Photographs).

ELLA'S usefulness was not over following withdrawal from service on the R.&E.R. in 1926. For a further two years the side mainframes of this locomotive were incorporated into the R.&E.R.'s I.C.L. No.2, which was powered by an in-line six cylinder Lanchester car engine. Although satisfactory in terms of power output, the resultant conversion proved to be accident-prone in service and was therefore destined to be short-lived. (Courtesy P. Van Zeller ex-Mary Fair Collection).

boiler (supplied by Yorkshire Engine Co. Ltd in 1927), with a depending firebox, and a cab with 'scale model' pretensions were fitted and a tender added. The resulting locomotive was renamed RIVER IRT and entered service on AUGUST 1ST 1927. It has remained a valuable part of the Ravenglass and Eskdale's motive power fleet ever since, although a new and larger cab was fitted during the Winter of 1971/2 and a new boiler in 1978 following a borrowed boiler from RIVER MITE in 1977. During 1981-2, RIVER IRT appeared at the National Railway Museum as part the 'Minimum Gauge Railways' Exhibition staged to celebrate the centenary of ELLA's completion and the engine has also appeared at the Liverpool (1984), Stoke (1986) and Gateshead (1990) Garden Festivals and on the R.H.&D.R. in 1991.

Despite its age ELLA put in much useful work on the R.&E.R. during the early 1920's and several photographs survive of the engine working trains of Heywood and Heywood type passenger stock, and also on stone workings from Beckfoot quarry. On one occasion, during Whitsun 1920, ELLA is recorded as taking a train with 265 passengers, rather more than the customary loads at Duffield Bank! Plans were discussed for the conversion of the engine to oil-firing, and even to a petrol electric unit but neither of these came to fruition. At one stage during the early 1920's the firebox crown suffered low water damage and was restored to a rough approximation of its manufactured shape by the application of a jack (a practice hardly conducive to the safety of the driver or close bystanders). Eventually the condition of the engine, its operational limitations and the desire on the part of the R.&E.R.'s proprietors for their steam locomotives at least to outwardly resemble standard gauge main line practice all combined to ensure ELLA's withdrawal from service on SEPTEMBER 5TH 1926.

During the following Winter, ELLA's chassis was lengthened by two feet at each end and converted to a 2-6-2 wheel arrangement. A Lanchester Model 38 touring car six cylinder engine provided the new source of motive power and this was mounted on part of the original car chassis. The car's original gearbox was retained, but fitted with a Parson's Marine direct reverse gear in order to provide the full range of gears in either direction of travel. The transmission was then taken via a Cardan shaft to a countershaft with final chain and sprocket drive to the coupled wheels. A wooden box-like teak superstructure with vertical planking was added as shelter for the driver. The resultant creation, christened 'I.C.L. NO. 2', entered service in spring 1927 and proved to be a good performer. Its

CHAPTER 12

I.C.L. No.2 is seen here at Ravenglass, probably during the late Summer of 1927. The final drive, from a counter shaft via a chain and sprockets, is shown to advantage in this view. (Courtesy P. Van Zeller ex-Mary Fair Collection).

operational career was destined to be a short one, however, as damage to the chassis was sustained during a collision on OCTOBER 2ND 1928 and in the following year a big-end on the six cylinder engine was pushed through a crank case resulting in the engine's final withdrawal from service. Today, ELLA's rather battered side mainframes are preserved as part of the R.&E.R.'s Museum Collection whilst the side tanks are now to be found on BONNIE DUNDEE, a regauged and modified ex-Dundee Gasworks tank locomotive of Kerr, Stuart parentage which entered service on the R.&E.R. following conversion in 1981-2.

Other miscellaneous Heywood relics survive in the Ravenglass Museum and these include a wooden casting pattern for the standard Heywood dry firebox backhead and another pattern for part of a point assembly.

HEYWOOD EQUIPMENT ON THE R.&E.R.

Above: The destruction of Heywood equipment on the R.&E.R. was a protracted process with Murthwaite often proving to be the final 'port of call'. This 1951 view shows the remains of Heywood's last carriage to be completed (which was unfinished at the time of his death). This vehicle was identical as built to the still-extant 1904 carriage supplied to Eaton Hall but the latter has undergone much alteration since 1947.

Right: Following MURIEL'S conversion to the 0-8-2 tender locomotive RIVER IRT, its 1908 boiler was used for a few months at least at Beckfoot Quarry to provide steam to power the quarrymens' drills. It was mounted on a flat wagon and supplied with water from one of the R.&E.R.'s Theakston wagons. (R.&E.R. Co.).

CHAPTER 12

Above: Muir Hill 4wPM 'QUARRYMAN' (Muir Hill No2 of 1926) seen on 25th of May 1951 (while the standard gauge Kerr Stuart diesel was stripped down awaiting a major overhaul) approaching Ravenglass with a loaded train of Theakston built wagons. (Brian Hilton).

Right: Although after 1929 much of the R.&E.R. stone traffic from Murthwaite crushing plant was transferred direct to L.M.S. metals by means of a standard gauge branch from Ravenglass to Murthwaite and a six wheel Kerr, Stuart diesel, the 15 in. gauge line (laid for the most part between the standard gauge rails) between Ravenglass and Murthwaite was still used for some stone traffic, which was transferred to motor lorries be means of a stone chute behind the locomotive shed at Ravenglass. Heywood's view that 15 in. gauge was suitable for mineral carriage was therefore vindicated but by this time none of his locomotives remained intact on the R.&E.R.

CHAPTER THIRTEEN
THE EATON RAILWAY AFTER 1916

THE PERIOD BETWEEN THE WARS – apart from the attention paid to it by celebrities over the years, the Eaton Railway's 51 year period of operation was largely uneventful with even the same driver, Mr. Harry Wilde, remaining in office for over 37 years. Mr. Harry Wilde had been Sir Arthur's assistant engineer at Duffield Bank from the late 1880's until 1895 when he went to Eaton Hall to assist with construction of the railway there. During the following year he assumed the position of driver on the Eaton Hall Railway. Mr. Wilde was a keen bell-ringer (his obituary appeared in 'The Ringing World' for NOVEMBER 4TH 1932) and whilst working on the Eaton Railway he compiled a record of 'Notable Passengers and Visitors' from OCTOBER 1895 to NOVEMBER 1911. He also amassed a collection of photographs of the railway, some of which appear in this book.

From DECEMBER 1916 until the cessation of hostilities, Eaton Hall was used as a hospital for wounded officers and the railway experienced a corresponding increase in traffic. This period of the Eaton line's history was recalled in a letter from a Mr. A. C. Hyde Parker in 'The Model Engineer and Practical Electrician' for MAY 7TH 1936. Mr. Hyde Parker stated that whilst at the hospital he had had several rides on the railway and had conversed with the engineer in charge (presumably Mr. Harry Wilde) about the Duffield Bank Railway. As events had turned out, Mr. Hyde Parker's grandmother's residence had adjoined Duffield Bank and he had often watched the Duffield Bank line in use as a boy.

Following the loss of Duffield Bank Works as a base for repairs, the two Heywood 0-6-0 tank locomotives at Eaton Hall fell out of favour within a few years. The difficulties associated with the fireboxes on the Heywood locomotives at Ravenglass and Fairbourne were also evident with KATIE and URSULA, particularly as a result of the decision not to fit firebox stays to the 1914 boilers to counteract differential expansion of the rear tubeplate and associated tube leakage.

With the expertise necessary to keep the unorthodox steam locomotives in working order no longer readily available, a more reliable source of motive power was desired during the post-World War One era. During the war, the second Duke of

URSULA seen with bogie brake van (brake column end trailing), again circa 1921. (F. Wilde Collection).

CHAPTER 13

Above: 0-6-0T KATIE (alias SHELAGH) shown from a rear three-quarter angle, again for the 1929 feature. Beneath the footplate can be seen four pipes. From left to right these were the steam brake control chest waste outlet; the connection from the brake control chest to the front of the steam brake cylinder, the injector waste outlet and the steam supply to the injectors. The steam brake lever actuated a slide valve within the chest and when positioned vertically connected the two rear pipes together, thereby allowing steam to escape from the brake cylinder and for its associated piston to be returned to the 'off' position by means of a light return spring within the steam brake cylinder. Pushing the lever forward admitted steam to the rear intermediate pipe and the brake cylinder and blanked off the waste pipe. This was the 'on' position for the brake. (Real Photographs).

Opposite – top left: A rear head-on view of KATIE (nee SHELAGH) taken for the 1929 'Meccano Magazine' feature. From left to right can be seen the tank water gauge (in shadow); the handbrake column; the left hand boiler water gauge; the firebox backhead, steam regulator handle and boiler pressure gauge; the right hand boiler water gauge; the upper parts of the control levers for the blast nozzle and sanders; the reversing lever and associated handwheel; the steam brake lever and the control tap for the steam supply to the injectors. The relief inscription on the cast firebox backhead read: 'Duffield Bank Works 1903'. An important point to notice is that two longitudinal stays are visible on the backhead of the engine in this view. So far as is known, no such modification was made to URSULA and this difference between the two locomotives proved to be of major importance. (Real Photographs).

Opposite – top right: The date of this previously unpublished photograph is something of an enigma. Two details identify the subject as URSULA. The most significant of these is the lack of the longitudinal stays fitted to KATIE'S boiler by 1929, whilst the other is the lack of a date in relief on the cast dry firebox backhead (KATIE, as we have seen, bore the relief date 1903). The track configuration identifies the location as immediately in front of the carriage shed at Eaton. The near-pristine condition of much of URSULA'S paintwork, and absence of a driver's seat suggest that the engine was stored out of use by this stage in the carriage shed. This view is further supported by the fact that the cab of the 1922 'Simplex' is visible behind the engine. The waste and brake pipes from the steam brake control valve are visible beneath the right hand rear portion of the bufferbeam.

Westminster had held the position of Assistant to the Controller of the Mechanical Warfare Department at the Ministry of Munitions. It seems likely that during this period he would have become familiar with the 'Simplex' petrol tractors then in use on the 60 centimetre gauge light railways of the Western front. For this reason, it came as no surprise that a 20 H.P. Motor Rail 'Simplex' petrol-mechanical locomotive was delivered to Eaton Hall in 1922 (Works No. 2099). This locomotive was propelled by a Dorman 2JO two-cylinder engine, with transmission effected via an inverted cone clutch, Dixon-Abbott patent two-speed gearbox and final drive consisting of roller chains and sprockets to both axles.

In order to adapt this basic design for 15 IN. gauge, it was necessary for the final drive sprockets to be located closer to the longitudinal centreline of the locomotive, than on its 60 CM. gauge counterparts. This in turn resulted in the need for the engine and gearbox to occupy a 4½ IN. 'off-centre' position, with a balance weight protruding this amount from the other side thus increasing the width of the locomotive by approximately 9 IN. on a reduced gauge!

By 1929, when an article on the Eaton Railway appeared in 'The Meccano Magazine', URSULA was out of service, for reasons which were not specified. The relevant passage in the article reads: The whole system, including track, rolling stock and two locomotives – only one of which is now in service – was entirely designed by Sir Arthur P. Heywood'. Further light appears to be shed on this matter by close examination of rear photographs of both KATIE and URSULA dating from the 1920's, however. The 1929 photograph of the former clearly shows that two longitudinal stays had been fitted to the upper part of the boiler, and a later photograph showing this engine's front tubeplate indicates a pair of lower stays, almost certainly anchored at their rear ends to the front end of the firebox barrel. Just who carried out this boiler repair is unclear, but it certainly helped to relieve the stresses on the tubeplates and tubes, thereby lengthening the working life of the engine.

The arrival of the petrol locomotive removed the need to carry out this modification to URSULA and consequently it would appear that this locomotive was simply consigned to the carriage shed after 1922, only to be towed outside on a few

CHAPTER 13

This photograph of KATIE with a mixed train was first published in 'The Meccano Magazine' for July 1929. (Real Photographs).

occasions for the benefit of privileged visitors. URSULA's apparent early withdrawal from service would appear to account for the fact that the locomotive's existence went largely unnoticed by commentators of the period; photographs of the engine in ordinary operational service are extremely difficult to find!

It would appear that post-1922 steam locomotive use was largely confined to special occasions, such as the 1925 visit of representatives of the Central Council of Church Bellringers to Eaton Hall for a meeting. With the petrol locomotive in demand for duties requiring immediate attention (no time being lost for steam-raising), there would appear to have been little justification for the maintenance of two steam locomotives in working order. KATIE appears to have remained in service until around the time of Mr. Wilde's death, thereafter a major personal link with Sir Arthur was gone and KATIE joined URSULA in the carriage shed. Mr. Wilde's place was taken by Mr. Harry Morgan, who remained responsible for the running of the railway until its eventual closure.

The first 'Simplex' was replaced by another 20 H.P. locomotive from the same maker in MARCH 1938 (Works No. 7059) and this was generally similar to its predecessor, save for the fact that the 'channel section' form of chassis construction used on the earliest 'Simplexes' had given way by 1938 to a simpler 'plate-framed' chassis configuration.

The Last Years

On JANUARY 15TH 1940 both Heywood locomotives were noted out of use by Mr. J. G. Vincent in the carriage shed at Eaton, with KATIE at the front of the shed and URSULA at the rear. Both locomotives faced Balderton at this time. Wartime drives for metal salvage appear to have prompted the decision which was taken during summer 1942 to scrap the Heywood engines. As a result the two locomotives were towed to Balderton during July or August of that year. It would seem, from their final positions at Balderton Siding, that the locomotives were towed one at a time and that they were each reversed on the triangular junction of the Cuckoo's Nest branch, possibly to enable a visit to Belgrave Lodge for removal of name and works plates. A subsequent visit by Mr. Vincent on SEPTEMBER 4TH revealed that cutting up work was almost complete on KATIE and well advanced on URSULA. So far as is known, the only items which survive from these locomotives are a toolbox, the nameplates, one pair of works plates (from URSULA) and two gunmetal spectacle rims, 8 IN. in diameter, ¾ IN. wide and a little under ⅛ IN. thick. One of these latter items bears the number '2', and the other '3', but precisely what significance these numbers have does not appear to have been recorded.

The 'Railway Magazine' for September and October 1944 recorded that Mr. Robin Butterell (wrongly credited as 'J. D. Buttrell') had supplied information concerning the current state of the Eaton Hall Railway. By this time the Heywood coaches, although in good condition, were seeing use merely 'from time to time'. The permanent way was in good order and trains were run regularly on weekdays, carrying coal for the estate's lighting and heating needs and timber for the sawmills adjoining the engine sheds. The section of the branch between the sawmills and the Cuckoo's Nest estate works had apparently fallen out of use during the intervening period after compilation of an article featured in the 'The Locomotive' for MARCH 14TH 1942.

Mr. Butterell's 1944 visit also revealed that in addition to rails and sleepers specifically made for the Eaton line (some of which bore the relief lettering 'E.R. 1895, B.') there were some bearing the legend 'D.B.R. 1897, B.' indicating that these were intended originally for the Duffield Bank system, or even possibly for Doveleys. The date of 'migration' of these latter items to Eaton Hall is not known for certain.

A modification to the track plan at the Eaton end of the line, which had certainly been carried out during its operational period, was that the enclosed part of the carriage shed eventually sported two running roads instead of one. Two long wheelbase four wheel wagons had been 'improvised' at Eaton using original Heywood wheel and axle components, and these remained in use until the end of normal operation.

The end finally came for the Eaton Hall line in 1947. Following the end of World War Two, a lease of Eaton Hall was granted to the War Department and the greater part of the Hall was used for much of the remaining fourteen years of its existence as a National Service training establishment for Officers. The War Department possessed its own road transport facilities and consequently the little railway was no longer required. The 'Railway Magazine' for May and June of that year carried news from a Mr. J. T. White that the Duke

This previously unpublished view is of considerable historical interest as it is the latest known view showing the Heywood 0-6-0T locomotives KATIE and URSULA intact. The photograph shows these locomotives on January 15th 1940 in store in the carriage shed at Eaton Terminus. KATIE displays two features of interest, namely the unsprung coupler (secured from beneath) and the internally hinged smokebox door (an early Heywood feature first seen on ELLA in 1881).
(Courtesy J. G. Vincent).

CHAPTER 13

THE EATON RAILWAY AFTER 1916

Above: This view shows the remains of the Heywood locomotive KATIE (the erstwhile SHELAGH) on September 4th 1942 at Balderton. On the right is shown the boiler, from which it is possible to discern the tube arrangement and the tubeplate exit position of the blower pipe. In addition two of the four stays fitted to the boiler during the 1920's in order to prolong the engine's working life can be seen. The remains of the internally mounted smokebox door hinge do not at first sight reveal its modus operandi, but examination of the boiler drawings reveals a generous clearance between the inner disc of the smokebox door and the smokebox front aperture. It is therefore seems certain that the swinging arm of the hinge was a truncated spherical segment in profile and bore against the inner curved surface of the door. A slot arrangement (almost certainly incorporating one of the smokebox door rivets and the door locking pin) would have allowed the door to slide to the left (looking frontwards) whilst being opened, and eventually for the extreme right of the door to lie just to the left of the hinge fulcrum when the door was fully open. The door handle was on a pin which passed through both discs of the door and would have worked the locking catches via bellcranks. As with the 18 in. gauge Manning Wardle locomotives of the Royal Arsenal, there was no need for any fixed bars across the smokebox front aperture. On the left of the picture a portion of the mainframes can be seen. This incorporates the rear axle sleeve and its associated linkage hoops. Two of the seatings for the secondary suspension on the upper portions of the hoops can be seen clearly, as can two of the attendant bearing surfaces on the lower part of the rearmost frame stretcher casting. The pipe shown leading from the 'blow off flange' area of the boiler was the supply to the steam brake control valve situated under the footplate to the rear of the boiler backhead. In the foreground can be seen the handwheel from URSULA'S reverser, together with the inside left hand face of the reversing pedestal with its sector guide, and (on the extreme right) the handle for the steam brake. Other debris includes several firebars. (Courtesy J. G. Vincent).

Opposite page – Upper: The Eaton Railway closed carriage and four wheel brake van are seen outside the carriage shed on January 15th 1940. The windows of the carriage are misted up by condensation. (Courtesy J. G. Vincent).

Lower: Photographs of the second Motor Rail 'Simplex' petrol locomotive on the Eaton Railway are rare, but it is fortunate that a few views have survived. The locomotive is seen here on January 15th 1940 at Balderton siding in company with the bogie brake van. Note the more angular cab on the locomotive when compared with its 1922 predecessor. Unlike the 1922 locomotive, this 'Simplex' was fitted with the more modern Dorman 2JOR engine, which incorporated detachable cylinder heads. (Courtesy J. G. Vincent).

CHAPTER 13

Above: A frontal view of the chassis of URSULA, with the right hand side tank in the foreground. The portion of the tank normally visible was actually the 'cosmetic' valence; the tank proper (seen here) being a galvanised component with snap head rivets. The aperture visible in the underside of the upper face of the tank is for the filler cap. The bars for operating the sandpipes and the draincocks can be seen between the cylinder ends. Other components visible in this view (from front rearwards) are the leading guard iron; the truncated remains of the smokebox front plate; the leading cast frame stretcher; the rods for the adjustable blast pipe (lower) and front sanding gear (upper) passing through a bracket on the right hand mainframe; the rear right hand brake hanger; part of the equalising pipe; the trailing cast frame stretcher and the severed rear portion of the chassis. (Courtesy J. G. Vincent).

Opposite page. A rear overhead shot of URSULA during scrapping at Balderton on September 4th 1942. From this view, the position of the sandboxes can be made out, as can the steam brake cylinder (centrally placed and bolted to the rear bufferbeam casting). The two water pipes to the injectors can been seen with their forward ends leading to the site of the tank water level equalisation pipe (three sections bolted together). The injector bodies can be seen immediately to the left of the steam brake cylinder, in conjunction with the delivery flow combination manifold (from which the pipe to the right hand 'clack' valve has been cut away). The tap visible to the right of the remains of the reverser/steam brake pedestal controlled the steam inlet to the injectors. Examination of the remaining portion of the right hand running plate suggests that a small aperture was necessary in order to allow for the requisite degree of rotation of the linear linkage body when 'notching up'. To the right of the chassis can be seen the remains of the right hand tank valence, and (resting on the frontal portion of the valence) the middle frame stretcher. Also resting on the frontal portion of the valence is the pipe which led from the 'blow-off' flange to the steam brake control valve. The broken structure seen between the rear of the chassis and the middle frame stretcher is believed to be part of the steam brake control valve, hence the fact that the injector steam supply control spindle has fallen through its attendant hole in the running plate. Behind the chassis, to the rear centre of the picture, is the part of the reverser pedestal carrying the leadscrew. Landmarks visible in this view include the E.R./G.W.R. intersection (and gates protecting the G.W.R siding), the transfer crane and the weighbridge hut. (Courtesy J. G. Vincent).

of Westminster had decided to close the line (replacing it with lorries for coal and timber transportation) and offer the equipment for sale by private treaty. The edition of the same journal for September and October of that year recorded the sale of the entire plant to the Romney, Hythe & Dymchurch Railway.

Surviving Relics of the Eaton Railway

After its acquisition by Captain Howey the 1938 'Simplex' locomotive was soon at work hauling ballast trains on the R.H.&D.R. This engine is still in use at the time of writing although it has received many modifications during the intervening years, including conversion to diesel hydraulic propulsion.

Comparatively little use was made by the R.H.&D.R. of the Eaton Hall track, which was confined to sidings, or of the four wheeled wagons which were mostly scrapped after only a few years. The bogie stock, however, proved to be a better buy and this comprised the open coach of 1896 and parcels van of the same year, together with a bogie brake van (which was not mentioned in the 1898 Edition of 'Minimum Gauge Railways') and the closed carriage supplied in 1904. These

CHAPTER 13

A rear three-quarter view of the coal store showing the site of the two flanking sidings and the incline into which the road wagon would be run so that the coal could be emptied into it. (Author).

vehicles were all cut down to a loading gauge of 5 FT. 3 IN. in 1947 and subsequently fitted with Gibbins bogies and Marillier couplings in place of their original running gear. Numerous other modifications were carried out including the roofing over of the open coach and open end seats on the closed coach and bogie brake van. The closed coach also lost its doors and internal blue upholstery and curtains. The bogie brake van was adapted for passenger use by means of the provision of further windows and increasing the seating capacity from eight to ten, although the parcels van remained a non-passenger vehicle despite the provision of small side windows. This latter vehicle was scrapped in 1966 but the erstwhile open coach, closed coach and brakevan (latterly numbered 409, 699 and 698 in the R.H.&D.R. register) remain in existence. These vehicles were returned in 1980, together with an ex-E.R. 'improvised' wagon to the Eaton Hall site and are normally kept in the old Carriage Shed there, having outlasted most of Eaton Hall itself, which was demolished in 1961 leaving only the stable block and clock tower from the Victorian structure. The open coach and bogie brake van were loaned for the National Railway Museum's Minimum Gauge Railways Exhibition of 19TH OCTOBER 1981 to 28TH FEBRUARY 1982 and the latter of these items, together with the closed coach, were loaned to the R.&E.R. in 1990 for the celebrations of the 75TH anniversary of the line's conversion to 15 IN. gauge.

Today, the sites of the Eaton Terminus and Belgrave Engine Shed are still recognisable. The Engine Shed is now an office at the Grosvenor Garden Centre and a chimney now covers the site of the roof ventilator. The Carriage Shed and Coal Store buildings at Eaton are both very much in the condition which they started life in 1895-6, an enduring memorial to Sir Arthur Heywood and the Eaton Railway. No trace now remains of the level crossing over the main road.

Two Heywood relics currently to be found at New Romney are the four wheeled Eaton Hall brakevan and the Eaton snowplough. The brakevan, which featured in photographs of the LITTLE GIANT locomotive trials of 1904, was one of the exhibits in the National Railway Museum's 'Minimum Gauge Railways' Exhibition previously mentioned. At New Romney, the roof and attendant pillars had been removed when the van was first purchased but these were re-instated by 1981. From 1966 to 1972 the vehicle ran on the private 15 IN. gauge line belonging to Mr. Michel Jacot, before returning to New Romney.

THE EATON RAILWAY AFTER 1916

Above: Although the surviving ex-Eaton Railway bogie rolling stock is normally kept in the old carriage shed at Eaton Hall, the closed bogie carriage remained on loan to the R.&E.R. at the time of writing. The vehicle is seen on display at Ravenglass in July 1993 showing the mutilation which it suffered during its spell under R.&D.R. ownership. (Author).

Right: The Eaton Railway four wheeled brakevan on display at New Romney in June 1989. When first sold to the R.H.&D.R. in 1947, it was found to be necessary to remove the roof and cut down the pillars to waist height, but the original outline was restored in time for the vehicle to appear at the National Railway Museum's Minimum Gauge Railways' Exhibition of 1981-2. (Author).

CHAPTER FOURTEEN
THE HEYWOOD LEGACY AND RENAISSANCE
THE WORK AND VIEWS OF HENRY GREENLY

ALTHOUGH THE HEYWOOD RAILWAY as exemplified by the systems at Duffield Bank and Eaton Hall could not be described as a major success in terms of commercial adoption, certain important lessons in small gauge locomotive and carriage design were to be learned from Sir Arthur's efforts, particularly from the use of some of his railway equipment on the Ravenglass and Eskdale Railway during the decade following 1916.

The most well-known influence during the first three decades of the twentieth century upon the direction taken by British small gauge locomotive design is that of Henry Greenly (1876-1947) and it is significant to note that during the period in which he studied engineering and architecture in the evenings at London's Regent Street Polytechnic, the Principal (a Professor Henry Spooner) had decided upon the construction of an 18 IN. gauge semi-scale replica of a Great Northern Railway Stirling single as a practical project for his students. Castings and a boiler were supplied by Bagnalls of Stafford (who had constructed a similar locomotive for a private customer in 1893 as their Works No. 1425). Henry Greenly is believed to have worked on the construction of this engine, which today survives at the Sandy Bay Countryside Museum near Exmouth, and his interest in model engineering was to continue with his taking up an appointment to the position of Technical Editor of the 'Model Engineer' magazine in JULY 1901 (following a period of four years spent in the Metropolitan Railway's Drawing and Architectural Offices). During that year both he and his superior on the magazine, Percival Marshall saw the 15 IN. gauge Cagney-McGarigle locomotive in use at the Glasgow International Exhibition. The Northampton based modelmaker, W. G. Bassett-Lowke was also present at the Exhibition and as we have seen the result of the identification of a home based market for 15 IN. gauge locomotives of 'main line' appearance was the construction by the Northampton maker of several such locomotives of Greenly design during the period leading up to World War One. These included the first example, LITTLE GIANT, referred to previously in connection with the Eaton locomotive trials. In order to manufacture the Greenly designed locomotives and operate them on railways in the United Kingdom and Europe, Bassett-Lowke had formed another company, Miniature Railways of Great Britain Ltd. immediately prior to LITTLE GIANT's construction.

The 18 in. gauge 'Stirling Single' built at Regent Street Polytechnic led a chequered career including service on the Fairborne, albeit with the aid of a third rail! Here she is seen, circa 1953 in the garden of her then owner, Mr A. L. Bird. A full history of this locomotive can be read in Issue No 76 of 'The Narrow Gauge' – Journal of the Narrow Gauge Railway Society. (Bassett-Lowke Archive).

Miniature Railways of Great Britain Limited re-laid their line at Sutton Coldfield to 15 in. gauge during the winter of 1907/8. To work the new line a second 'Little Giant' class 4-4-2 'MIGHTY ATOM' was constructed. This 1908 scene shows the locomotive coupled to a train of three Greenly designed 12 seater bogie open coaches. Run round loops were provided at each end of the line and the driver could couple and uncouple without leaving his position on the footplate. (Bassett-Lowke Archive).

Despite the success during the Edwardian era of his 'main line' style locomotives on railways at such places as Blackpool, Sutton Coldfield, White City, Halifax Zoo, and on exhibition lines at such European venues as Nancy and Brussels, Greenly was not totally convinced that locomotives of 'scale model' appearance were right for every 15 IN. gauge application. He is believed to have visited the Duffield Bank Railway in 1904-5 and during or slightly before 1904 he had laid down a proposal for what he described as a locomotive specially designed for estate work. This little tank engine had a cylindrical firebox, four coupled wheels, a trailing two wheeled radial truck and cylinders 3½ IN. diameter and 5 IN. stroke. The major point of interest is that provision was made in the basic specification for the driver actually to sit on the engine (as opposed to a tender) and for the footplate to be given a well configuration to facilitate this possibility.

Although Henry Greenly is recorded as saying, in relation to the Heywood locomotives when they were in use at Ravenglass, that he admired their use of all of the engine's weight for adhesion, it was clear from the choice of wheel arrangement for his early estate locomotive proposal that he did not consider that upholding this principle justified the use of a sleeved axle flexible wheelbase. So far as is known, he did not again propose a design for a 15 IN. gauge locomotive with a cylindrical firebox and by 1921 he had certainly realised the shortcomings of such boilers. Of the Heywood engines at Ravenglass, he said: 'Although they embody many interesting and ingenious features, users of these engines find that they are not really so economical as the model express engines employed on this line, more especially with regard to the working of passenger services. While there is more stuff in them, the defects in the boilers of the Heywood engines are very apparent to the most casual observer'.

It was clear, therefore, that Greenly admired the relatively large cylinders and bearing surfaces of the Heywood engines for work on 15 IN. gauge railways, but not their boiler design or high coal consumption when compared with the coke burning Bassett-Lowke locomotives. His views on the aesthetic properties of 15 IN. gauge locomotives were stated in the JULY 1916 issue of Models, Railways and Locomotives: 'While the engines at Ravenglass are doing excellent work on, the writer understands, a rather rough track with heavy grades, we must confirm our reader's opinion that such engines will not, on a five year basis, show themselves an economic investment. Possibly not one person in ten who uses the line is interested in the fact that the locomotive hauling him is a model of what would be the largest British express locomotive, if it were a 'real one'. He arrives at Ravenglass and wants to get to Boot and vice versa'.

Despite this expressed viewpoint, four locomotive design proposals which accompanied the 1916 article all had an element of 'main line' practice about their aesthetic properties and these included an outside framed 0-6-0 (possibly styled after the Beyer Peacock locomotives for the Stratford-upon-Avon and Midland Junction Railway and intended for Blakesley Hall) and three very ungainly proposals for swivelling power bogie locomotives. In the FEBRUARY 1918 issue of 'Models, Railways and Locomotives', Greenly outlined a further design proposal for 15 IN. gauge 2-6-2 locomotive. Although some element of 'main line' aesthetics was still present in this design, the boiler was comparable with some 2 FT. gauge locomotives and with outside frames for all wheels except those on the leading pony truck, 2 FT. diameter coupled wheels, 6 IN. by 9 IN. cylinders and a length over frames of 15 FT. 6 IN. this engine would have been the largest British single wheelbase 15 IN. gauge locomotive ever built. Heywood valve gear was suggested, of the type originally fitted to MURIEL in 1894; Greenly did not care for the Brown-inspired linear linkage, saying that: 'it had too many pin joints to be a real success'.

Although not stated in the 1918 article as the design proposal was in reply to an enquiry from an 'A. J. (Winnipeg)', it seems certain that the 2-6-2 proposal was intended for Ravenglass. Sadly the engine never saw the light of day but the necessity for 'overscale' proportions on main line style 15 IN. gauge locomotives constructed for serious work was not lost on Henry Greenly. His subsequent RIVER ESK of 1923 for Ravenglass, and other locomotives for the Romney, Hythe and Dymchurch Railway all display this characteristic of construction. Perhaps the closest that was got to Greenly's 1918 2-6-2 proposal in retrospect was NORTHERN ROCK with 6½ IN. by 8½ IN. cylinders and 20 IN. diameter coupled wheels completed at Ravenglass in 1976, although this has a Wootton-type firebox, Walschaerts valve gear and a Cartazzi trailing truck (all characteristics taken from RIVER ESK in its post-1927 condition). The success of this locomotive has resulted in the export of two similar examples to Japan in recent years.

As a variant of the 1894 pattern Heywood valve gear, Greenly laid out a version in which the swinging link, vibrating link and slide/die block assembly were located forward of the driving axle. This gear was originally specified for RIVER ESK but later dropped in favour of the unsuccessful Paxman-Lentz poppet valve gear used on the engine as built. When used on model locomotives, Greenly's variant of Heywood valve gear generally gave poor steam distribution characteristics (owing to the short valve rod) and for 15 IN. gauge purposes it was quietly forgotten.

Figure 39. Henry Greenly's proposal of 1918 for a 15 in. gauge 2-6-2 tender engine for heavy duties. As can be seen from the diagram, Greenly proposed to fit the 1894 pattern of Heywood valve gear to this engine. The locomotive, which was probably intended for use on the R.&E.R., was never constructed although its design showed a considerable degree of foresight as an engine of the same wheel arrangement and similar proportions was eventually completed at Ravenglass in 1976. (Models, Railways and Locomotives).

THE HEYWOOD LEGACY & RENAISSANCE

At first sight Henry Greenly's 2-8-2 RIVER ESK for the R.&E.R. would appear to have little connection with Sir Arthur Heywood's principles as it has a definite 'main line' appearance. By 1923, the date of the engine's construction, however, Greenly had at least appreciated that an 'overscale' boiler, cylinders and other bearing surfaces were necessary on a 15 in. gauge locomotive intended for serious work. As originally designed, RIVER ESK would have had Greenly-Heywood valve gear but this proposal was dropped in favour of the unsuccessful Paxman-Lenz gear fitted to the engine when first completed. This picture was taken at Ravenglass in September 1989. (Author).

0-8-2 RIVER IRT taking water at Fisherground (between Eskdale Green and Beckfoot) on the Ravenglass and Eskdale Railway in September 1989. Beneath the footplate, much of the chassis is MURIEL as received by the R.&E.R. in 1917, although the flexible wheelbase linkages were removed in 1921, the cylinder bore reduced by half an inch in the same year, and modifications made to the rear of the mainframes in 1927 and 1977. (Author)

CHAPTER 14

Minimum Gauge Renaissance

For the ensuing years until the 1960's, 'main line' aesthetic properties were to be the norm for steam locomotives used on British small gauge leisure orientated railways. In more recent times, however, there has been a retreat from this philosophy and steam locomotives have been constructed to gauges as low as 7¼ IN. with a non-scale narrow gauge 'functional' appearance. A detailed consideration of these locomotives and their associated railways is outside the scope of this present volume, but it should be mentioned that Heywood's valve gear has found favour on some examples, particularly on the 7¼ IN. gauge Moors Valley Railway and the 10¼ IN. gauge Mull and West Highland Railway.

Full Size Heywood Replicas

The evolution of functional steam locomotives for use on small gauge leisure orientated public railways has been one of the welcome developments of the period following the end of revenue earning steam operation of British Railways, but there remained some enthusiasts who wished to re-create the Heywood era in its former glory, complete with replica locomotives. At first, this was accomplished in model form and a fine 3½ IN. gauge quarter scale model of ELLA was constructed by Basil Markham, with construction being serialised in the 'Model Engineer' from 6TH FEBRUARY 1976 to 7TH JANUARY 1977. Following on from this exercise, an equally fine 7¼ IN. gauge model of MURIEL (with some dimensions 'eased' from their half scale equivalents in order to allow the driver to sit on the footplate) was constructed by Anthony Harris from Redditch and this was exhibited at the 1988 Midlands Model Engineering Exhibition.

The natural progression from recreating Heywood locomotives in large scale form was the construction of full-size replicas. At the time of writing a replica of 0-4-0T KATIE has recently been completed by Messrs. Paul Stileman and Anthony Reen at Thursley, near Basingstoke, Hants. Whilst this replica has many mechanical differences from the original, its external appearance is a reasonable likeness to the engine which first saw the light of day in 1896.

The initial work on Paul Stileman's locomotive and three more KATIE replicas was undertaken by F.M.B. Engineering Ltd., a small Hampshire-based concern founded in 1989 and now principally owned by Brian Gent (the Hon. Secretary of the Narrow Gauge Railway Society of Great Britain). Work on the other three replica locomotives is still proceeding as the availability of time and customer funding permits.

With KATIE's side frames currently extant at Ravenglass, there was little surprise that moves would be made to build a replica around these which would be more faithful to the original from the mechanical point of view. Fundraising for such a project has already commenced, with the construction of a 'rolling chassis' being the immediate priority, the 'boiler' initially being a hollow shell. The project is being undertaken by the R.&E.R. Heritage Group and the desire has been expressed to replace the dummy boiler with a working one in time for KATIE's centenary in 1996. Such a goal may prove optimistic, but the result would certainly make an interesting addition to the attractions currently on offer on the R.& E.R.

THE HEYWOOD LEGACY & RENAISSANCE

Above: The first working replica of KATIE was completed in early 1995 by Messrs. P. Stileman and A. Reen. Although this engine differs greatly in several details from the original it serves to perpetuate the memory of Sir Arthur's endeavours at Duffield Bank. The engine was photographed at Thursley, Hants in February 1995. (P. Stileman).

Right: A working model, constructed to 7.25 in. gauge by Mr. A. F. Harris, of Heywood's 0-8-0T MURIEL. In order to accommodate a driver on the footplate, the front and rear overhangs have been lengthened in relation to the scale dimension, and the boiler shortened. (Courtesy A. F. Harris).

APPENDICES

APPENDIX ONE

A letter to the Editor of 'The Times' concerning light railways and written in anticipation of the Board of Trade Conference of 1896:

Light Railways

Sir, – The movement in favour of secondary railways has evoked from your numerous correspondents widely divergent views. This want of accord is more apparent than real, and it would facilitate the proceedings of the approaching conference if conflicting opinions could be partially reconciled beforehand.

The causes to which these differences are due may be summarised under three heads:-

1. The absence of a defined terminology of the distinctive heads of railways.

2. The failure to appreciate that a scheme which is good for one locality is not of necessity the best for all.

3. The apparently meagre acquaintance on the part of those who state their views with the practical working of any but the standard railways of the country.

Under the first head, some confusion has arisen in consequence of the application of the term 'light railway' now to lines of the standard gauge only, and again to narrow gauge lines also. Similarly, with other expressions. It may be pointed out that the term 'light railway' is properly applicable and should be confined to a line of standard gauge, of which the entire construction is lighter, cheaper and simpler than is obligatory where weighty engines, heavy traffic, and high speeds are dealt with. Any line of less than standard gauge is correctly described as a 'narrow gauge railway', and such lines, when not of a permanent character, come under the title, simply, of 'portable railways', for these are invariably of less than the normal width. The term 'tramway' should be restricted to its modern meaning of a line laid in the metalled or paved surface of a road or street. Finally, the not unfamiliar appellation of 'secondary railways' might be fitly adopted as generally descriptive of all lines not amenable to the standard railway regulations of the Board of Trade. It would be well that the conference should pronounce on these points.

In regard to the second head, needless controversy is engendered by attempting to assume that, because a light railway is right here, therefore a narrow gauge railway is wrong there, or vice versa. In estimating the transport requirements of any particular locality, if connection is to be made with the railway system, the applicability of a light railway, as above defined, should first be considered. By its adoption the use of existing rolling stock is secured, transhipment is avoided, and the line can subsequently and without difficulty transformed, if necessary, into a railway of standard construction – advantages for which much may be sacrificed. But as it would be almost invariably essential to build a light railway of sufficient strength to carry the 15 TONS gross weight of a standard coal wagon, the permanent way would be of a somewhat costly character, and, in the case of severe gradients, considerable difficulty would arise in providing locomotive power.

Where the impediments in the way of a light railway branch are insuperable or where the proposed line has no connection with the railway system, the advantages of a narrow gauge railway may properly be weighed – such as the smaller width occupied, the sharper curves admissible, the lighter, cheaper, and more easily handled permanent way and rolling stock, the absence of much of the unsightliness of a line of standard gauge, the ease with which, in the case of gauges under 2 FT., the rails can be laid among and into existing buildings, and lastly, the convenience of being able to load and unload small wagons at the exact point required without the intervention of carts or barrows.

In regard to the third head, it may be noticed as a curious fact that the strong and commendable predilections of English engineers for the standard gauge, whenever obtainable, appear to lead them, where circumstances compel the adoption of a narrower one, to advocate as little reduction as possible. Now, the general result of foreign experience goes strongly to show that narrow gauges exceeding 30 IN. approximate so closely to a full-size line as to forfeit, to a considerable extent, the advantages of either system. This attitude is probably due to ignorance of what can be done on the narrowest gauges, for, in spite of the fact that many hundreds of miles of lines of less than 2 FT. gauge are at work abroad, our professional advisers persist in regarding such railways as mere toys. Yet a line of 15 IN. gauge has been at work in this country for twenty years, on which thousands of passengers have been carried without a single accident, as many as 120 in one train, over gradients as steep as 1-IN-20, the goods traffic being worked in all weathers up a long gradient of 1-IN-11 without difficulty.

It would be well that our railway engineers should inform themselves more fully on the subject, as otherwise their valuable assistance, which would insure that narrow gauge railways were constructed in a solid and reliable manner, will be thrust on one side by the requirements of the times, and the work will be wholly in the hands of the many manufacturers of narrow gauge plant, whose designs, being chiefly of what is known as the 'portable' class, are for the most part, ill adapted for locomotive traffic. If so, it is likely that, in the push that may very possibly be presently made for secondary railways, the results will not be so satisfactory as would be the case if the work were carried out under the direction of professional advisers.

Under the same head, attention may be directed to the fact that it is entirely unnecessary to urge the adoption of a standard narrow gauge. The circumstances of each case will decide the most suitable gauge, and it is only where there is a possibility, as in the North Wales district, of a wide ramification of connected narrow gauge lines that the adoption of a particular standard is of any importance.

I am, Sir, your obedient servant, *ARTHUR PERCIVAL HEYWOOD.*

APPENDIX TWO

A letter to the Editor of 'The Times' following the 1896 Board of Trade Conference on Light Railways (N.B.: this letter discusses the course of action taken by Heywood in relation to the Eaton Railway's crossing of a public highway. He brought to bear all of the influence that he could obtain in an attempt to secure the insertion in the 1896 Light Railways Act of a clause protecting private railways requiring public road crossings from the possibility of unjustified revocation of the crossing concession. This attempt proved to be unsuccessful):

PRIVATE LIGHT RAILWAYS

Sir, – May I, through your columns, draw attention to a class of light railway which does not apparently come within the purview of the Bill now before Parliament – that of lines constructed by private individuals or firms for their own purposes? These will usually confer advantage upon the district in which they may be situated by relieving the roads of a more or less heavy traffic, and in some cases by offering facilities of transport to a section of the neighbourhood.

In the proposed route two difficulties may arise. in the first place, land not in possession of the proprietor may have to be invaded, and way-leaves obtained by a judicious tact in selecting the ground and in approaching the owners, since private interest is properly debarred from invoking customary powers. This problem, then, may frequently be satisfactorily solved. The second and more common impediment is the crossing or skirting of highways, and it is to this point that my letter is specially directed. The county and district councils are usually ready in their own interest to permit a private line to cross a road on the level – an over or under bridge is almost invariably impossible by reason of the expense – or to make use for a short distance of waste space by the road side. But – and here is the crux – no permanent agreement is obtainable, because councils have apparently no power to bind their successors in office, and without such guarantee the projector is naturally unwilling to risk his capital when the possible rescinding of the concession would render his entire outlay abortive.

The Light Railway Bill contains, apparently no provision under which this disability can be remedied, for it is improbable that the Commissioners would take action in respect of a private concern. The above difficulty was lately met with in the construction of a private narrow gauge line for the Duke of Westminster, which crosses a main road. The matter was ultimately compromised by the insertion of a clause in the agreement to the effect that, should the county council give notice to discontinue the crossing, the Duke should be entitled to appeal to the Board of Trade for arbitration. There is, however, no assurance that the Board would consent to appoint an arbitrator if called upon, but it is very certain that if a provision legalising such a appeal could be incorporated in the Bill a serious hardship would be thereby removed, and some encouragement given to private persons to embark capital in enterprises of the kind.

As a case in point, and doubtless there are plenty of others, a quarry owner of my acquaintance is at the present time conveying some 30,000 TONS of stone annually by means of traction engines from his works to the railway along 2 ½ miles of highway. The road authorities, levying £400 a year for extraordinary traffic, are utterly incapable of coping with the destructive action of heavy loads, and the roads are in a state of disintegration that baffles description. The proprietor of the quarry would at once set about making a narrow gauge line at his own expense, with the cordial goodwill of the county and district councils and his neighbours generally, could he only obtain some guarantee that the permission to cross and, in some parts, run alongside the road, which today would be gratefully accorded, would not be suddenly revoked at a future date.

Perhaps those in charge of the Bill will see their way to give this point their consideration.

I am, Sir, your obedient servant, *ARTHUR PERCIVAL HEYWOOD.*

This letter received comment in a Manchester newspaper:

According to a correspondent in yesterday's 'Times' projectors of private light railways have hitherto been very chary of risking their capital owing to the precarious nature of their running powers. In nine cases out of ten the light railway proposes to cross or skirt the highways at certain points, and the permission which may be given by one district council in such cases is revocable by the next. This must be so inevitably, for circumstances might well arise under which a level crossing, for instance, would become a public danger. The difficulty might well be met by an appeal to arbitration in all cases of proposed revocation of the running powers; and if the Board of Trade were to undertake to nominate the arbitrator, the projector ought to have no reasonable ground for timidity. The present Bill can only be regarded as proposing to set an example and provide occasional assistance to the construction of light railways. Seeing, therefore, that its chief result, if successful, will be to encourage a more extensive construction of railways, it is important that all obstacles in the way of private enterprise in this direction should at once be removed. The 'Times' correspondent suggests that the insertion of a clause providing for arbitration in all cases of dispute with the highway authorities would meet this difficulty.

APPENDIX THREE

EATON RAILWAY
Regulations in Force in 1898

General Regulations

1. All persons connected with the Railway shall be held responsible for making themselves acquainted with such of the regulations as apply to them, and acting in accordance therewith.

2. All workmen on the Estate shall be liable to such fines for infraction of the Railway Regulations as are herein set forth, and as the Estate Office may see fit further to order.

3. All men employed on the Railway Staff shall promptly report any infraction of the Regulations as are herein set forth, and as the Estate office may see fit further to order.

4. All workmen on the Estate are particularly requested to remove any impediment, such as sticks or stones, which they may see on the line; and in case of any serious block, such as a tree fallen across the rails, to give prompt notice to one of the Railway Staff.

5. No wagon or car shall (under a penalty of 1s.) be moved by hand on to or along the main line, except by special arrangement with the engine-driver; and the term 'main line' shall be understood to include every part of the railway not being a siding or within a terminal yard.

6. Hand shunting of vehicles on sidings shall be done carefully, so as to avoid injury to the rolling stock; but no vehicle shall be moved at all except by an authorised person.

7. No vehicle shall (under a penalty of 1s.) be left in such a position on a siding as to interfere with the free passage of other vehicles along adjoining rails.

8. If it is necessary to throw over the weight of any point lever, this shall be done gently, and the weight shall be returned as soon as possible to the position in which the white bar thereon is uppermost. Point levers of which the weights are pinned in one direction shall not (under a penalty of 1s.) have the locking pins tampered with.

9. No material of any kind whatever shall (under a penalty of 1s.) be deposited within a distance of two feet from the rail on any part of the main line or sidings.

10. No heavy weight shall be dropped upon the rails or sleepers, and no carts shall cross any part of the line except where a proper crossing of double rails is provided. But in the terminal yards light loads may cross the rails where the ballast is for that purpose made level with the top of the metals. Any unintentional damage to rolling

stock or the line shall be at once reported to the engine-driver or foreman platelayer.

11. No unauthorised person shall ride on any part of the train, and those having permission shall, whenever possible, travel in vehicles provided with seats.

12. It is desired that all workmen on the Estate should understand that there exists the same liability to accident on a narrow gauge line as on one of full size, and that it is only by similar careful observation of proper regulations that serious mishaps will be avoided.

Regulations for Yardmen

13. Yardmen shall carefully observe the General regulations for the safe conduct of traffic comprised in Rules 1 to 12 inclusive.

14. The yardman at each terminus shall clean and oil all points in or near his yard at least once a week, and keep them perfectly free from grit, leaves etc..

15. In frost or snow the points shall receive daily attention, and great care shall be taken in releasing frozen switches not to strain them. Salt, for this purpose, shall, on account of its injurious effect on the rails, be used only as a last resource.

16. Yardmen shall take care that the loads on wagons are securely placed, evenly balanced, and not in excess of the specified weight.

17. Lengthy articles shall be loaded on a sufficient number of wagons to ensure that the ends thereof do not catch against other wagons.

18. All vehicles shall be loaded to the satisfaction of the engine-driver.

19. Yardmen shall give the earliest possible intimation to the engine-driver of the nature and quantity of the material requiring transport from their respective yards, that he may provide the necessary wagons at the proper time.

20. Yardmen shall take care that the wagons and cars are not roughly handled, and shall see that heavy lumps of coal or other material are not thrown carelessly on to the wagon bottoms.

21. The yardman at Balderton shall be responsible for the washing of all wagons when necessary, and the yardman at Eaton Hall shall similarly see to all the bogie cars. Care shall be taken in washing that no water is allowed to run into the axle boxes.

22. Yardmen shall use their best endeavours to get the rolling stock in their respective yards promptly unloaded, and also put under cover at night and in wet weather.

Regulations for Platelayers

23. Platelayers shall carefully observe the General Regulations for the safe conduct of traffic comprised in Rules 1 to 12 inclusive.

24. The foreman platelayer shall be responsible for keeping the whole of the permanent way, bridges, cattle stops, banks, road crossings, etc. in proper repair.

25. He shall see that every set of points on the line is kept in good working order, but he shall only be responsible for the oiling and cleaning (as under Rules 14 and 15) of such points as are not under charge of a yardman. He shall report to the engine-driver any set of points not under his personal charge which he finds neglected, as also any defect which he himself is unable to repair.

26. He shall keep clear all road and field crossing grooves, and shall at once acquaint the engine-driver when repair to the surface of any road crossing is necessary.

27. At least once a week he shall walk over the whole length of the main line and sidings, observing carefully that the keys, bridge bolts, fish bolts and sleepers are in order.

28. He shall, at the same time note, and as soon as possible rectify, all loose sleepers, crooked rails, and defective superelevation.

29. He shall pay particular attention to the prompt repair of all parts of the line marked by the engine-driver as defective, but, independently of such notice, he shall be responsible for detecting such places.

30. In regard to any special repairs, or other emergencies of the traffic, he shall be under the direction and obey the instructions of the engine-driver.

31. When any part of the line is under repair, care shall be taken that the surface of the rails is kept clear of ballast grit, and that the free passage of trains is in no way obstructed.

32. When it is necessary to remove a sleeper, a red flag shall be set up between the rails in such a position that the engine-driver can discern it from a distance of at least 150 yards in each direction. Such flag shall remain until the line is made good. On no account shall the engine or a loaded wagon pass over any rail from which a sleeper is removed.

33. If from any cause it is necessary to remove a rail, or otherwise block the line, the foreman platelayer shall previously notify the engine-driver, and arrange with him a convenient time for the work to be done; and without such notification the line shall under no circumstances whatever be so blocked. A red flag (as directed under Rule 32) shall remain exhibited until the line is clear.

34. No platelayer other than the foreman shall be authorised to undertake any work interfering with the free passage of trains.

35. If, for ballasting or other purposes, wagons are left by the engine-driver at any point on the main line, such wagons shall on no account be subsequently moved by hand to any point on the main line, except by special arrangement with the engine driver.

36. The platelayer's trolley shall under no circumstances be left standing on the main line; and when not in use, or unattended, the trolley shall always be put at a safe distance from the line, with the wheels padlocked.

37. The foreman platelayer shall report to the engine driver any case of material found deposited within two feet of the rails, and likewise any other infraction of Regulations which may come to his notice.

Regulations for Engine Driver

38. The engine-driver shall be responsible for the efficient working of the line, and shall use the utmost promptitude in dealing with the traffic as notified to him by the yardmen.

39. He shall be responsible also for the care of the locomotive, rolling stock, and fittings appertaining thereto, any defect in which that is beyond his own power to rectify he shall at once notify to the Superintendent, with whom any further responsibility in regard to such defect will then rest. But the washing of the wagons and cars shall be done by the yardmen as set forth under Rule 21.

40. He shall, further, be responsible for the proper oiling of the axle boxes, spring slides, swivelling forks, and brake gear of the whole of the rolling stock; and shall on no account run on the train a loaded wagon having a hot axle box or a bent axle.

41. He shall see that all rolling stock is kept, as far as possible, under cover at night and in wet weather.

42. He shall watch carefully that the whole of the line and its accessories are kept in thorough working order, and shall direct the foreman platelayer in regard to any part requiring attention.

43. He shall put down white marker pegs, of which he shall at all times carry a sufficient supply in the brake van, at all points of the line which he may notice to be in special need of repair.

44. He shall arrange with the foreman platelayer, as set forth under Rule 33, in regard to the time of execution of any work requiring the blocking of the line.

45. He shall promptly enquire into, and report to the Superintendent, any case of material left within two feet of the rails, as also any other infraction of the Regulations which may be brought to his notice. He shall take care that Rule 11, in regard to passengers by the train, is strictly observed, and shall allow no person to ride on the engine without permission of the Duke from the Estate Office.

46. He shall carefully observe the following County Council Regulations in regard to crossing the public roads, and shall be personally liable to the County and District Councils for the consequences of any infraction thereof:-
(a) Every train about to cross the road shall be brought to a stand at a point not less than 10 yards therefrom, and the brakesman shall proceed to the centre of the road with a red flag, and shall, as soon as any approaching vehicles have crossed the

railway, wave the said flag as a warning to distant vehicles and as a sign to the engine-driver to proceed; and shall continue to wave until the whole of the train shall have passed over the road. After dusk a red lamp shall be used in place of a flag (but a green light shall be momentarily shown to the driver when the road is clear).

(b) No train shall cross the road at a greater speed than five miles an hour, nor shall any train impede the traffic along the road further than is necessary for the crossing thereof, which shall in no case exceed three minutes.

(c) Every train crossing the road shall be in charge of a competent engine-driver and brakesman, and shall consist of not more than twenty-five vehicles, exclusive of the engine.

47. He shall take care to run no train without a brake-van at the rear end, and a brakesman in attendance.

48. He shall at all times whistle before putting his engine in motion, and also on approaching all road crossings, termini, and other points where a warning may be desirable. He shall, during fog, proceed with the utmost caution, particularly in crossing roads, and shall be ready to stop promptly where cattle may be on the line.

49. He shall approach all facing points with caution, especially after dark, and shall see that his train is well under control in descending inclines, particularly the gradient by the Eaton cricket ground.

50. He shall cross the Great Western siding at Balderton only when the yard gates are closed, and at dead slow speed, and shall be personally responsible for any mishap resulting from neglect of this rule.

51. He shall perform no fly-shunting with the engine pushing, and in draw shunting he shall proceed with the utmost caution.

52. He shall take care to avoid injury to the rolling stock from shocks, careless usage, or foul shunting.

53. He shall, between September and February inclusive, carry on the train all necessary lamps ready trimmed.

54. He shall take care that the breakdown tackle is always kept ready on the brake van in case of emergency.

55. He shall under no circumstances leave his engine with the steam up without the hand brake hard down, the lever out of gear and the cylinder cocks open.

56. He shall take care that the spark arrester is kept effective, the sand boxes full, and that, in conveying passengers, condensed water is cleared from the cylinders before starting.

57. He shall keep his engine in good working order, clean, and smart; executing all necessary repairs at the earliest possible opportunity.

58. He shall keep a careful watch that point lever weights are left in the right positions, and that the white bars thereon are kept clearly painted.

59. He shall notify the Superintendent at the earliest possible time any requirement for the rolling stock or line, such as coal stores, material for repairs, oil, waste, etc., etc., and keep such booked records of the working as are required.

60. He shall impress upon the brakesman the following orders:-
   (a) To travel always in the brake-van; to keep a sharp look-out and promptly put down his brake should occasion require, or on receiving a signal from the engine.
   (b) To carefully watch the loaded wagons, and in the event of any part of the load appearing unsafe, to signal at once to the engine-driver to stop the train.
   (c) To carry always on the van a red flag, and, between September and February inclusive, a hand lamp ready trimmed, which latter, in travelling after dusk, shall show a red light at the back of the train.
   (d) To perform shunting operations with caution, taking care that all point lever weights are left in their proper position.
   (e) To keep his van clean and smart, washing it when required.
   (f) To carefully observe such of the Railway Regulations as apply to the brakesman's work.

Signalling Regulations

61. The engine-driver shall give three short whistles when he requires the brake-van brakes to be put down, and one short whistle when they are to be released. When he requires facing points to be set for the main line he shall give two, and for a branch or siding three medium whistles. A whistle continued for several minutes is a call for assistance and workmen within hearing shall at once proceed to the spot.

62. A red light is a signal to stop; a green light, to proceed cautiously; a white light to go ahead. In shunting, a green light, if waved up and down, is a signal to move ahead; if from side to side, to back.

63. It is important that all persons having to do with shunting operations should understand that if an engine is either in contact with no vehicles, or has vehicles in front and behind, it is said to go ahead when it moves chimney first, and to back when it moves fire-box first. If in contact with vehicles at one end only, it is said to go ahead when it draws and to back when it pushes such vehicles, without regard to its own direction.

APPENDIX FOUR

Abbott & Co. Boiler Details 1903-1924

Drawing No.	Order No.	Drawing Date	Delivery Date	Customer	Cost	Locomotive		
187D	6203	11.06.1903	?	Heywood	£84	SHELAGH	(B)	
187D	9837	?	23.01.1908	Heywood	£89	MURIEL	(B)	
408D	5454	27.07.1914	24.12.1914	Heywood	£86	SHELAGH	(B) (1) (2)
408D	5454	27.07.1914	21.01.1915	Heywood	£86	URSULA	(B) (1)
187D	697-1	29.01.1921	?	R.& E.R.	?	MURIEL	(F) (3)
187D	3611	22.08.1924	02.09.1924	R.& E.R.	?	MURIEL	(F) (3)

Notes: (B): boiler replacement; (F): firebox replacement;
(1) these two boilers could each have gone to either of the locomotives covered by this note;
(2) this locomotive renamed "KATIE" during 1914-15 rebuild; (3) fireboxes fitted at Workington.

APPENDIX FIVE

DISPOSAL SUMMARY FOR HEYWOOD LOCOMOTIVES & ROLLING STOCK

Duffield Bank Equipment

Item	Date Completed	Disposal
Locomotives:		
EFFIE	1875	Withdrawn from ordinary usage on completion of 'Muriel'. To Doveleys(?) and dismantled circa 1905.
ELLA	1881	To Hill Bros. May 1916, Gretna(?) shortly afterwards and R.&E.R. in 1917. Withdrawn October 1926 and some parts still extant.
MURIEL	1894	Most details as for above engine. Withdrawn 1926 and much of chassis incorporated into 0-8-2 locomotive 'River Irt'.
Bogie Stock:		
Open 12 seater	1875 or 1876	Scrapped by 1894.
Closed 16 seater	1881	To R.&E.R. 1915, scrapped by 1934.
Open 16 seaters (4)	Between 1882 and 1894	To Hill Bros. May 1916 and R.&E.R. shortly afterwards. Scrapped by 1934.
Passenger brakevan	As above	To R.&E.R. 1915, grounded by 1925, body destroyed in 1940.
Sleeping Car	As above	To Hill Bros. May 1916 and R.&E.R. shortly afterwards. Scrapped after 1949.
Dining Car	As above	To R.&E.R. 1915, scrapped after 1949.

Item	Date Completed	Disposal
3 ton Open Wagon	Between 1894 and 1916	To R.&E.R. 1916 (?) scrapped after 1925.

Four Wheeled Stock

Item	Date Completed	Disposal
Standard Wagons	Between 1875	Some to R.&E.R. in 1916, others to Eaton Hall and at least two early examples to Doveleys. These latter two possibly extant in private hands, along with one larger example in R.&E.R. Museum and one at New Romney.
Dynamometer Car	Between 1881 and 1894	To R.&E.R. 1916, withdrawn during 1920's. A few components still exist.
Permanent Way Wagons	As for standard wagons	At least one vehicle to R.&E.R. 1916, believed scrapped by 1920's.
Pedal Trolley	Circa 1888	Ex-'Dove Bank Railway', to R.&E.R. 1916, scrapping date unknown.
Bucket Tip Wagons (2)	1903	To R.&E.R. in 1916 (?) and Fairbourne prior to 1922. One example now preserved in the Narrow Gauge Railway Museum, Tywyn.
Braked Top	Between 1875 and 1916	Lot 430 in 1916 Auction. To R.&E.R. via a Mr. J. Parker (?) and subsequently scrapped.
Flat Topped Shop Bogie	?	To Hill Bros. 1916, then to R.&E.R. (?).
Box Shop Bogie	?	To Hill Bros. 1916, then to R.&E.R. (?).

Eaton Hall Railway Equipment

Item	Date Completed	Disposal

Locomotives

Item	Date Completed	Disposal
KATIE	1896	To R.&E.R. 1916, Southport Miniature Railway 1919, Fairbourne Miniature Railway 1923 and scrapped in 1926. Frames now at Ravenglass.
SHELAGH/KATIE (2)	1904	Scrapped September 1942.
URSULA	1916	Scrapped September 1942.

Bogie Stock

Item	Date Completed	Disposal
Open 16 seater	1896	To R.H.&D.R. 1947, given stock no. 409 under 1952 numbering scheme. Returned to Eaton Hall in 1980.
Bogie brakevan	1896	To R.H.&D.R. 1947, numbered 207 under 1952 scheme (later 698). Returned to Eaton Hall in 1980.
Parcels Van	1896	To R.H.&D.R. 1947, scrapped after withdrawal from service in 1966.

Item	Date Completed	Disposal
Closed 16 seater	1904	To R.H.&D.R. 1947, numbered 8 under 1952 scheme (later 699). Returned to Eaton Hall in 1980.
Closed 16 seater	1916	Same design as above, but never delivered to Eaton Hall. To Hill Bros. 1916 and R.&E.R. shortly afterwards. Scrapped by 1934.

Four Wheeled Stock

Item	Date Completed	Disposal
Standard Wagons	Between 1896 and 1916	Most (Approximately 36) to R.H.&D.R. in 1947 and scrapped during 1947-60 period. At least two examples still extant of which one is in the R.& E.R. Museum.
Large 2 ton Wagons (2)	1896	To R.H.&D.R. 1947 and used latterly as flat wagons. Scrapped by 1980.
Tipper Wagons (6)	1896	Four withdrawn by 1898, returned to Duffield Bank and sold to Hill Bros. (?) in 1916. The remaining two scrapped by 1947.
Brakevan	1896	To R.H.&D.R. 1947 and private ownership 1966. Returned to R.H.&D.R. in 1972 and now on display there.
Permanent Way Wagon	1896	Possibly adapted from standard wagon chassis. Final disposal unknown.

APPENDIX SIX

The Klien-Lindner System of Sleeved Axle Articulation

Although strictly speaking outside the scope of this book, it has been decided to incorporate some notes relating to the use of sleeved axles on locomotives built by commercial manufacturers, principally in Germany.

In 1892 the Klien-Lindner system of articulation was patented, and by 1901 600 MM. gauge eight coupled locomotives utilising this system were seeing use on the State Northern Railway in German colonial South West Africa (now Namibia). No proof has yet come to light to show that the German system was in any way inspired by Heywood's efforts and it is important to note that unlike the Heywood principle, the Klien-Lindner system did not employ sliding sleeves on its intermediate axles. Instead, the Klien-Lindner system employed sleeves on the extreme end axles which could both pivot and slide within limits, and which were fitted with internal side control springs. By this means, the leading pair of wheels could impart a measure of guidance to the main bulk of the locomotive whilst entering a curve.

In contrast to the reception given to Heywood's efforts by the Royal Engineers, the Klien-Lindner system enjoyed much popularity with the German military authorities, and from the designs used in South West Africa were developed the well known 'Feldbahn' 0-8-0T's of the First World War. Examples of this class survive in preservation in Britain, France, Germany and elsewhere today. Other Klien-Lindner 0-8-0T designs found their way to such diverse locations as Java and the Philippines and representatives remain extant, at the time of writing, in both these locations. The most recently built examples to have come to the author's notice were completed in Rumania as late as 1987.

It is an open question as to whether Sir Arthur Heywood knew of the German system. The fact that he followed French and German developments in narrow gauge military railway construction is revealed from his writings in 'Minimum Gauge Railways', but these predate the widespread adoption of Klien-Lindner articulation. Sir Arthur's presence at the opening of the Leek and Manifold line and probable acquaintance with E. R. Calthrop is suggestive that the former may have known of the German system by 1904, particularly in the light of the 'hybrid' system which was later employed on the Matheran Hill locomotives, but the evidence is not conclusive.

Sleeved axle articulation was adopted by only one British Commercial manufacturer for a small number of locomotives. In 1909 John Fowler & Co. Ltd. completed an eight coupled locomotive for T. Leach's Argentine Estates which employed a modified Klien Lindner articulation system. Surviving correspondence shows that T. Leach requested a locomotive of this design as a result of experiences with a German-built Klien-Lindner locomotive on a nearby system. Sir Arthur, despite retaining his ties with the R.A.S.E, had no influence over Fowler product policy by this time.

The Leach class possessed a conventional firebox and an unequally divided wheelbase, both features of which Sir Arthur would have heartily disapproved, but unlike the 'Feldbahns', was able to contain the firebox within the wheelbase limits. Between 1909 and 1920, six locomotives of this design were supplied to the Argentine customer (Maker's No's. 11944 of 1909; 13208 of 1913; 13645 and 13646 of 1913; 14175 of 1914 and 15511 of 1920).

Although the Klien-Lindner system theoretically allows for a smoother passage into curves than its Heywood counterpart, it has a major weakness inherent in the linkage joining the yokes on the end axles. This has to cope with the variable distance between the inner ends of the yokes whilst in operation and more than one design of intermediate linkage was used during the era of construction of revenue earning Klien-Lindner locomotives.

The Fowler locomotives employed a modification of the Klien-Lindner system which dispensed with the need for an intermediate yoke linkage and instead reverted to the Clark principle of using divorced yokes for the end axles (albeit with oval rather than circular holes for the pivots at their apices). The side control springs were mounted outside the sleeves, rather than within them, as is the case with normal Klien-Lindner practice.

At least one of the Leach locomotives is believed to have survived as a stationary boiler into the 1960's. Despite the fact that Fowler catalogues of the relevant period offered 'radial driving axles' as a standard optional extra, the Klien-Lindner system was not destined to make a major contribution to British steam locomotive locomotive practice, either from the point of view of construction for export or domestic usage. Only one further similar locomotive was constructed by Fowler, this being supplied under Works No. 14744 of JULY 1916 via Leslie & Co. for Kalgoorlie & Boulder Firewood Co., Australia. This engine, which was described as having $9\frac{1}{2}$ IN. by 12 IN. cylinders, is believed still to be in existence at the time of writing.

APPENDIX 6

Figure 40 – Above: The Klien-Lindner system. The ball jointed axle sleeves on axles 1 and 4, which incorporated lateral play and side control springs, are shown to advantage along with the yokes and crude centre joint linking these latter components.

Figure 41 – Below: The Fowler-Klien-Lindner articulation system used on Fowler's 2ft gauge 0-8-0's for T. Leach's Argentine Estates Ltd., and Kalgoorlie & Boulder Firewood Co., Australia. This plan view shows the divorced yokes and (for the leading axle) the external side control springs. Compare with Figure 40.

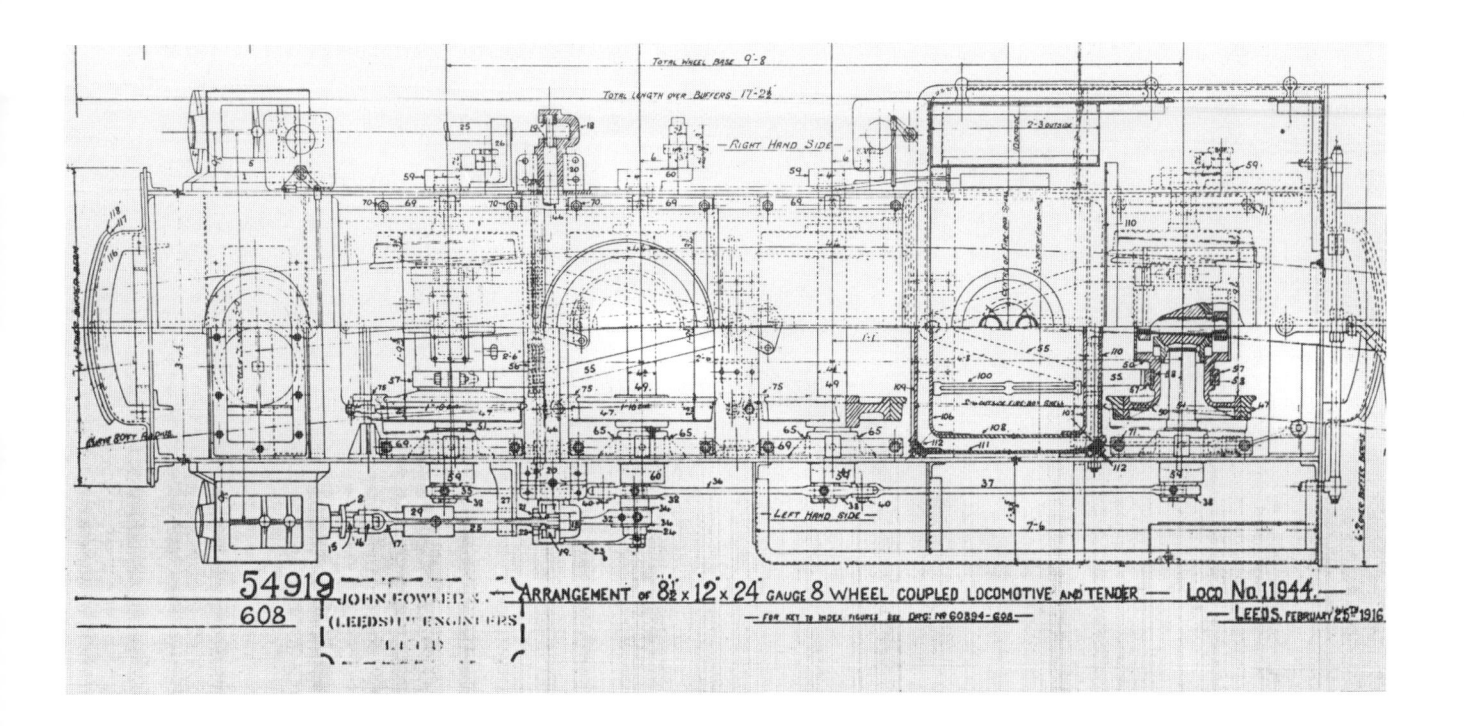

APPENDIX SEVEN

This parody of the Light Railways Act appeared in a London newspaper in 1896, and was reproduced two years later in 'Minimum Gauge Railways'. It highlights its writer's view that the Light Railways Act would bring little benefit to British farmers

THAT TIGHT LITTLE, LIGHT LITTLE RAILWAY

You farmers who lately
Have suffered so greatly
From agricultural depression,
Shake off gloom and sorrow,
A brighter tomorrow
Will dawn in the course of the session.
By no relaxation
Of rates or taxation,
By a certain sure never-to-fail way
Through Government's pleasure
To bring in a measure
For giving some districts a railway:
A tight little, light little railway
A nice little, light little railway,
O think of the joy
Of that exquisite toy,
A tight little, light little railway.

Your wheat may grow cheaper,
The pay of your reaper
May rise to a figure outrageous;
The weather may lay all
Your crops and your hay all
Be ruined by tempests rampageous
Your stock mayn't grow fatter,
But that does not matter,
Except in a bargain and sale way:
What are these to the blessing
Of really possessing
A tight little, light little railway?

(Chorus)

146

You may not have a fraction
Of produce for traction,
Not a stone's weight to put in a wagon,
Not a horse in your stable,
No bread on your table,
Not a shoe to your feet, not a rag on:
All this would be frightful
Were it not so delightful
To see in as-slow-as-a-snail way
The trucks all go gliding
From track into siding,
From siding to track on your railway.
(Chorus)

Then oh *fortunati*
Agricolæ, wait, aye
Wait for the clouds to roll by you:
Your troubles are over;
To-morrow in clover,
You'll laugh at the ills that now try you.
'*Ex machinâ Deus*
Is coming to free us
Not in an old-fashioned or stale way'
Let this be your chorus –
'A future's before us ;
Three cheers for the light little railway!'

APPENDIX EIGHT

COMPARATIVE TABLE OF DIMENSIONS OF HEYWOOD LOCOMOTIVES

	EFFIE	**ELLA**	**MURIEL**	**KATIE**	**SHELAGH**	**URSULA**
Building Date	1875	1881	1894	1896	1904	1916
Engine No.	1	2	3	4	5	6
Cyl. Bore	4 in.	4⅞ in. (5 in. before 1898)	6¼ in.	4⅝ in.	5½ in.	5½ in.
Cyl. Stroke	6 in.	7 in.	8 in.	7 in.	8 in.	8 in.
Wheel Dia.	15¼ in.	13½ in. (14 in. before 1889)	18 in.	15 in.	16 in.	16 in.
Wheelbase	2 ft. 6 in.	4 ft. 6 in.	6 ft.	3 ft.	5 ft.	5 ft.
No. of Wheels	4	6	8	4	6	6
Length over Bufferbeams	7 ft.	8 ft. 8 in. (9 ft. before 1898)	10 ft. 9 in.	8 ft.	10 ft.	10 ft.
Overhangs	2 ft. 3 in.	2 ft. 1 in. (2 ft. 3 in before 1898)	2 ft. 4½ in.	2 ft. 6 in.	2 ft. 6 in.	2 ft. 6 in.
Width over Bufferbeams	2 ft. 3 in.	3 ft. 10 in. (3 ft. 9 in. before 1898)	3 ft. 10 in.	3 ft. 10 in.	3 ft. 10 in.	3 ft. 10 in.
Boiler Length	4 ft. 6 in.	6 ft. 6 in.	8 ft. 3 in.	5 ft. 8 in	7 ft. 8 in.	7 ft. 8 in.
Boiler Dia. (External)	1 ft. 10 in.	2 ft. 1 in. (2 ft. before 1889)	2 ft. 1 in.	2 ft. 1 in.	2 ft. 1 in.	2 ft. 1 in.
Length of Firebox (Internal)	1 ft. 9 in.	2 ft. 3 in.	3 ft.	2 ft. 3 in.	3 ft. (3 ft. 3 in. after 1914-5)	3 ft. 3 in.
Firebox Dia. (Internal)	11 in.	15½ in. (14½ in. before 1889)	15¼ in.	15¼ in.	15¼ in.	15¼ in.
No. of Tubes*	23 (brass)	57 (brass: 42 before 1889)	57 (brass)	57 (brass)	57 (brass) (steel after 1914-5)	57 (steel)
Heating Surface (sq. ft.)*	23.00	70.14 (approx. 56 before 1889)	91.15	52.88	80.06 (75.98 after 1914-5)	75.98

148

APPENDIX 8

	EFFIE	**ELLA**	**MURIEL**	**KATIE**	**SHELAGH**	**URSULA**
Grate Area (sq.ft.)	1.25	2.12 (2.00 before 1889)	3.00	2.12	3.00	3.00
Tank Cap. (Galls.)	18	50	84	49	77	77
Boiler Pressure (p.s.i.)	125	160 (150 before 1889)	160	160	175 (†)	175 (†)
Weight (W.O.)	1t. 3c.	3t. 15c. (3t.6c. before 1898; 2t.10c. as built)	5t.	3t. 5c.	4t. 10c.(†)	4t. 10c.(†)
Adhesion Factor @145 p.s.i.	3.6	4.7	4.5	4.9	4.6	4.6
Tractive Effort per p.s.i.	6.2 lb	12.3 lb	17.3 lb	9.9 lb	15.1 lb	15.1 lb
Net loading On Level	15t.	35t.	49t.	28t.	44t.	44t.
Up 1 in 100:	9t.	21t.	30t.	17t.	27t.	27t.
Up 1 in 50:	6.4t.	14.6t.	21t.	11t.	18t.	18t.
Up 1 in 25:	3.8t.	8.3t.	12t.	6.5t.	11t.	11t.
Up 1 in 12:	1.8t	3.4t.	4.9t.	2.5t.	4.4t	4.4t.

N.B. The basis of Heywood's tractive effort calculations was not specified.

* The heating surface figures calculated by Heywood for the first five locomotives appear to have been calculated on the assumption that the lower part of the firebox (i.e. the portion below the grate) contributes towards the heating process, despite the fact that it admits cold air. The tube length used in these calculations appears to have been inclusive of tubeplate thicknesses although this approach is theoretically unsound. Despite these reservations, it has been decided to calculate the heating surface figures for URSULA on the same basis for the purposes of producing this table. The tubes on EFFIE and on the first boiler used on ELLA were 1.25 in. outside diameter, whereas those on subsequent boilers were 1.375 in. The quoted heating surface figures also show that the internal smokebox length was an inch shorter on the boilers of ELLA and KATIE than on those of MURIEL, SHELAGH and URSULA.

† The figures for No.5 were given respectively as 160 p.s.i. and 4 t.5c. in 1898: the 'Model Engineer' in 1905 gives amended data for No. 5, namely weight 4 t.10c. in working order and boiler pressure 175 p.s.i.

APPENDIX NINE

MAXIMUM LOAD ON FIFTEEN INCH GAUGE?

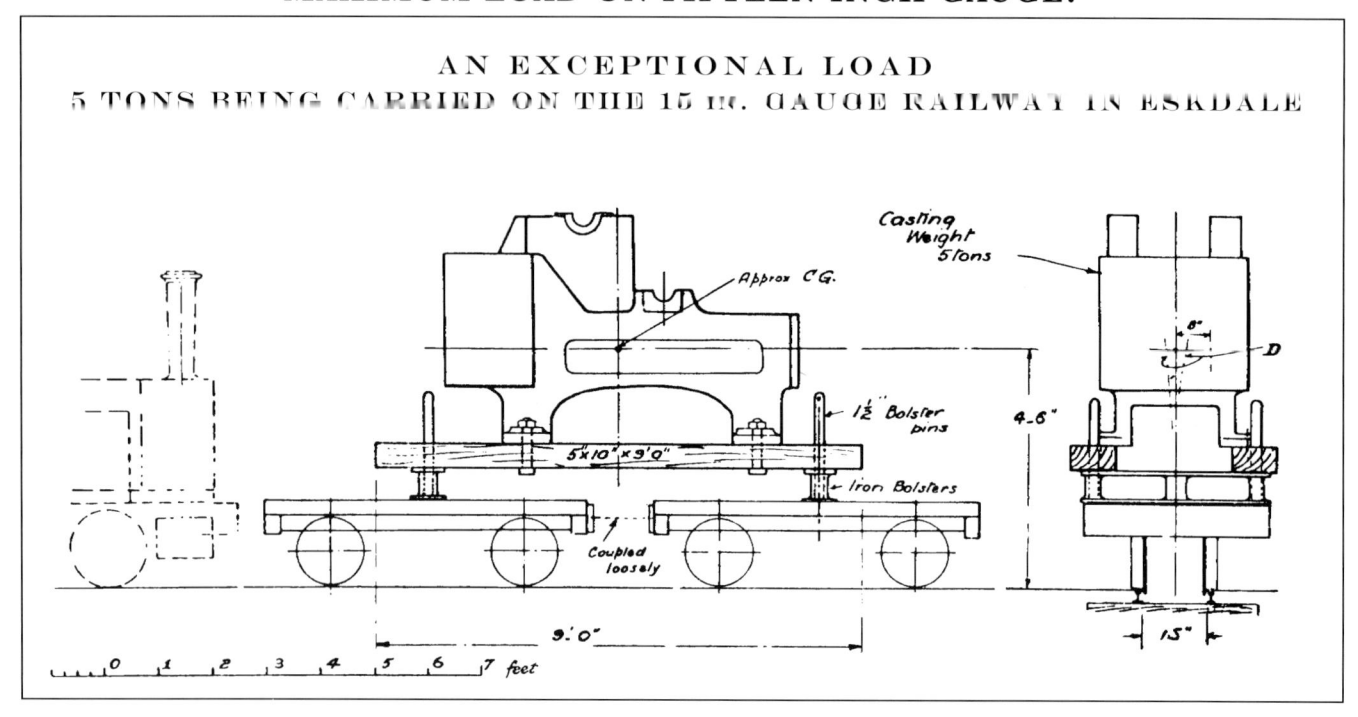

An Exceptional Load for the 15 in. gauge Miniature Railway at Eskdale

BY HENRY GREENLY, A.I.LOCO.E.

We have all heard of and seen the exceptional loads which model locomotives have been called upon to haul at exhibition and society's meetings, and further from time to time accounts of how 'over gauge' loads are carried on full size lines. Quite recently the Eskdale 15 IN. gauge railway authorities were called upon to perform a similar feat. In connection with the new work at Murthwaite a large casting, weighing just on five tons, had to be conveyed from the terminus to the above-named place – a distance of nearly three miles. This was done quite successfully in a running time of 25 minutes. The casting was previously bolted to two longitudinals of 10 INS. by 5 INS. section timber and slewed and jacked up on to the swivelling bolsters of a pair of single-bolster trucks, as indicated in the sketch herewith. When in place the longitudinals were bored and the 1½ IN. diameter steel bolster pins inserted. The unstable angle would have been obtained with a lateral movement of the centre of gravity of 8 INS. or a track deflection of 2 INS., but during the run not more than 2 INS. side movement, out of centre, was observed, and this meant that a track deflection of only ½ IN. had taken place. The size of the engine (one of the large goods type used on the line, not the model engines) is indicated on the drawing. Taking the tonnage co-efficient to be 30 for this engine the load represents 150 TONS in real practice.

A week later or so another large consignment was tackled i.e., the carcase of a 24 H.P. Tangye oil engine.

Figure 42. The 'Model Engineer' for June 7th 1923 carried this drawing, together with a small article by Henry Greenly about the movement of a five ton casting from Ravenglass to Murthwaite (which was to form part of the stone crusher there). The drawing shows two Heywood four wheel wagons fitted with iron bolsters in order to carry the longitudinal planks supporting the casting. Unfortunately, as has been said before, no details survive as to how the bolsters were secured to the wagons.

APPENDIX TEN
HEYWOOD WORKS & NAMEPLATES

ONE THIRD FULL SIZE

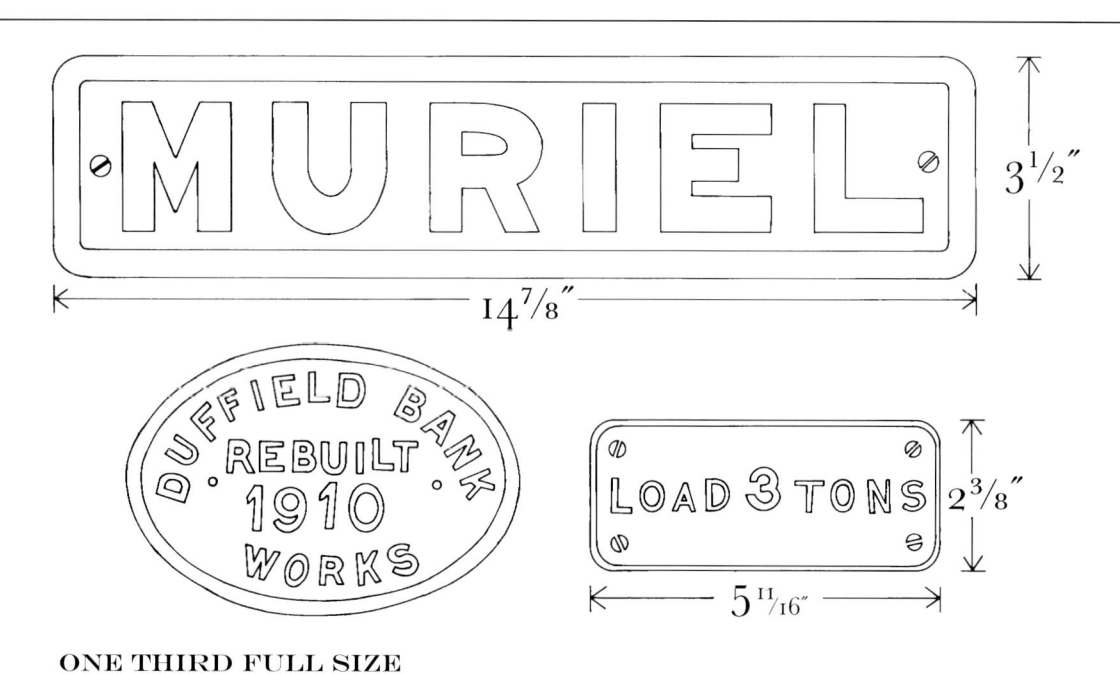

Figure 43. These three drawings are made from rubbings of plates surviving in the museum at Ravenglass. MURIEL'S nameplate is self evident but the other two plates are of considerable interest. The first is a 1910 rebuild plate presumably intended for MURIEL but never fitted. Precisely how and why this item found its way to Ravenglass is a mystery. The other plate is from the 3 ton capacity Heywood bogie wagon which ran on the Ravenglass and Eskdale Railway into the mid-1920's. This item was not mentioned in any edition of 'Minimum Gauge Railways', nor did it appear in the 1916 Auction Catalogue. The only plausible explanation appears to be that it was constructed after 1898 and that it passed to the R.&E.R. prior to the auction, possibly with 0-4-0T KATIE in the spring of 1916. (Author).

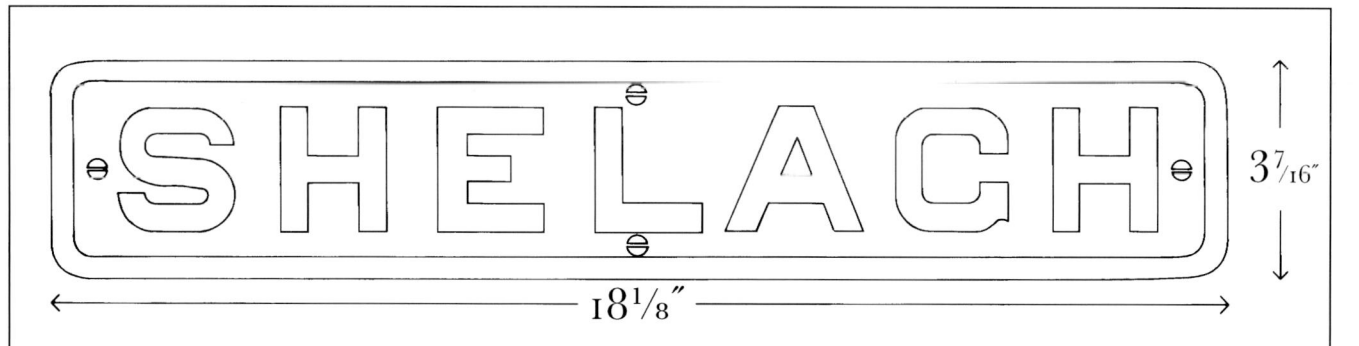

ONE THIRD FULL SIZE

Figure 44. Above and page 152. These drawings have been produced from rubbings of surviving Eaton Railway name and builders' plates in the museum at Tywyn. The earliest plate appears to be that for SHELAGH, and this would have been cast in 1904. The brass on this plate is of a noticeably different quality (more akin to gunmetal) to that of the other two. KATIE and URSULA appear to be of the same age, probably early 1916, and were the plates carried by both the 0-6-0T's shortly before scrapping. The background on all of these plates is black and the letters are virtually all of uniform height (1 15/16 in.), although there are noticeable imperfections in the configuration of some of them. The fixing screws for KATIE are out of horizontal alignment. The builders' plate is from URSULA. The date figures appear to slope slightly to the right and the letter 'D' of Duffield is slightly lower than the 'K' of Bank in relation to the date. The background once again is black. The back of the plate was originally concave to fit the smokebox, but was flattened to facilitate mounting on display in the Narrow Gauge Railway Museum. (Courtesy J. G. Vincent).

APPENDIX 10

URSULA — 3 7/16"
— 15 1/8" —

ONE THIRD FULL SIZE

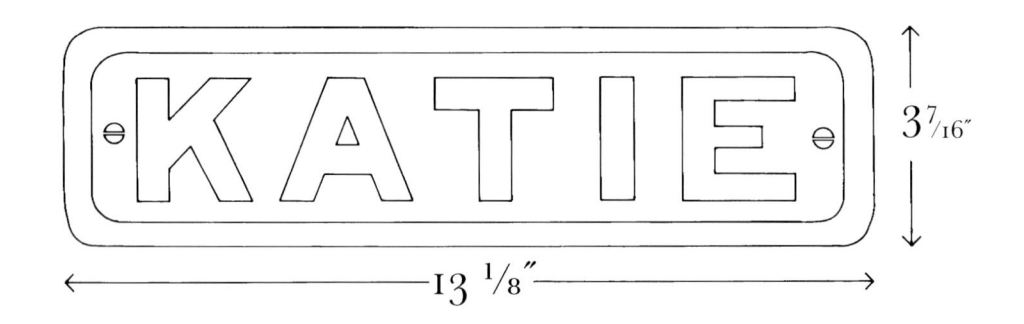

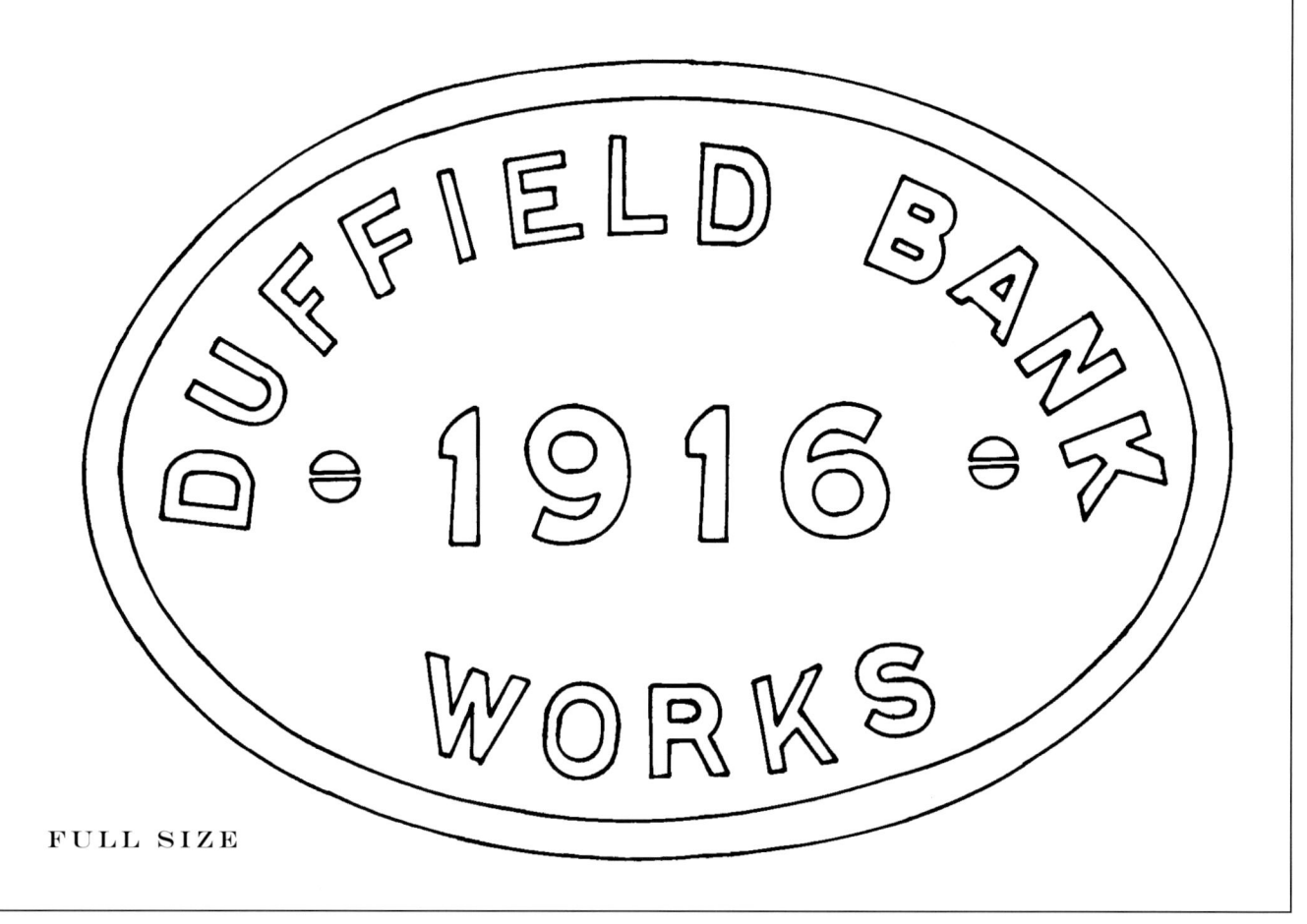

KATIE — 3 7/16"
— 13 1/8" —

DUFFIELD BANK 1916 WORKS

FULL SIZE

152

An... EATON HALL Album

… AN EATON HALL ALBUM

BALDERTON JUNCTION

Above: A view of Balderton siding showing timber being loaded onto two 'top' wagon underframes fitted with bolsters, along with several other 'top' wagons. This view dates from circa 1905. (Courtesy F. Wilde Collection).
Below: The channel frame Simplex i/c loco and brakevan at Balderton. (L&GRP).

155

AN EATON HALL ALBUM

BALDERTON

Above: KATIE is seen leaving Balderton with a mixed train circa 1922. (Courtesy F. Wilde Collection).

Below: KATIE standing in almost the same position as the Simplex (lower - page 155). The 'Tarmac' wagon in the background however is not the same! (Courtesy F. Wilde Collection).

156

BALDERTON
0-4-0T KATIE pauses just outside Balderton with a goods train circa 1915. (Courtesy F. Wilde Collection).

THE FIRST KATIE

At Belgrave shed when new and without any surrounding personnel. The lack of any visible pipework for the steam brake control is strongly indicative of the proposition that the control valve was located forward of the rear axle, rather than to the rear of the reversing/steam brake column (as was the case on all of the other Heywood locomotives in service in 1916). This proposition is supported by other evidence, as is discussed elsewhere in this book. (Courtesy F. Wilde Collection).

AN EATON HALL ALBUM

THE FIRST KATIE

Above: Driver Wilde posed next to KATIE with a train of 4 wheel 'top' wagons. Below: KATIE waits with a passenger train at the Hall. (Both: Courtesy F. Wilde Collection).

SNOW ON THE LINE

Above: A Wintry scene from between the two World Wars, with channel-framed Simplex petrol locomotive (2099 of 1922) on snow plough duty in company with a four wheeled wagon and the bogie brake van.
(Courtesy F. Wilde Collection).

Opposite page: The E.R. snowplough in use circa 1909. The snowplough is seen here attached to the front of the permanent way wagon, whilst SHELAGH provides the motive power and the bogie brake van is drawn behind.
(Courtesy The Grosvenor Estate).

AN EATON HALL ALBUM

BELGRAVE SHED

Above: The Belgrave Engine Sheds of the Eaton Hall Railway in 1896. These were situated in a small siding leading from the Cuckoo's Nest (Estate Works) branch. The provision of a two road shed at this stage suggests that two locomotives were then envisaged for Eaton Railway, although SHELAGH did not arrive until 1904.
(Minimum Gauge Railways Plate XI).

Opposite page – upper: KATIE, seen again circa 1898 in front of the Belgrave locomotive shed with a train consisting of the open carriage, four wheeled brake van and two four wheeled wagons. This view also shows the protective tarpaulins originally fitted to the brake van for use in bad weather.
(Courtesy F. Wilde Collection).

AN EATON HALL ALBUM

*KATIE with loaded 'top' wagons outside Belgrave shed circa 1899.
(Courtesy F. Wilde Collection).*

*An impressive view showing KATIE and SHELAGH together in front of Belgrave shed circa 1908.
The pipework for the injector steam supply and steam brake control valve on SHELAGH is shown to advantage in this view.
(Courtesy F. Wilde Collection).*

Belgrave locomotive shed seen on 31st March 1947 with the bogie brake van, standard four wheel wagon and large four wheel wagon outside. By this stage, the railway had less than six months to live in its integral form, and the external condition of much of its infrastructure emphasised this fact. (Courtesy J. G. Vincent).

Belgrave locomotive shed viewed at the same time as the previous photograph. The building is now the offices of the Grosvenor Garden Centre. (Courtesy J. G. Vincent).

CUCKOO'S NEST

Above: Estate Works sidings at Cuckoo's Nest. (Minimum Gauge Railways - Plate X).

Page opposite – Upper: A front three-quarter view of SHELAGH at the Estate Works, taken circa 1910. This view illustrates the front end characteristics of the Heywood locomotive design and also shows three Estate employees of the period. From left to right, these were Driver Wilde, Mr. Morgan and Mr. King. (Courtesy The Grosvenor Estate).

Page opposite – lower: A good view of SHELAGH at the Estate Works circa 1910. Many constructional features of the locomotive can be seen to good advantage in this particular view, and a feature of particular interest is the straight intermediate valve rod, a feature of all of the Heywood locomotives with the exception of MURIEL. (Courtesy The Grosvenor Estate).

AN EATON HALL ALBUM

ALONG THE LINE

Above: SHELAGH seen circa 1910 with a train of seventeen four wheeled 'top' wagons and the bogie brake van. Driver Wilde is once again on the footplate and in this view he has just released the steam brake, hence the steam emission beneath the rear right hand side of the locomotive. This photograph epitomises the normal pattern of working for the line during the first quarter century of its existence, with goods traffic providing the "bread and butter" and steam being the source of motive power.
(Courtesy The Grosvenor Estate).

Opposite page – upper: A fine view of SHELAGH with the closed passenger coach, some wagons loaded with stone (presumably bound for the Estate works) and, almost certainly, the bogie brake van. The photographer has presumably left the coach in order to take his photograph, hence the stationary train and open carriage door!

Opposite page – lower: SHELAGH leaving the Eaton terminus with a train consisting of nineteen empty four wheeled 'top' wagons (not all apparently of the same capacity) and the bogie brake van.
(Both: Courtesy F. Wilde Collection).

AN EATON HALL ALBUM

AN EATON HALL ALBUM

AN EATON HALL ALBUM

Above: The channel-framed Simplex is seen on a Summer children's special, probably during celebrations of the Silver Jubilee of King George V in 1935, or at the time of the Coronation of King George VI in 1937.
(Courtesy F. Wilde Collection).

Opposite page — upper: A specially posed Edwardian view of SHELAGH with closed and open passenger vehicles on the E.R. 'Main Line'. Apart from special occasions such as shoots and fete days, full employment for the passenger vehicles seemed the exception rather than the rule.

Opposite page — lower: A rather faded view of SHELAGH posed stationary in the pushing mode with Harry Wilde standing at ground level. So far as can be seen, this appears to have been an 'empties' working.
(Both: Courtesy F. Wilde Collection).

0-4-0T KATIE with a train comprising six 4w 'top wagons' and the bogie brake van – circa 1915. (Courtesy F. Wilde Collection).

AN EATON HALL ALBUM

A VISIT FROM A 'LITTLE GIANT'

Above: SHELAGH and LITTLE GIANT posed for the camera immediately in front of Belgrave shed.
Below: LITTLE GIANT with only the four wheel brake van as a train approaching the park gates prior to entering the Hall grounds proper.
(Both: Courtesy Bassett-Lowke Archive).

175

SHELAGH & URSULA

Above: This view shows SHELAGH circa 1910 with Mr. Harry Wilde on the footplate. During the period from 1904 to 1914, this engine appears to have borne the brunt of the E.R. traffic as it had the twofold advantages over the four coupled KATIE of lower axle loading and greater power output.

Opposite page: A head on view of one of URSULA in front of Belgrave locomotive shed, note that the front Heywood coupling has been supplemented with the addition of a chain and hook. The identity of this locomotive can be verified by the pattern of paint scratches on the bufferbeam.
(Both: Courtesy The Grosvenor Estate).

AN EATON HALL ALBUM

AN EATON HALL ALBUM

Views of URSULA in ordinary service are not easy to find, owing to the the engine's exceptionally short operating career, but this is one such view, showing the engine simmering at rest circa 1921. This engine was named after Lady Ursula Mary Olivia Grosvenor (1902-1978). Harry Wilde is once again in evidence on the footplate.
(Courtesy F. Wilde Collection).

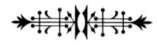

AN EATON HALL ALBUM

BELGRAVE
AN
ARCHITECTURAL STUDY...

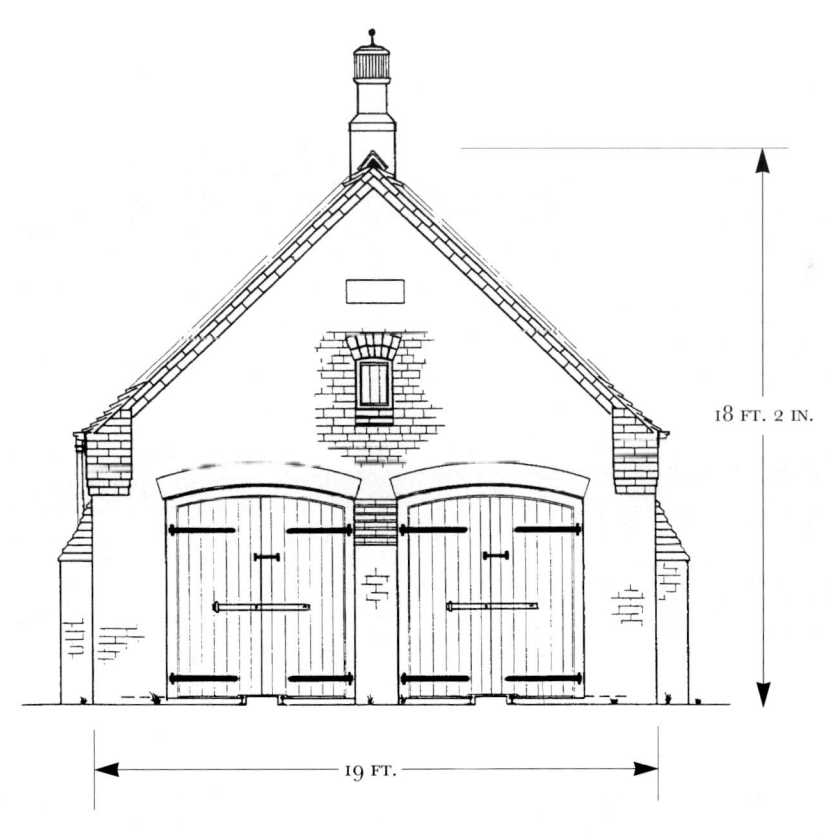

FRONT ELEVATION

SCALE 1:76.2 © J. M. KIMBER 03/95

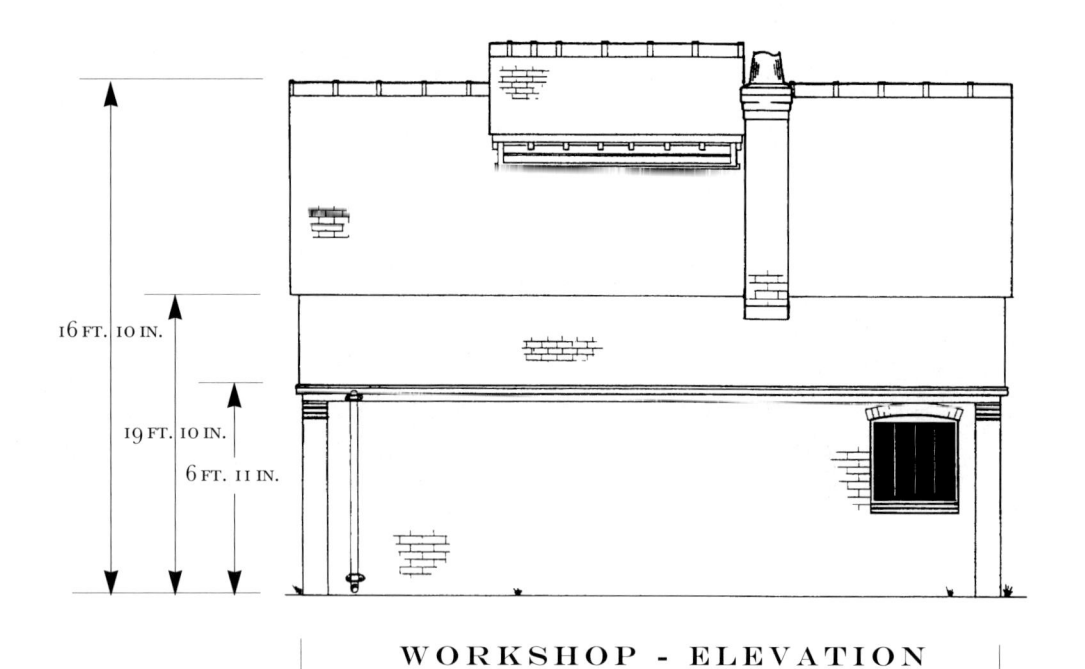

AN EATON HALL ALBUM

16 FT. 10 IN.
19 FT. 10 IN.
6 FT. 11 IN.

WORKSHOP - ELEVATION

23 FT. 4 IN.

23 FT. 6 IN.

16 FT.

BELGRAVE SHED & WORKSHOP BUILDING

COMPILED FROM SITE MEASUREMENTS - DETAILS TAKEN FROM PHOTOGRAPHS

SCALE 1:76.2

© J. M. KIMBER 03/95

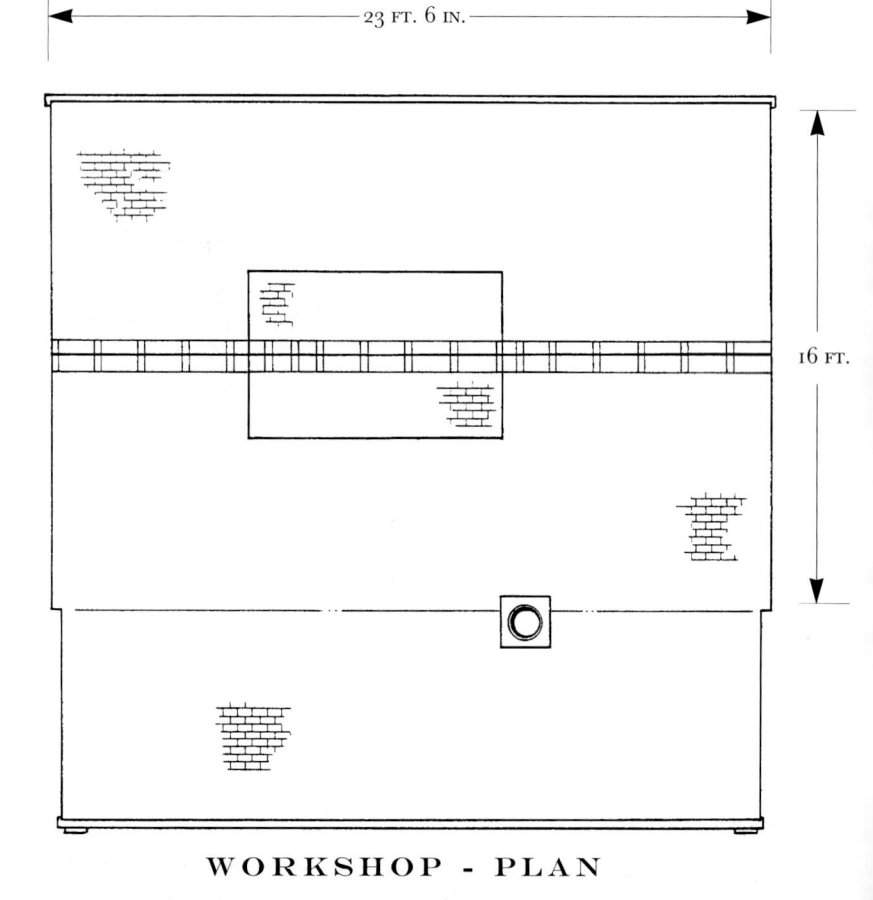

WORKSHOP - PLAN

180

AN EATON HALL ALBUM

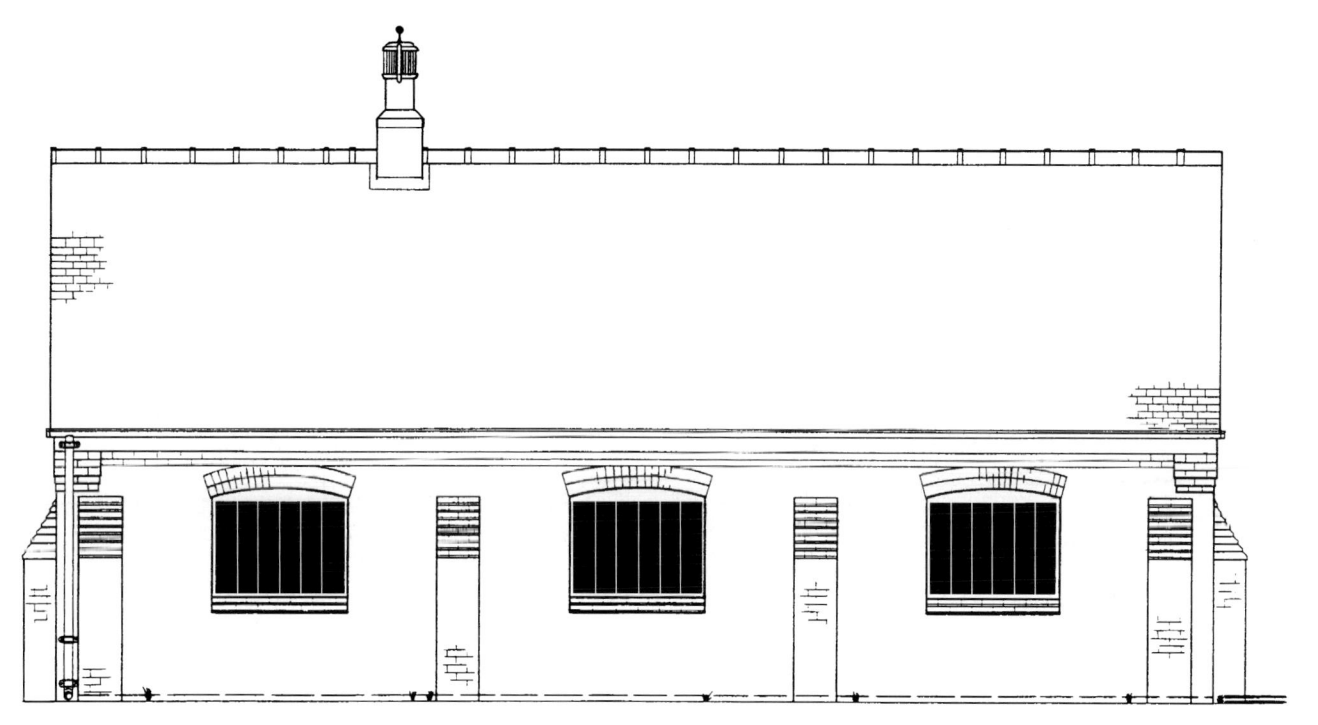

BELGRAVE SHED - SIDE ELEVATION

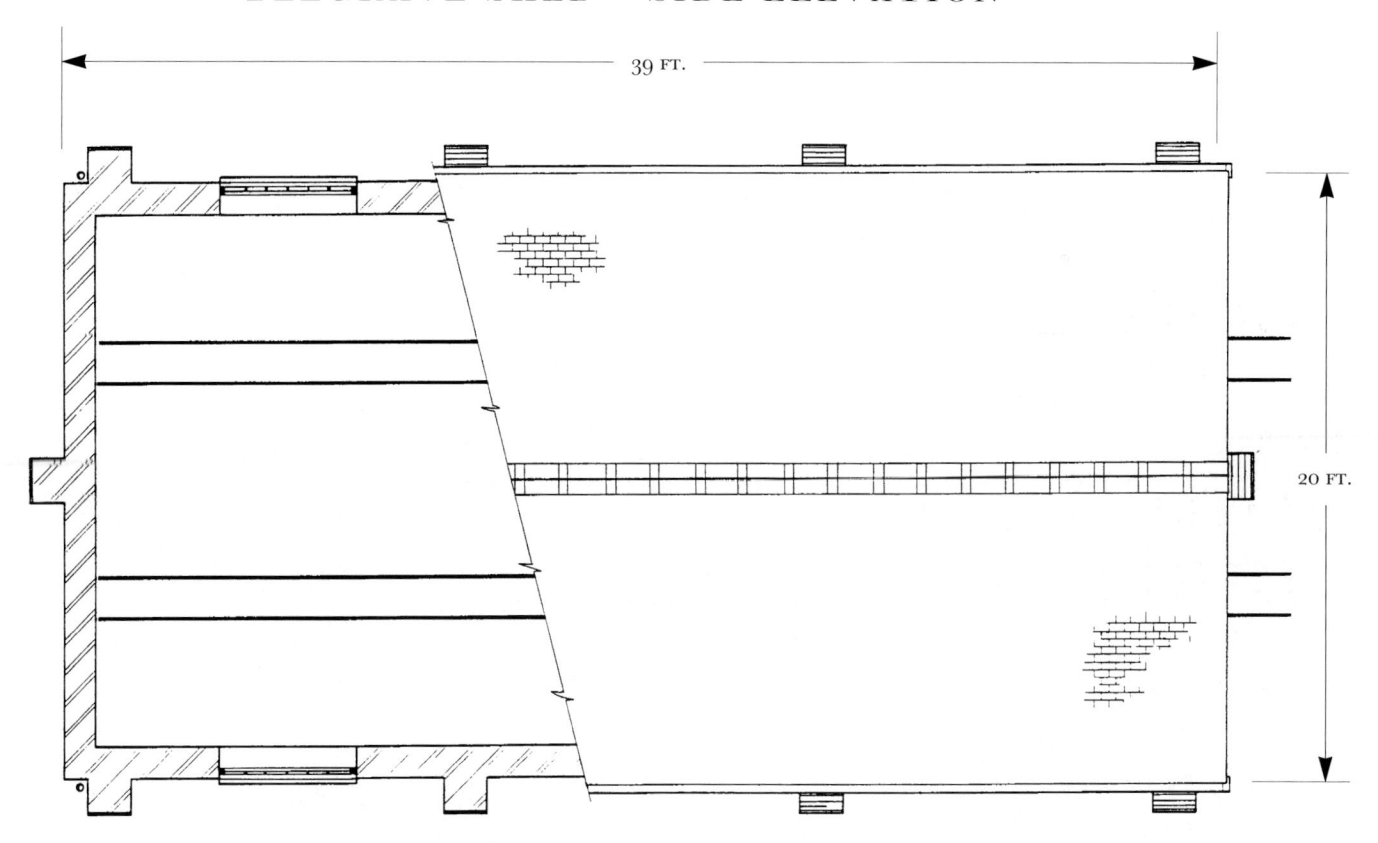

BELGRAVE SHED - PLAN

39 FT.

20 FT.

181

INDEX

Abbott & Co., Newark *23, 28-29, 37, 39, 51, 65, 68-72, 84, 99, 141*
Acresfield (Heywood family residence) *3*
Adamson, Daniel (Patent No. 1377 of 1869) *51*
'An Illustrated History of 18 inch Gauge Steam Railways'
    (M. Smithers – Haynes/OPC 1993) *22*
Architectural Study, Belgrave, Eaton Railway *179-181*
Afon Wen-Carnarvon section, L.&N.W.R. *91*

Bagnall, W. G. & Co. Ltd., Stafford *51-52*
Baguley, Ernest *51*
Barclay, Andrew & Co. Ltd. *97*
Bartholomew, Charles *93*
Bassett-Lowke & Co. Ltd., Northampton *68, 73, 92-97, 99, 103, 104,
    122-123, 175*
Big end bearing, cylindrical cross-section *27*
Blackpool Miniature Railway *92-93, 123*
Blakesley Hall *93*
Boilers
    (Heywood):
        General – (R.&E.R.) *99-100, 123*
        EFFIE *20, 148-149*
        ELLA *28-31, 33, 35, 50-51, 99, 148-149*
        MURIEL (built by Abbott) *39, 99, 109, 141, 148-149*,
            (built by J. Fowler & Co. Ltd.) *51, 148-149*
        KATIE (1) *5, 99, 101, 119, 148-149*; replica *126*
        SHELAGH [187D] *37, 65, 68-71, 141, 148-149*
        KATIE 2) [408D] *68-72, 84, 111-113, 117, 141, 148-149*
        URSULA [408D] *68-72, 84, 111-113, 141, 148-149*
    (Other):
        Ardkinglas locomotive *6*
        Bagnall 'Bullhead' *51-52*
        Fowler 500 mm. gauge locos *48, 50-51*
        Guinness Brewery locos *28-29*
        LAVINIA *5*
        Matheran Hill locomotives *29*
        Ramsbottom design *20*
        R.&E.R. locos: RIVER ESK *125*, RIVER IRT *107*,
            RIVER MITE *107*
Bouch, William *31*
British Association, Sheffield *85*
British Railways *126*
Brocklebank, Sir Aubrey *98*
Bullock, H. C. S. *5*

Callander, George Frederick William *5-6*
Calthrop, Everard Richard *27, 144*
Cauchi, William F. *101*
Cavendish, Lady Katherine
    (later Duchess of Westminster) *62*
Central Council of Church Bellringers *55, 114*
Chatham Dockyard *41-42, 63*
Chattenden & Upnor Railway, Chatham *91*
Churchill, Winston *57*
Church's patent slide valve *49*
Claremont (Heywood family residence) *3*
Clark, John *24, 144*
Clark & Webb 'chain brake' *24*
Cleminson, James *23-25, 30*
Cliffe Hill Granite Co. *52*

Conference on Light Railways, 1896, Board of Trade *89, 131, 133-134*
Cornwallis-West, Lady Edwina 'Shelagh'
    (later Duchess of Westminster) *66*
Crewe Works, L.& N.W.R., *20-21, 30, 41, 99*

De Beers diamond mines, Kimberley, South Africa *51*
Decauville, Paul *7, 31, 48-49*
'Derbyshire Advertiser', The *96*
Dove Bank Railway *46, 81-84, 96, 142*
Doveleys *3, 6, 40, 46, 48, 53-55, 81-84, 89, 115, 141*
Du Cane, Major (Royal Engineers) *3*
Duffield Bank Auction (1916) *14-15, 18, 45-46, 96, 141-143, 151*
Duffield Bank (Heywood family residence) *1, 4, 7, 14, 15, 45, 55*
Duffield Bank Railway *1-5, 7-19, 21-22, 30-32, 35-38, 40-49, 52,
    55-57, 59 60, 62-63, 66-69, 72-73, 75-77, 81-86, 88-89, 92, 94,
    96-100, 102-103, 107, 111-112, 115, 122-123, 127, 132, 141,
    143, 151*
Duke of Sutherland *8*
Duke of Westminster:
    General *138*;
    1st: Hugh Lupus Grosvenor *2, 62*;
    2nd: Hugh Richard Arthur Grosvenor, known as
        'Bend-Or' *66, 95, 111-112, 115, 119*

Eaton Hall & Railway *2, 30-32, 35, 40-42, 45, 51, 54, 56-64, 66-69,
    72-81, 83-84, 87-89, 92-97, 99-100, 109, 111-115, 117,
    119-122, 133, 135-140, 142-143, 151, 153-181*
Edward VII, King *57*
'Engineer', The *19-25, 42, 48, 81, 85, 92*
'Engineering' *19-21, 31-32, 42-44, 85*
Estate Duty (Inheritance Tax) *91*
Exceptional load on 15 in. gauge *150*

Fairbourne Railway *99-103, 142*
Fell, John Barraclough *13-14, 21*
Festiniog Railway *1, 4, 8-9, 13, 91*
F.M.B. Engineering Ltd. *126*
Fowler, John & Co. (later Ltd.), Leeds, *5, 20, 48-51, 57*
Furness Railway *99*

Galloway, Lt. J. J. *11, 15, 18, 32, 35*
Geoghegan, Samuel *28, 32, 39*; (Patent 3296 of 1879) *33*
Gibbins bogie *29, 120*
Great Eastern Railway *4*
Great Western Railway *56, 58, 61, 92, 119, 139*
Greenly, Henry *5, 93-94, 99, 103-104, 122-125, 150*
Green, Revd. Sidney *53-54*
Greig, Alfred (portable track) *48-49*;
    (and Beadon, Patent 402 of 1880) *51*
Grosvenor, Lady Ursula Mary Olivia *178*
Groudle Glen Railway *52*

Hadfield Steel Foundry Co., Sheffield *30*
Hawthorn, R. & W. Ltd. *27, 38*
Heywood, Sir Benjamin Bart. *3*
Heywood, Arthur Percival (later Sir) *1-15, 18-25, 27-33, 35, 37-46,
    48-60, 62-64, 66-75, 77, 81-93, 96-102, 104, 107-111, 113-115,
    117, 120, 122-127, 132-134, 141, 144, 148-151, 168, 176*

INDEX

Heywood, Isabel Effie *21, 53, 82, 84*
Heywood, Sir Thomas Percival *3, 4, 6, 48, 53-55, 82*
Hill Bros., Messrs., Derby *96, 141-143*
Hogg, Major J. R. (Royal Engineers) *21, 85, 91*
Holden & Brooke, Salford *32-33*
Horwich Works, L.&Y.R., *28, 30*
Howey, Capt. J. E. P. *94-95, 119*
Huddersfield tram disaster *31*
Hunslet Engine Co., Leeds *52*

Injectors *32-33, 37, 66, 70, 103, 112, 119, 165*
Inspector-General of Fortifications *21*
Institution of Mechanical Engineers *15, 18, 23, 29, 38-39, 86, 89*

Kerr, Stuart & Co. Ltd. (Stoke-on-Trent) *21, 28, 57, 108, 110*
Klien-Lindner sleeved axle system *24, 26-27, 144-145*

Lancaster Wagon Co. *43*
Leek & Manifold Valley Light Railway *27, 91, 144*
Light Railways Act 1896-60 *133-134, 146*
Llewelyn's Miniature Railway, Southport *100-101, 142*
'Locomotive Magazine', The *26, 33, 96, 99, 115*
Locomotives –
    (*Heywood*):
      General – E.R. *138-140*; R.&E.R. *99-101, 123, 150*
      EFFIE *7-10, 16, 19-21, 28-29, 35, 41, 42, 46, 48-49, 52, 62,*
        81-82, 85, 141, 148-149
      ELLA *8, 10-11, 13-15, 18, 20-25, 27-33, 35, 37-39,*
        49-51, 57, 62-63, 66, 70-71, 83, 85, 92, 96-99,
        101-104, 106-108, 115, 126, 141, 14-149
      MURIEL *12, 17-18, 22-23, 27, 31-39, 51, 56,*
        62-64, 66-67, 69-71, 83, 96-99, 101, 103-104, 106,
        109, 124-127, 141, 148-149, 151, 168
      KATIE (1) *27, 31, 35, 60, 62-66, 68, 72-73, 84, 87,*
        94-96, 98-104, 126-127, 142, 148-149, 151, 155-159,
        162, 164-165, 174, 176
      SHELAGH/KATIE (2) *37, 65-68, 71-72, 75, 77, 79, 83,*
        92-93, 111-115, 117, 141-142, 148-149, 151-152, 160,
        162, 65, 168, 170, 173, 175-176
      URSULA *31, 37, 69-72, 75, 77, 83, 111-115, 117, 119,*
        141-142, 148-149, 151-152, 176, 178
    (*Other*):
      Ardkinglas Railway *6*
      Bassett-Lowke:
        JOHN ANTHONY/COLOSSUS *68, 94-95, 104*
        LITTLE GIANT *73, 92-95, 120, 122, 175*
        MIGHTY ATOM *123*
        SANS PAREIL *97, 104*
      Bagnall/Regent Street Polytechnic *122*
      Beyer Peacock 18 in. gauge for Horwich Works *28*
      Brotherhood three cylinder steam motor *30*
      Brown's tramway *27, 38*
      Cagney 4-4-0 *93, 122*
      Charles Fildes LAVINIA *5*
      Clark, John, sleeved axle *24*
      Crewe Works 18 in. gauge *20, 30, 99*
      Eaton Railway Motor-Rail 'Simplex' petrol: (1922)
        112-114, 155-156, 160, 173; (1938) *114, 117, 119*
      Feldbahn 0-8-0T *144*
      Festiniog Railway *1, 4*
      Fowler, John & Co. (later Ltd.): Fairground *5*;

      500 mm. gauge *20, 28, 48-51, 57*; 2 ft. gauge 0-8-0 *144-145*
      Fox Walker 0-4-0T, Crewe design *30*
      Geoghegan patent, Guinness tramway, Dublin *28-29, 32-33,*
        39
      Greenly, H. proposals: estate 0-4-2T *123*;
        R.&E.R. 2-6-2 *124*
      Groudle Glen Railway Bagnall 2-4-0T SEA LION *52*
      Handyside design for trench tramways:
      0-4-4-0 proposal rejected by R.E.C. *21-22*
      2-4-2T built by Fox, Walker & Co. in 1878 *1, 21-22, 32, 35*
      Hunt & Co., Bournemouth 4-6-2 SIR AUBREY
        BROCKLEBANK for R.&E.R. *99*
      Manning Wardle 18 in. gauge 0-4-0ST BURGOYNE for
        S.M.E., Chatham *19-20*; for Royal Arsenal *117*
      Matheran Hill Railway 0-6-0T *25-27, 144*
      Midland Railway, S. W. Johnson's 'Spinner' 4-2-2 *31*
      John Ramsbottom's L.&N.W.R. standard gauge 0-4-0ST *20*
      Ravenglass & Eskdale Railway:
        BONNIE DUNDEE *108*;
        I.C.L. No. 2 *107-108*;
        Muir-Hill QUARRYMAN *110*;
        NORTHERN ROCK *124*;
        RIVER ESK *124-125*;
        RIVER IRT *37-39, 49, 107, 109, 125, 141*;
        RIVER MITE *107*;
      Standard gauge Kerr, Stuart diesel-mechanical *110*
      Spary, William, miniature locomotives at Alresford *5*
      Spooner, C. E., 'slate quarry' 0-4-0T design *41*
Locomotive trials:
    Fell's Railway (Aldershot) *87*;
    Handyside *21*;
    ELLA *30, 85*;
    KATIE (1) *64, 68*;
    SHELAGH *68*;
    JOHN ANTHONY *68, 94*;
    LITTLE GIANT *73, 94*
London, Midland & Scottish Railway *110*

Manning Wardle & Co. Ltd., Leeds *19-20, 52, 117*
Manx Northern Railway *30*
Matheran Hill Railway *25 27, 144*
'Meccano Magazine', The *93, 112-114*
Metropolitan Railway *122*
Midgely, William *66, 92, 96*
Midland Railway *14, 31, 52, 56*
Miles Platting affair *53-54*
Miniature Railways of Great Britain Ltd. *122*
'Minimum Gauge Railways' (Sir A. P. Heywood in three Editions:
    1881, 1894 and 1898) *4, 8-13, 21-22, 24, 27-28, 30-32, 38,*
    43-46, 49, 51-52, 59, 62-63, 65-66, 70, 81, 83, 86, 87, 91, 119,
    142, 146
'Minimum Gauge Railways Exhibition', N.R.M. York *107, 120-121*
Ministry of Munitions *96-98*
'Model Engineer', The *68, 93, 111, 122, 149-150*
'Models, Railways and Locomotives' *124*
Moors Valley Railway *126*
Mull and West Highland Railway *126*

Narrow Gauge Railways Ltd. *84, 94-98*
Narrow Gauge Railway Museum, Tywyn *102-103, 142, 151*

x

INDEX

'Narrow Gauge Railways, Two Feet and Under'
(Leslie S. Robertson, 1898) *15, 89-91*
North Staffordshire Railway *83*
North Wales Narrow Gauge Railway *91*

Parker, Hon. Cecil *56*
Proctor-Mitchell, R. *96*

Radiating gear, Heywood (articulation):
derivation of *24-25;*
general *29, 63, 66, 123, 144;*
ELLA *22-25, 27, 28, 32, 66, 70, 103;*
MURIEL *32, 34-35, 66, 70, 103, 125;*
SHELAGH *66, 117;*
URSULA *70* (See also Klien-Lindner system)
Rail bending *12-13, 59, 81, 84*
'Railway Magazine', The *96-97, 115*
Ravenglass and Eskdale Railway *25, 30, 37, 39-41, 44-46, 49, 69, 71, 74-75, 77, 94-104, 106-110, 120-126, 141-143, 150-151*
Reen, A. *126-127*
Rhyl Miniature Railway *101*
Romney, Hythe and Dymchurch Railway *29, 41, 75, 94, 107, 119-121, 124, 142-143*
Rodney, Admiral *5*
Rodney, Capt. Robert *5*
Rolling stock
(Heywood):
Doveleys *40, 46, 48-49, 81-82, 84;*
D.B.R. *8-13, 15-16, 18, 37, 38, 40-48, 59, 72-73, 77, 81, 88, 96-98, 102, 109, 141-143, 150-151;*
E.R. *18, 29, 40-42, 45, 58-60, 64, 68, 72-81, 87-88, 95-97, 109, 111, 115, 117, 119-121, 135-140, 142-143, 155-157, 159-160, 162, 164, 166, 170, 173-175*
(Other):
Capt. Rodney's *5;*
Ardkinglas *6;*
Festiniog Railway *13, 42;*
Cleminson's proposals *24-25;*
Chatham Dockyard *41;*
Crewe Works *41;*
C. E. Spooner's Indian proposal *42-43;*
N.W.N.G.R. *42*

R.E., Chatham fortifications *43*
Royal Agricultural Society of England: *3, 144;*
Derby Show (1881) *30;*
Kilburn Show (1879) *48, 49*
Royal Arsenal, Woolwich, *42, 62-63, 86, 117*
Royal Engineers:
(General matters)
1, 3, 13, 15, 17, 21-22, 30, 32, 35, 85, 91, 144
(J. B. Fell's railway at Aldershot) *13-14, 19, 21*
(School of Military Engineering & Committee minutes, Chatham) *1, 9, 12, 14, 19, 21, 24-25, 30, 32-33, 35, 51, 64, 91*
'Royal Engineers Journal', The *21-23, 34-35, 37, 42, 46-47, 65, 83-84*

Savage & Co., King's Lynn *5*
Scott, G. D. *58*
'Scottish Field', The *6*

Signalling:
D.B.R. *7-8, 10, 14, 17, 62;*
E.R. *62, 140;*
Dove Bank Railway *81*
Smithies, Fred *94*
Smokebox door, Heywood, post-1881 *71, 106, 115, 117*
Spary, Henry *5*
Spary, William *5*
Spooner, Charles Easton *1, 13, 21, 40-43*
State Northern Railway, German S.W. Africa *144*
Staughton Manor Railway *94-95*
Steam brake & linkage:
ELLA *29-31, 103, 106*
MURIEL *35*
KATIE (1) *62-63, 158*
SHELAGH *66, 112, 117, 165, 170*
URSULA *66, 70, 72, 112, 119*
Steam sanding *31*
Stileman, P. *126-127*
Stockton & Darlington Railway *31*
Stratford-upon-Avon & Midland Junction Railway *93*
Suakin Expedition 1885 *51, 58*
Sumner, George Henry, Revd. *3-4*
Sumner, Margaret Effie (later Lady Heywood) *4, 19, 53, 55*
Sutton Coldfield Miniature Railway *123*

Tay Bridge Disaster *6*
'Times', The *89, 91, 131, 133*
Travis/Day cast-iron sleeper *12*
Trinity College, Cambridge University *4*

Uttoxeter Advertiser, The *84*

Valve gears:
Brown *27-28, 38-39, 62, 124*
Hackworth *23, 28*
Heywood *22-23, 27-28, 35, 38-39, 62, 70, 106, 119, 124-125*
Joy *28*
Paxman-Lenz *124-125*
Stephenson/Howe *21, 28, 48, 50, 62*
Walschaerts *28, 124*
Vignes 'Technical Study' *24*

War Department Light Railways *35, 87*
Warner & Co., J., London *5*
Water lifter, MURIEL *33, 35, 37, 39*
Webb, Francis William *24, 30*
Welsh Highland Railway *91*
Wilde, Frank *60, 63-64, 67-68, 72, 73, 75, 79, 111, 155-160, 162, 164-165, 170, 173-174, 178*
Wilde, Harry, *63-64, 87, 95, 111, 114, 159, 168, 170, 173, 176, 178*
'Windsor Magazine', The *85*

Yorkshire Engine Co. Ltd., Sheffield *107*